The Politics of Mental Health and Illness

Series Editor

Bruce M. Z. Cohen, Sociology, University of Auckland,
Auckland, New Zealand

The Politics of Mental Health and Illness conceptualises the western mental health system as a social, economic, political, and cultural project which cannot be adequately theorised without considering wider societal and structural issues such as professional power, labelling and deviance, ideological and social control, consumption, capital, and self-governance. Engaging with both social theory and empirical evidence, and situated at the intersections of critical psychiatry, sociology, anthropology, social psychology, social work, history, media studies, and the health and education sciences, the series offers academics, researchers, postgraduate students, and practitioners new and innovative monographs and edited collections with which to contest and challenge the taken-for-granted understandings of psychiatry and the mental health system currently progressed in western society. Research topics for the collection may include: aspects of the medicalisation and/or pharmaceuticalisation of everyday life; psy-professional power and knowledge production; psychopolitics and the expansion of talk therapies; the biomedical model and the future of psychiatric nosology; the marketisation of mental health discourse; social media and self-diagnosing behaviour; capitalism and psychiatric violence; and specific analyses of psy-professionals and their practices from a variety of locations (including prisons, workplaces, addiction clinics, the military, schools, the home, and general hospitals). As the first book series to explicitly encourage critical contributions in the area of mental health and illness, we welcome scholarship from a wide range of different theoretical and empirical perspectives.

If you would like to discuss a book idea prior to submitting a proposal please contact the Series Editor, Dr. Bruce M. Z. Cohen, via the Commissioning Editor, Beth Farrow (beth.farrow@palgrave.com).

Emmanuelle Bernheim

Therapeutic (In)justice and the Shadow Carceral State

An Ethnographic Study in Mental Health Courtrooms

palgrave
macmillan

Emmanuelle Bernheim
Faculty of Law, Civil Law Section
University of Ottawa
Ontario, ON, Canada

ISSN 2731-5266 ISSN 2731-5274 (electronic)
The Politics of Mental Health and Illness
ISBN 978-3-032-16185-7 ISBN 978-3-032-16186-4 (eBook)
https://doi.org/10.1007/978-3-032-16186-4

This work was supported by Social Sciences and Humanities Research Council of Canada.

Cover credit: smartboy10

This Palgrave Macmillan imprint is published by the registered company Springer Nature Switzerland AG
The registered company address is: Gewerbestrasse 11, 6330 Cham, Switzerland

This book is dedicated to all survivors of judicial violence.

Acknowledgments I express my deepest appreciation to the participants in my research, who made this work possible. First and foremost, I thank those who have been involved with the justice system—people I met in courtrooms, encountered in courthouse corridors, shared conversations with over coffee, or interviewed in my office at university. I am deeply grateful for your time, your generosity, and your trust in sharing your most private and difficult stories. I hope this work honors your lived experiences.

I extend my gratitude to the judges who granted me access to their courtrooms and agreed to discuss the cases we observed together. I value your openness and the trust you placed in me. These conversations were pivotal in shaping and advancing my research and continue to inform my work today. I also wish to recognize the judges, attorneys, and psychiatrists who generously provided their experiences and professional perspectives through interviews.

I want to emphasize the vital role played by multiple individuals and organizations in supporting these research endeavors, particularly in facilitating courtrooms access and recruitment processes. My appreciation goes to the Chief Justices of the Court of Quebec (Honorable Guy Gagnon and Honorable Lucie Rondeau), Quebec Superior Court (Honorable François Rolland) and Quebec Court of Appeal (Honorable Michel Robert), the coordinating judges of Civil (Honorable Michel Simard) and Youth Divisions (Honorable Robert Proulx) of the Court of Quebec, the Montreal Community Legal Centre (Me Marie-Laure Braun and the lawyers from the health law office), Action Autonomie-Le Collectif de défense des droits en santé mentale de Montréal (Nicole Cloutier), the Association des groupes de défense des droits en santé mentale du Québec (Doris Provencher), and the Front commun des personnes assistées sociales du Quebec. I appreciate your time, your accessibility, and your support.

I want to recognize the significant contribution of discussions I conducted with Quebec Court and Superior Court judges, along with defense lawyers, especially those from the Montreal Community Legal

Centre and the Legal Services Commission, during ecological validation phases of my projects, working meetings, and training or workshop sessions. I also wish to express my heartfelt gratitude to Action Autonomie-Le Collectif de défense des droits en santé mentale de Montréal and the Association des groupes de défense des droits en santé mentale du Québec members who contributed feedback, shared their insights and reflections during various conferences and workshops. I also thank the various groups with which I have collaborated in recent years—l'Avant-garde (Connie Bleau and Haleema Rashid), the Collectif de défense des droits de la Montérégie (David-Alexandre Grisé), the Mouvement Jeunes et santé mentale (Myriam Lepage-Lamazzi) and the Clinique interdisciplinaire en droit social de l'Outaouais (Anne Thibault, Sara Lambert). These meaningful dialogues have been tremendously enriching and have facilitated the continuous refinement of my analytical framework over the years.

I acknowledge with gratitude those individuals, including people with lived experience and legal professionals, who shared their insights and recommended research avenues or investigation sites over these years. These contributions have consistently proven relevant and enriching, ensuring that my research remained anchored to on-the-ground realities.

Some of these studies were collaborative efforts with colleagues and students to whom I am profoundly appreciative for our shared work and enriching exchanges: Alexandra Bahary-Dionne, Dominique Bernier, Florence Brosseau, Guillaume Chalifour, Valérie Costanzo, Marilyn Coupienne, Édith Perrault, Delphine Gauthier-Boiteau, Dalia Gesualdi-Fecteau, Marcio Gutierrez, Richard-Alexandre Laniel, Guillaume Ouellet, Claire Lebeke, Pierre Pariseau-Legault, Karen Rakotonorina-Razafimanantso, Nicolas Sallée, and Maxine Visotzky-Charlebois.

This work has been substantially improved through the generous feedback of many people. I am particularly indebted to those who reviewed this manuscript and offered commentary, or who engaged in productive discussions about this book project, especially Bruce Cohen, series editor of Politics of Mental Health and Illness at Palgrave Macmillan. My sincere thanks go to Gefen Bar-On Santor, Cristina Ferreira, Meghan

Guerreiro-Blaise, Emmanuel Nwatu, and Naïm Ounis, for their invaluable input. I also express my gratitude to the anonymous peer reviewers who provided constructive feedback on the book proposal.

I acknowledge with great appreciation the meaningful support for my work provided in different ways by many people over the years: Jeffrey Ansloos, Benoît Bastard, Jean-Guy Belley, Kevin Boire, Jude-Mary Cénat, Jacques Commaille, Lucy Costa, Mathias Couturier, Salvio Digesto, Agnieszka Doll, Jean-Laurent, Domingue Laure Donskoy, Véronique Fortin, Dave Holmes, Jean-François Gaudreault-Desbiens, Eugène LeBlanc, Monique Lefebvre, Bren Lefrançois, Nancy Melançon, Christopher McAll, Dahlia Namian, Marcelo Otero, Cintia Quiroga, Maxime Raymond-Dufour, Annie Rochette, Sébastien Saetta, Jacob Saumure, Sophie Thériault, Rob Wipond. Particular acknowledgment is due to Pierre Noreau and Marie-Ève Sylvestre; I am grateful for your confidence and faith in me. Crossing your path has been both a privilege and an invaluable opportunity. I am also grateful to my colleagues and the administrative collaborators at the University of Quebec in Montreal and the University of Ottawa for their support over the past fifteen years, and to the many scholars I have met at conferences and events who have contributed to my intellectual development through their ideas and commentary.

My heartfelt thanks go to my husband Hakim and my sons Naïm, David, and Axel for their incredible support, generosity, and patience throughout the realization of this work in recent years. These projects would never have been possible without your understanding and joyful companionship in my life.

I finally want to emphasize the essential contribution of the academic and funding institutions that have supported my work in the last several years: the University of Montreal and the Centre de recherche en droit public (CRDP), the École Normale Supérieure de Cachan, the Department of Legal Sciences at the University of Quebec in Montreal, the Centre de recherche de Montréal sur les inégalités sociales (CRÉMIS), the Centre for Health Law, Policy and Ethics, the Interdisciplinary Centre for Black Health the Civil Law Section of the Faculty of Law at the University of Ottawa, the Canada Research Chairs Program, and the Social Sciences and Humanities Research Council of Canada.

Competing Interests This research was undertaken, in part, thanks to funding from the Canada Research Chairs Program [grant number: 950-233192 and CRC-2025-00059] and the Sciences and Humanities Research Council of Canada:

- Doctoral scholarship [grant number: 752-2009-1293],
- Insight Development Grant [grant number: 430-2011-489],
- Partnership Grant [grant number: 201-2017-057] and
- Insight Grant [grant number: 435-2017-1150].

The author has no conflicts of interest to declare that are relevant to the content of this book.

Ethics Approval The studies presented in this book were performed in line with the principles of the Declaration of Helsinki and the Canadian Tri-Council Policy Statement. Approval was granted by the Ethics Committees of University of Montreal, University of Quebec in Montreal, and University of Ottawa. Written informed consent was obtained from all participants through signed consent forms.

Praise for *Therapeutic (In)justice and the Shadow Carceral State*

"A pathbreaking contribution to the literature that is grounded in thorough and rigorous research, *Therapeutic (In)justice and the Shadow Carceral State* provides the first systematic accounting of coercive practices within the mental health courtroom, opening up for inspection the magnitude of psychiatric authority within the judiciary.

In a world of escalating coercive containment, with the expansion of carceral legislation and the rise in forced psychiatric incarceration, Bernheim leaves us with no doubt that psycho-political surveillance and medico-legal coercion is an entrenched form of neoliberal institutional power that is working in tandem with the erosion of our human rights. This book is a must-read for lawyers, judges, mental health workers and social scientists looking to understanding how the law/psychiatry interface is perpetuating social inequities and increased marginalization, including with the targeting of people primarily based on race, class and gender through a child welfare-psychiatry-prison pipeline.

Based in civil law commitment proceedings in Québec, this research extends the boundaries of our understandings of the workings of medical coercion within the policing/psychiatry/law interface within Québec as well as other jurisdictions and legal systems whether based on statutes or judicial precedents. This knowledge is transferable because the fundamental issue in all jurisdictions is the presence and practice of institutional power. It is this institutional power through psychiatric coercion that needs to be scrutinized and abolished."

—Prof. Bren Lefrançois, *Memorial University of Newfoundland, Canada*

Contents

About the Author

Emmanuelle Bernheim is a full professor at the Civil Law Section of the Faculty of Law at the University of Ottawa and holds the Canada Research Chair in Mental Health and Access to Justice. She is a member of the College of New Scholars, Artists and Scientists of the Royal Society of Canada.

Grounded in sociological and legal scholarship, her research investigates how legal institutions and judicial practices generate and reproduce patterns of social inequality. Her research agenda aims to deepen understanding of how marginalized populations become subject to serial judicialization through the intersection of police, social, and health interventions.

Among her latest publications:

Bernheim, E. (2025). Rights against Abolition: how Law and Rights perpetuate Psychiatric Coercion. *Social Science and Medicine, 384*, 118509. https://doi.org/10.1016/j.socscimed.2025.118509

Bernheim, E., Ferron-Parayre, A. & Gauthier-Boiteau, D. (2025) To consent and to refuse electroconvulsive therapy: a study of consent documents and court orders in Quebec, Canada. *Ethical, Human,*

Psychology and Psychiatry, 27(1), 25–45 https://doi.org/10.1891/EHPP-2024-0011
Bernheim, E., Namian, D., Lambert, S., Thibault, A., & Fortin-Boileau, P. (2025). Collective advocacy in the age of neoliberalism: Getting political in an interdisciplinary social law clinic. *International Journal of Clinical Legal Education, 32*(2), 20–36. https://doi.org/10.19164/ijcle.v32i2.1690
Bernheim, E. (2024). Extending the boundaries of the psychiatric hospital: The use and misuse of psychiatric coercion during the Covid-19 pandemic in Quebec and Ontario. In Flood, C., Chen, Y.Y. B., Deonandan, R., Halabi, S. & Thériault, S. (Eds.), *Borders, Boundaries and Pandemics* (pp. 273–280). Routledge. https://doi.org/10.4324/9781003394006

List of Tables

1

Introduction. Rethinking Psychiatric Coercion

> I'm not just talking about my wife, I'm talking about my life. I can't seem to get that through to you. I'm not just talking about one person, I'm talking about everybody, I'm talking about form, I'm talking about content, I'm talking about interrelationships. I'm talking about God, the devil, hell, heaven.—Harding in One Flew Over the Cuckoo's Nest.

At the time of my initial encounter with Amélie[1] in 2012, we found ourselves at the same life stage—both thirty-five years old, both mothers, both living in Tiohtià:ke, also known as Montreal, Canada, and both bearing the weight of multiple psychiatric diagnoses received since our early twenties. Yet, while we shared several significant experiences, our trajectories were markedly different.

Amélie worked as a high school teacher, a profession she found fulfilling and had practiced for over ten years. She stated that she "loves working with young people," and described engaging in numerous activities with them. Following her father's suicide during her early childhood,

[1] All names are pseudonyms to ensure anonymity.

E. Bernheim, *Therapeutic (In)justice and the Shadow Carceral State*, The Politics of Mental Health and Illness, https://doi.org/10.1007/978-3-032-16186-4_1

her mother raised her and her four siblings as a single parent in conditions of "severe poverty." She had sustained a first severe depressive episode during her early twenties, associated with Accutane, a treatment for acne. This episode resulted in a 53-day involuntary commitment. This initial hospitalization was followed by multiple subsequent involuntary admissions due to depression or burnout, each accompanied by medical leave of varying duration. During one such commitment, a psychiatrist modified her diagnosis to bipolar disorder and restructured her pharmacological treatment. The revised medication protocol generated numerous adverse effects, including compromised concentration, sleep disturbances, and significant weight increase. Since that time, Amélie had further been assigned diagnoses of post-traumatic stress disorder and borderline personality disorder.

Amélie recounted that she discovered "by chance" her right to contest her involuntary commitments through judicial proceedings. This information was provided by a fellow involuntary committed person. From that point forward, she consistently "held firm." She appeared in court at every opportunity and prepared her own legal proceedings. She noted that the legal counsel assigned to her over the years provided minimal assistance. While she refused to take psychiatric medications, her attorneys attempted to persuade her to comply with treatment. Nevertheless, she persisted in her refusal. Until this point.

Amélie had a four-year-old son, Paul, and resided with the father in a small two-bedroom apartment in proximity to her place of employment. She experienced financial difficulties as her partner was unemployed and appropriated portions of her earnings for cocaine use. This circumstance generated considerable stress for her. She maintained regular consultations with her psychiatrist despite her continued refusal of psychopharmacological treatment. She reported feeling compelled to attend these appointments. During her most recent consultation, she requested two weeks of medical leave, citing exhaustion. The physician informed her that without medication compliance, he could not authorize sick leave, as she was not engaging in "all recommended therapeutic measures." Upon observing her resistance, he threatened to file a report with child welfare services. He subsequently carried out this threat.

Under this pressure, Amélie complied with the medication regimen. She also received home visits from a social worker who monitored her interactions with her child and took "extensive notes." She feared the consequences and remained uncertain about her future circumstances.

I encountered Amélie on two additional occasions during the subsequent two-year period. Her son had been removed from her custody and initially placed with his father, from whom she had meanwhile separated, before being transferred to a foster family residing at a considerable distance from her residence. The child commenced his education in a neighborhood remote from her own, leading Amélie to question how circumstances would unfold should she regain custody. This goal represented her overriding life priority: she expressed absolute determination to pursue any necessary actions to secure her son's return. In pursuit of this objective, she exhibited exemplary adherence to psychiatric treatment appointments and prescribed pharmacotherapy. She sought to "position herself as favorably as possible."

During this two-year period, Amélie "participated in 20 judicial proceedings, creating such stress that I experience memory blackouts." When Paul was initially removed, the psychological impact was so profound that she experienced mutism for several days. "I attempted to maintain composure before my child. I permitted his departure, then experienced intense grief. I was beyond comfort." Despite a judicial order granting visitation rights, she was denied contact with Paul for six months because child welfare services failed to arrange visits, alleging she displayed a poor attitude for refusing psychiatric medication. In court, the social worker had declared that Amélie "is well when compliant to her medication regimen, but when non-adherent, she could pose a danger to her child." While recounting the hearing, Amélie had exclaimed: "To say I could be a danger to my child! It's terrible." Her psychiatrist—the professional who had initiated child welfare involvement—advocated for her and ultimately secured supervised visitation arrangements. This experience struck Amélie as both incomprehensible and morally reprehensible: "What function do judicial orders fulfill?" Since then, notwithstanding legal representation, she questions both her understanding of her rights and their practical utility. She additionally wonders about Paul's rights and, should they exist, their nature.

Would not access to his mother be included among them? From Amélie's perspective, the core issue centers on power dynamics rather than legal rights:

> They [the child welfare system] constitute an overwhelming institutional force, while I remain virtually powerless. Strategic approach is imperative. Direct opposition is untenable. Potential retaliation must be calculated. They possess comprehensive advantages: legal resources, financial capacity, everything. This reality manifested during six months of enforced separation. However, confronted with identical circumstances, I would likely respond identically. The same approach would be justified, as such power abuse requires resistance.

The Genesis and General Direction of this Work

During my mid-twenties, concurrent with physical health issues including severe anemia and joint pain, I encountered periods of acute depression and suicidal ideation. Following referral to a psychiatrist by my family physician, I received sequential diagnoses of premenstrual syndrome, bipolar disorder, and schizoaffective disorder. Like Amélie, I underwent trials of multiple medications, each producing increasingly troublesome adverse effects: sedation, cognitive impairment, severe headaches. And like Amélie, my psychiatrist cautioned that medication discontinuation would precipitate severe depression risk; I had to accept that I would need to take medication for the remainder of my life. Contrary to Amélie's situation, however, I received psychiatric care in an office-based setting rather than in a hospital environment; my psychiatrist had specifically advised me never to present to the hospital, even in urgent circumstances, to avoid both the trauma I would inevitably experience there and the creation of psychiatric records that could be accessed during future medical consultations for physical health issues. He had underscored the imperative to conceal psychiatric diagnoses in both workplace and healthcare settings to mitigate stigmatization.

Despite these warnings, I ceased taking the medication due to adverse effects that impeded my ability to study and maintain presence with my children. Following years of diagnostic wandering (Zingone et al., 2021) and one year before I met Amélie, I had been diagnosed with celiac disease, an autoimmune gluten-triggered condition affecting digestive function and preventing nutritional absorption. Within weeks of gluten elimination, my depressive ideation and mood disturbances resolved completely without recurrence. This experience appears commonplace (Ciacco et al., 2024a), as psychiatrists represent the most frequently consulted specialists during celiac diagnostic processes, reflecting nutrient deficiency consequences and gluten protein blood infiltration (Ciacco et al., 2024b; Clappison et al., 2020).

This experience transpired during the final stages of my doctoral research on judicial procedures governing involuntary commitment and involuntary treatment, precipitating numerous theoretical and personal questions. My research had brought me into contact with women who had undergone involuntary commitment and who reported difficulties maintaining custody of their children due to child welfare services involvement (Hammond et al., 2017; O'Donnell et al., 2015). Some articulated their need for support, describing feelings of depression, isolation, and being overwhelmed. Others, by contrast, condemned this intrusion into their family lives, asserting they required no assistance. I understood that maintaining presence could be challenging when experiencing depressive ideation. Nevertheless, my personal trajectory—receiving multiple psychiatric diagnoses over several years and experiencing debilitating medication adverse effects, only to find rapid resolution through a physical illness diagnosis—compelled me to consider that my experience was likely not unique. I was certainly not the only person for whom the underlying issues were simultaneously more complex and more straightforward than pharmaceutical intervention.

Moreover, my family physician and psychiatrist demonstrated complete indifference toward this situation. As though sequential diagnostic assignment and withdrawal, alongside threatening predictions regarding medication cessation, represented routine, ordinary, habitual practice. As if these circumstances were inescapable, providing no learning opportunities to shield future persons in crisis from diagnostic inaccuracies and, especially, from unnecessary and burdensome treatments.

For me, this experience challenged and continues to profoundly challenge the utilization of psychiatric coercion. The disparity between the casualness with which diagnoses are assigned, altered, and rescinded stands in stark contrast to the gravity of the authority that underpins coercive practices. Coercion represents substantial power that cannot be wielded carelessly within contexts of uncertainty or indifference. It demands serious consideration and must be acknowledged for what it fundamentally represents: the exercise of institutional power.

The open discussion of institutional power becomes these days increasingly crucial, as psychiatric coercion is typically normalized through multiple ways and contexts. This realization struck me years ago as a law student. Legal training marginalizes involuntary commitment and treatment, relegating these to footnote status—as if they represented merely routine departures from healthcare consent requirements. It glosses over criminal non-responsibility and trial fitness questions while largely ignoring post-verdict consequences (Johnston & Sheldon, 2024). Rights considerations within these extraordinary legal circumstances receive scant attention. The coercive dimension is generally obscured by a legal fiction wherein liberty deprivation arising from administrative or civil decisions is considered merely collaterally coercive, absent punitive purpose.

It bears noting that mental health law lacks the prestige that would attract substantial student or practitioner interest. This phenomenon extends beyond mental health to encompass housing law, social assistance, and child welfare, for example—areas that receive similarly limited attention and minimal curricular coverage (Hornstein, 2008). This systematic marginalization of law serving marginalized groups, combined with the normalization of coercive mechanisms within legal training, creates a fundamental contradiction with the proclaimed emphasis on mental health rights. This raises critical questions about how legal progress can be achieved, when so few legal professionals are motivated to engage seriously with these issues.

This limited interest among legal practitioners is compounded by the political context. Over recent years, involuntary mental health and addiction treatments are increasingly promoted as solutions to growing homelessness in North American cities (Conservative Party of Canada, 2025; White House, 2025; Bernheim, 2024a). Given the proliferation of encampments and the inadequacy of existing services and shelter capacity, involuntary treatments are positioned as responses to public safety concerns and criminal activity, despite the absence of supporting scientific evidence. Multiple jurisdictions have enacted legislation or adopted policies reflecting this approach, with some explicitly targeting homeless populations (*Community Assistance, Recovery and Empowerment (CARE) Court Program Act*; New York State, 2025). While framed as compassionate and protective measures, the coercive nature of involuntary treatments is typically obscured or ignored (Kisely et al., 2024).

The suppression of coercive dimensions within legal and political narratives concerning involuntary admission, involuntary treatments, detentions, seclusion, and restraints is rendered feasible through the deliberate marginalization of those who undergo these experiences. Authority over narrative construction is customarily assigned to mental health and public safety professionals. This dynamic produces the familiar pattern whereby psychiatrists and police officers routinely discuss mental health and coercive practices without incorporating the perspectives of individuals who possess lived experience of such interventions. This imposed exclusion privileges psychiatric, legal, and law enforcement narratives over other perspectives on psychiatric coercion (Legghio, 2012; Foucault, 2006). The relations of power that authorize and sustain coercion are manifest in public discourse, mirroring coercion's central issue: determining who possesses speaking authority versus those compelled to silence, who holds knowledge versus those kept ignorant, and ultimately who exercises authority over whom and on what grounds (Adler-Bolton & Vierkant, 2022). This is what Amélie evoked when she spoke of "institutional force."

This book advances a critical analysis of how law, rights, and courts operate in psychiatric coercion contexts. Through empirical research conducted across various judicial mental health courtrooms, it reveals that therapeutic justice functions as one among several relays in an increasingly surveillant and coercive institutional continuum. The analysis contextualizes judicial practices within neoliberal political structures, illuminating the violence embedded within therapeutic apparatuses. It concludes that coercion in all its forms—psychiatric and beyond—represents purely a manifestation of power and should be analyzed as such.

I argue that legal systems, rights frameworks, and judicial institutions function as active contributors to coercive practices targeting marginalized communities (Rose, 1985). Rather than safeguarding against institutional violence, these systems currently facilitate serial judicialization of individuals increasingly marginalized through inequality-generating policies and deepening social crises. These institutions have additionally enabled coercive apparatus expansion beyond traditional involuntary commitment and detention, extending psychiatric control from institutional walls into community settings and intimate domestic spaces (Bernheim, 2024b). Today, coercion assumes increasingly covert manifestations, permitting hospitalization, medication, and monitoring within residential, shelter, and street environments. Judicial implementation mechanisms have correspondingly expanded, spanning from criminal diversion programs through civil diversion schemes to administrative tribunal systems. Rooted in therapeutic jurisprudence ideology, these judicial devices increasingly brand themselves as "compassionate" measures, masquerading as "consensual" while extracting agreement through involuntary commitment or detention threats. Although rights frameworks often represent individuals' primary, and often sole, defensive resources against coercive practices, they demonstrably fail to contain the current coercive expansion. Rising psychiatric coercion rates across global North jurisdictions provide unambiguous evidence of this failure (Kisely et al., 2024; Schölin et al., 2024; Wipond, 2023; Bernheim, 2022; Lee & Cohen, 2020; Rains et al., 2019; Light, 2019; Lebenbaum et al., 2018).

Such developments appear predictable when contextualized within prevailing political conditions. Across four decades of neoliberal ideological dominance (Harvey, 2005; Klein, 2007), free-market ideology has penetrated increasingly diverse spheres, encompassing healthcare services, education, and housing sectors (Schram, 2018; Davies, 2018;

Gilbert, 2013; Samson, 1994). In mental health, rights and justice markets have supplanted the aspirations advanced by civil rights defenders and psychiatric survivor liberation movements.

The argument presented here may appear counterintuitive, perhaps even disconcerting. Mental health rights represent hard-won victories achieved through sustained advocacy. The judicialization of coercive measures has been pursued through decades of reform efforts (Milner, 1986; Rose, 1985). Legal diversification strategies have sought to establish less restrictive forms of oversight that operate beyond traditional institutionalization and liberty deprivation. Therapeutic jurisprudence has attempted to enhance the outcomes of judicial processes (Wexler 2021, 2008, 1992, 1990). Contemporary evidence suggests not merely increased utilization of coercive practices and diminished mental health rights protections (Steele, 2020; Nolan, 2020; Doll, 2016; Case, 2016), but a broader pattern of expanding coercion alongside general rights erosion (Bernheim, 2025; Rossero, 2023; Series, 2022).

My proposal advocates neither regression nor maintenance of the status quo. It is necessary, I argue, to confront the limits of rights in a context of political instrumentalization, where rights lie at the heart of neoliberal ideology and culture (Samson, 2020; Moyn, 2014). I suggest that meaningful solutions must be pursued beyond legal paradigms, commencing with a critical rethinking of psychiatric coercion.

Rethinking Psychiatric Coercion: Structure of the Book

The book is structured in four parts.

The first part, comprising Chapters 2 and 3, lays out the theoretical framework that informs the entire book—namely, neoliberal thought as it relates to mental health, and the concept of therapeutic justice.

Rethinking psychiatric coercion must necessarily interrogate mental health itself. Contemporary scientific literature exhibits a pronounced dichotomy between a dominant paradigm asserting an unprecedented mental health crisis (Patel et al., 2023; Czulada et al., 2022; World Health Organization, 2016; Mnookin, 2016), and an alternative perspective that conceptualizes mental health as an instrument of colonial and epistemic domination (Malott et al., 2023; Adler-Bolton & Vierkant, 2022). Chapter 2 situates this opposition within neoliberal political frameworks, demonstrating that these ostensibly contradictory currents represent dual manifestations of a unified phenomenon. Regardless of whether social problems and inequalities undergo psychiatrization, diagnostic rates and psychiatric medication consumption continue to escalate, confirming the empirical presence of "crisis" indicators. These phenomena, however, emerge from an ideological framework positioning individuals as accountable for their wellness and personal achievement, thereby rendering them responsible for their own recovery (Cohen, 2025; Johansson & Holmes, 2024). More fundamentally, they constitute outcomes of policies characterized by neglect and structural abandonment of specific social groups, whose mental health status is instrumentalized to rationalize precarious economic circumstances. Consequently, deinstitutionalization initiatives spanning 1960–2000 are purported to account for contemporary homelessness rates (Winkler et al., 2016), while the statistic that 80% of individuals with mental illness reside in low- and middle-income countries (World Health Organization, 2008) circumvents structural analyses of colonial and neoliberal policy ramifications. Concerning psychiatric coercion, historical examination reveals its primary function as serving political objectives in population management of impoverished, racialized, and colonized communities (Studer, 2015; Fernando, 2014; Keller, 2001; Foucault, 1989; Fanon, 1986, 1963). The implementation criterion for psychiatric coercion—namely risk—has persisted generally unaltered since initial involuntary commitment legislation, with research demonstrating disproportionate representation of racialized, Indigenous, immigrant, and socioeconomically disadvantaged populations among targeted individuals (Moloney et al., 2022; Salam et al., 2022; Barnett et al., 2019), as well as extensive scientific controversies surround psychiatric practice (Paris, 2023)—particularly coercive interventions (Corderoy et al., 2024; Kisely et al., 2024; Iudici et al., 2022). Rights frameworks and judicialization processes are typically conceptualized as legitimate instruments for dignity preservation and abuse prevention.

Mental health rights recognition emerged primarily through judicial determinations that convicting accused individuals with mental health conditions or addictions constituted cruel and unusual punishment in the case *Robinson v. California* in 1962. While this case law facilitated critical examination of detention practices, it simultaneously legitimized the notion that involuntary hospitalization may not violate rights when pursued for therapeutic purposes. Courts could thereby assume functions beyond traditional adjudication and punishment, specifically that of therapeutic facilitation. Chapter 3 traces the evolution of therapeutic jurisprudence theory (Wexler 2021, 2008, 1992, 1990) and its operationalization through diversion programs (Steele, 2020; Nolan, 2020). It reveals the alignment between its foundational principles and neoliberal ideology (Nolan, 2003), particularly the conviction that social problems are due to individuals and can be resolved through responsibility and empowerment (Winick, 2003, 1997; Wexler, 1992). Therapeutic justice fundamentally transforms legal frameworks and judicial roles by incorporating them into therapeutic processes. Research consequently documents systematic rights violations across diverse mental health judicial settings spanning decades (Rusch & Banner, 2024; Collins, 2023, 2020; Steele, 2020). While criminal courts receive greater scholarly attention, therapeutic civil and administrative courts remain comparatively underexamined. Despite often incomplete data, studies increasingly demonstrate their emergence as control institutions within a "shadow carceral state" (Beckett & Murakawa, 2012).

The analytical frameworks of neoliberalism and the shadow carceral state, developed across the following two chapters, function as the conceptual organizing principles for the entire book. These frameworks support a reconceptualization of psychiatric coercion as both a political phenomenon and a control apparatus embedded within a broader continuum of interventions. They serve more precisely to interrogate judicial practices surrounding mental health coercion, revealing the underlying continuities with psychiatric paradigmatic structures and forms of institutional violence.

The second part, Chapter 4, details the ethnographic research I conducted in four mental health courtrooms in Tiohtià:ke (Montreal),

Canada. During the past fifteen years, I have undertaken multiple judicial ethnographies within civil and administrative courts adjudicating psychiatric coercion matters, specifically involuntary commitment, involuntary treatment, child welfare interventions, and the monitoring of individuals found not criminally responsible due to mental disorder or unfit to stand trial. I characterize these courtrooms as "mental health courtrooms" in contrast to "mental health courts," given that the courts I investigated possess additional jurisdictional powers, with mental health adjudication constituting one dimension of their broader mission. These ethnographic studies are connected through the involvement of the same defendants across various judicial processes. These research environments have provided extensive encounters with defendants, judges, attorneys, and psychiatrists. The cross-sectional analysis of the observational and interview data illuminates shared patterns concerning hearing procedures and content, judicial risk assessment approaches, and perhaps most significantly, the notable absence of law and rights in courtroom conversations. Consequently, despite substantially different procedural frameworks, hearings demonstrate striking similarities, particularly because the defendants appearing before them represent consistent demographics.

The third part, consisting of Chapters 5 and 6, offers a description of courtroom quotidian practices through extensive utilization of observational fieldnotes. These chapters attempt to concretize hearing proceedings, including their articulated and implicit dimensions, dramatic moments and silences, alongside perspectives of defendants, psychiatrists, judges, and attorneys. They illuminate risk management both as discursively constructed and practically implemented. They demonstrate how defendants' invocation of rights within courtroom settings is interpreted as evidencing mental illness denial, aggressiveness, and non-cooperation. Chapter 5 examines defendants' everyday experiences as scrutinized minutely during proceedings. It exposes the operationalization of social class adjudication, wherein defendants' precarity is conceptualized as lifestyle choices requiring justification, while social code differences are interpreted as incapacity or abnormality indicators. Chapter 6 employs intersectional analysis to detail poverty, gender, race, and ethnicity treatment within mental health courtrooms. It reveals extreme precarity situations that, while constituting sufficient risk to justify psychiatric coercion in judicial perspectives, remain unresolved post-hearing while defendants experience impoverishment through judicial processes. It illuminates gendered differential treatment wherein men are constructed as violent subjects requiring protective measures while women are positioned as fragile subjects requiring protection. Mothers receive specialized treatment as failure to embody expected loving, available, and protective roles renders them suspect of exposing children to partner violence or personal deviance. They experience the most intensive and intimate surveillance. Race amplifies masculine tendencies, with racialized men, particularly those from specific ethnicities or religious practices, typically perceived as more threatening by courts. For women, patterns appear reversed. While white women, predominant in observed mental health courtrooms, are characterized as fragile and vulnerable, racialized women are alternatively described as more aggressive, demonstrating inadequate parenting techniques indicating limited child dedication and endangerment. Similar to rights discourse, defendants' discrimination or profiling assertions are interpreted as paranoia or manipulation. These chapters demonstrate how judicial class, gender, and race blindness contributes to mental health courtrooms functioning as sites extending and amplifying power relationships.

The fourth part, composed of Chapters 7 and 8, advances deeper and less descriptive analyses of mental health courtrooms, with power relationships as a foundational analytical thread. Chapter 7 investigates ostensibly "therapeutic" practices within mental health courtrooms, revealing judicial actors' alignment with the psychiatric paradigm. Judges consequently maintain expectations of defendants that frequently transcend procedural objectives and jurisdictional authority. Treatment acceptance and adherence, particularly regarding medication compliance, are typically deemed indispensable, with adherence authenticity subjected to intensive judicial scrutiny. Despite defendants typically possessing exclusive experiential knowledge of psychiatric medication within courtroom contexts, their reasoning is systematically dismissed as inconsequential or disregarded entirely. Their requests for alternative treatment modalities, predominantly psychotherapy, are similarly ignored—defendants generally lacking private insurance coverage, they possess limited access beyond pharmacological interventions. Consequently, despite defendants' lived experiences and extensively documented adverse effects, diverse strategies are implemented to compel defendants to relinquish their consent rights—and refusal rights—regarding medication. The strategies employed by judicial actors—threat, undue pressure, paternalism, and confusion—mirror informal coercive practices documented within psychiatric institutional settings. Through mental health and therapeutic narratives, judicial processes normalize and conceal coercion. Coercion experienced by defendants within hospital environments is deemed necessary or justified based on mental health problem severity, risk assessment, or defendant incapacity, or alternatively because they purportedly merited such treatment. Conversely, under helping relationship pretenses, judicial process coercion itself is negated. Defendants are consequently conceptualized primarily as patients or individuals requiring assistance rather than parties within judicial proceedings.

Chapter 8 examines judicial violence, revealing a dichotomy between legal practitioners who regard mental health practice as distinctive specialized work and those who conceptualize it as conventional legal practice. The chapter discusses how judicialization of mental health coercive decisions has generated a mental health justice market, fostering judicial and legal specialization. Challenging practice conditions and defense-unfavorable hearing dynamics create differential attorney attraction and retention patterns. Research findings indicate that lawyers committed to advocating for client rights and following client instructions are typically perceived as failing to comprehend mental health courtroom defense practice specificities and are regarded as problematic by colleagues and judges. Alternatively, other lawyers characterize their roles as "hybrid" between legal and clinical functions. These practitioners typically advance minimal legal argumentation during proceedings, occasionally expressing opinions contradicting defendant preferences. Observational and interview data document multiple private attorney practices violating professional ethics, including courthouse hallway solicitation, strategic client acquisition, conflicts of interest, and illegal fee arrangements. These practices are not only frequently recognized by legal and judicial colleagues but have increased corresponding to recent judicial caseload expansion. Observational analysis suggests defendants benefit more from unrepresented appearances than representation by inadequately prepared lawyers or those advancing counter-preferential arguments, as judges demonstrate greater engagement with unrepresented defendants. Nevertheless, defendant arguments typically prove ineffective due to multiple judicial practices. Defendants must initially position themselves regarding their mental health conditions during testimony. Admission generally prompts judicial actors to encourage cooperation through best-interest arguments, while denial tends to trigger confrontational responses utilizing threats and pressure to secure cooperation and treatment acceptance. Additionally, elastic interpretations of substantive and procedural legal frameworks by numerous judges frequently contravene defense rights. Defendants experience judicial proceedings as generating powerlessness and predetermined outcome perceptions.

It is evident from my research that mental health courtroom procedures constitute merely one dimension of defendants' coercive and monitoring experiences. Multiple defendants have undergone serial judicialization processes, occasionally commencing in childhood. Some encounter repeated and deliberate judicial procedures initiated by their psychiatrists within different mental health courtrooms. Others confront judicial systems across multiple life domains: housing, family relationships, social benefits, immigration status, or healthcare access. Additional defendants have navigated criminal justice systems, frequently through specialized diversion programs addressing mental health, homelessness, substance dependency, or related issues. Those with child welfare system involvement may have appeared before courts repeatedly across decades. While subjected to continuous institutional monitoring by the courts and a network of organizations, many of which operate within community settings such as shelters and community groups, defendants describe feelings of systemic abandonment.

Drawing upon Michel Foucault's (2008) protective continuum concept, this analysis illuminates the fundamentally political dimension inherent in coercive practices. The book concludes with the proposal to frame coercion as a violent population management system targeting marginalized populations through a child welfare-psychiatry-prison pipeline. The ongoing coercive experiences that defendants navigate across multiple justice systems, and through an expanding array of institutions, indeed relativize any presumed specificity of psychiatric coercion.

This repoliticization of the conversation on coercion would allow circumventing the deficiencies of "reformist reforms" through which the status quo has been sustained over recent decades (Ben-Moshe, 2020) and which now supports its recrudescence. It also facilitates including power relationships within the analytical equation (Adler-Bolton & Vierkant, 2022)—a factor central to coercive practices and pivotal to mental health courtroom proceedings.

The power relations issue also interrogates research conducted frequently within disciplinary silos, circumventing economic and political analyses while failing to consider its own social and political implications. Research thereby contributes to psychiatrization and judicialization of social problems without revealing how policies of abandonment and structural neglect generate social crises or perpetuating an enchanted belief in rights and the judiciary, something this book seeks to correct.

References

Adler-Bolton, B., & Vierkant, A. (2022). *Health communism.* Verso Books.

Barnett, P., et al. (2019). Ethnic variations in compulsory detention under the mental health act: A systematic review and meta-analysis of international data. *The Lancet, 6*(4), 305–317. https://doi.org/10.1016/S2215-0366(19)30027-6

Beckett, K., & Murakawa, N. (2012). Mapping the shadow carceral state: Toward an institutionally capacious approach to punishment. *Theoretical Criminology, 16*(2), 221–244. https://doi.org/10.1177/1362480612442113

Ben-Moshe, L. (2020). *Decarcerating disability: Deinstitutionalization and prison abolition.* University of Minnesota Press.

Bernheim, E. (2022). The triumph of the "therapeutic" in Quebec courts: Mental health, behavioral reform and the decline of rights. *Windsor Yearbook on Access to Justice, 38*, 125–147. https://doi.org/10.22329/wyaj.v38.7779

Bernheim, E. (2024a, November 14). Why involuntary admission and treatment won't solve homelessness. *The Conversation Canada*. https://theconversation.com/why-involuntary-medical-admission-and-treatment-wont-solve-homelessness-243428 (accessed August 10, 2025).

Bernheim, E. (2024b). Extending the boundaries of the psychiatric hospital: The use and misuse of psychiatric coercion during the Covid-19 pandemic in Quebec and Ontario. In C. Flood, Y. Y. B. Chen, R. Deonandan, S. Halabi, & S. Thériault (Eds.), *Borders, boundaries and pandemics* (pp. 273–280). Routledge. https://doi.org/10.4324/9781003394006

Bernheim, E. (2025). Rights against abolition: How law and rights perpetuate psychiatric coercion. *Social Science and Medicine, 384*, 118509. https://doi.org/10.1016/j.socscimed.2025.118509

Case, P. (2016). Dangerous liaisons? Psychiatry and law in the court of protection—Expert discourses of "insight" (and "compliance"). *Medical Law Review, 24*(3), 360–378. https://doi.org/10.1093/medlaw/fww027

Ciaccio, E. J., Lee, A. R., Lebovits, J., Wolf, R. L., & Lewis, S. K. (2024). Physical and psychological symptoms and survey importance in celiac disease. *World Journal of Gastrointestinal Endoscopy, 16*(12), 632–639. https://doi.org/10.4253/wjge.v16.i12.632

Ciaccio, E. J., Lee, A. R., Lebovits, J., Wolf, R. L., Lewis, S. K., Ciacci, C., & Green, P. H. (2024). Psychological, psychiatric, and organic brain manifestations of celiac disease. *Digestive Diseases, 42*(5), 419–444. https://doi.org/10.1159/000534219

Clappison, E., Hadjivassiliou, M., & Zis, P. (2020). Psychiatric manifestations of coeliac disease, a systematic review and meta-analysis. *Nutrients, 12*(1), 142. https://doi.org/10.3390/nu12010142

Cohen, C. I. (2025). Neorecovery: A critical analysis of the relationship between neoliberalism and the recovery movement. *Community Mental Health Journal, 61*(2), 248–253. https://doi.org/10.1007/s10597-024-01275-6

Collins, E. (2023). Problem-solving courts and the outcome oversight gap. *University of Missouri-Kansas City Law Review, 92*, 533–554.

Collins, E. R. (2020). The problem of problem-solving courts. *University of California Davis Law Review, 54*, 1573–1630.

Community Assistance, Recovery and Empowerment Court Program Act, SB 1388.

Conservative Party of Canada. (2025). *Polievre Promises "Compassionate Intervention. To Help People Struggling with Severe Addiction.* https://www.conservative.ca/poilievre-promises-compassionate-intervention-to-help-people-struggling-with-severe-addiction/ (accessed August 10, 2025).

Corderoy, A., Kisely, S., Zirnsak, T., & Ryan, C. J. (2024). The benefits and harms of inpatient involuntary psychiatric treatment: A scoping review. *Psychiatry, Psychology and Law, 1–48.* https://doi.org/10.1080/13218719.2024.2346734

Czulada, L., Kover, K. M., Gracias, G., Kumar, K.-N., Desai, S., Stawicki, S. P., Costello, K. & Erickson-Parsons, L. (2022). Toxic stress affecting families and children during the COVID-19 pandemic: A global mental health crisis and an emerging international health security threat. In Stawicki, S. P., Izurieta, R. Firstenberg, M. S. & Galwankar, S. C. (Eds.), Vol. 3, *Contemporary Developments and Perspectives in International Health Security.* IntechOpen. https://doi:10.5772/intechopen.104991

Davies, W. (2018) The Neoliberal State: Power Against "Politics." In Cahill, D., Cooper, M., Konings, M. & Primrose, D. (Eds.), The SAGE handbook of neoliberalism (pp. 273–288). Sage. doi:https://doi.org/10.4135/9781526416001.

Doll, A. (2016). Lawyering for the "mad": Social organization and legal representation for involuntary-admission cases in Poland. In Burstow, B. (Ed.), *Psychiatry Interrogated: An Institutional Ethnography Anthology* (183–202). doi:https://doi.org/10.1007/978-3-319-41174-3_10.

Fanon, F. (1963). *The wretched of the earth.* Grove Weidenfeld.

Fanon, F. (1986). *Black skin, white masks* (first published in 1952). Pluto Press.

Forman, M. (1975). *One Flew Over the Cuckoo's Nest.* Fantasy Films.

Foucault, M. (1989). *Madness in Civilization: A History of Insanity in the Age of Reason.* Routledge.

Foucault, M. (2006). *Psychiatric Power: Lectures at the Collège de France, 1973–1974.* Picador.

Foucault, M. (2008). *The birth of biopolitics: Lectures at the Collège de France, 1978–1979.* Palgrave Macmillan.

Gilbert, J. (2013). What kind of thing is "neoliberalism"? *New Formations, 80*(80), 7–22. https://doi.org/10.3898/nEWF.80/81.IntroductIon.2013

Hammond, I., Eastman, A. L., Leventhal, J. M., & Putnam-Hornstein, E. (2017). Maternal mental health disorders and reports to child protective services: A birth cohort study. *International Journal of Environmental Research and Public Health, 14*(11), 1320. https://doi.org/10.3390/ijerph14111320

Harvey, D. (2005). A brief history of neoliberalism. Oxford University Press. doi:https://doi.org/10.1093/oso/9780199283262.001.0001.
Hornstein, R. (2008). Teaching law students to comfort the troubled and trouble the comfortable: An essay on the place of poverty law in the law school curriculum. *Wm. Mitchell L. Rev., 35*, 1057–1083.
Iudici, A., Girolimetto, R., Bacioccola, E., Faccio, E., & Turchi, G. (2022). Implications of involuntary psychiatric admission: Health, social, and clinical effects on patients. *The Journal of Nervous and Mental Disease, 210*(4), 290–311. https://doi.org/10.1097/NMD.0000000000001448
Johansson, J. A., & Holmes, D. (2024). "Recovery" in mental health services, now and then: A poststructuralist examination of the despotic state machine's effects. *Nursing Inquiry, 31*(1), e12558. https://doi.org/10.1111/nin.12558
Johnston, L., & Sheldon, T. (2024). " is mental health law a thing?": Why law schools should invest in teaching mental health law. *Windsor Rev. Legal & Soc. Issues, 44*, 1–8.
Keller, R. (2001). Madness and colonization: Psychiatry in the British and French empires, 1800-1962. *Journal of Social History, 35*(2), 295–326.
Kisely, S., Bull, C., & Gill, N. (2024). Extending the reach of involuntary treatment to substance use disorders: Is it "compassionate" or coercive care? *Australian & New Zealand Journal of Psychiatry, 58*(12), 1017–1019. https://doi.org/10.1177/00048674241299215
Kisely, S., Zirnsak, T., Maylea, C., Bull, C., & Brophy, L. (2024). Latest findings highlight the continuing uncertainty over the utility of compulsory psychiatric treatment in the community. *BJPsych Open, 10*(5), e133. https://doi.org/10.1192/bjo.2024.718
Klein, N. (2007). *The Shock Doctrine*. Penguin Random House.
Lebenbaum, M., Chiu, M., Vigod, S., & Kurdyak, P. (2018). Prevalence and predictors of involuntary psychiatric hospital admissions in Ontario, Canada: A population-based linked administrative database study. *British Journal of Psychiatry Open, 4*(2), 31–38. https://doi:10.1192/bjo.2017.4
Lee, G., & David Cohen, D. (2020). Incidences of involuntary psychiatric detentions in 25 U.S. *States. Psychiatric Services, 72*(1), 61–68. https://doi.org/10.1176/appi.ps.201900477
Leggio, M. (2012). A denial of being: Psychiatrization as epistemic violence. In B. A. LeFrançois, R. Menzies, & G. Reaume (Eds.), *Mad matters: A critical reader in Canadian mad studies* (pp. 122–129). Canadian Scholars.

Light, E. (2019). Rates of use of community treatment orders in Australia. International Journal of Law and Psychiatry, 64, 83–87. doi:https://doi.org/10.1016/j.ijlp.2019.02.006.

Malott, K. M., Barraclough, S., & Yee, T. (2023). Towards decolonizing diagnosis: A critical review and suggested alternatives. *International Journal for the Advancement of Counselling, 45*(1), 1–17. https://doi.org/10.1007/s10447-022-09501-0

Milner, N. (1986). The dilemmas of legal mobilization: Ideologies and strategies of mental patient liberation groups. *Law & Policy, 8*(1), 105–129. https://doi.org/10.1111/j.1467-9930.1986.tb00372.x

Mnookin, S. (2016, April 1st) *Out of the shadows: making mental health a global development priority.* Report 105052. World Bank Group. http://documents.worldbank.org/curated/en/270131468187759113 (accessed August 9, 2025).

Moloney, N., et al. (2022). Homelessness amongst psychiatric in-patients: A cross-sectional study in the mid-west of Ireland. *Irish Journal of Medical Science, 191*(1), 321–326. https://doi.org/10.1007/s11845-021-02546-x

Moyn, S. (2014). A powerless companion: Human rights in the age of neoliberalism. *Law and Contemporary Problems, 77*(4), 147–169. https://www.jstor.org/stable/24244651

New York State. (2025, May 9). *Governor Hochul Signs Legislation to Improve Mental Health Care and Strengthen Treatment for Serious Mental Illness as Part of FY 2026 Budget.* https://www.governor.ny.gov/news/governor-hochul-signs-legislation-improve-mental-health-care-and-strengthen-treatment-serious (accessed August 10, 2025).

Nolan, J. L., Jr. (2003). Redefining criminal courts: Problem-solving and the meaning of justice. *American Criminal Law Review, 40*(4), 1541–1566.

Nolan, J. L., Jr. (2020). The cultural constraints of legal transplantation a ten-year retrospective. *Cardozo Journal of Conflict Resolution, 21,* 641–662.

O'Donnell, M., Maclean, M. J., Sims, S., Morgan, V. A., Leonard, H., & Stanley, F. J. (2015). Maternal mental health and risk of child protection involvement: Mental health diagnoses associated with increased risk. *Journal of Epidemiology & Community Health, 69*(12), 1175–1183. https://doi.org/10.1136/jech-2014-205240

Paris, J. (2023). *Fads and Fallacies in Psychiatry.* Cambridge University Press.

Patel, V., Saxena, S., Lund, C., Kohrt, B., Kieling, C., Sunkel, C., et al. (2023). Transforming mental health systems globally: Principles and policy recommendations. *The Lancet, 402*(10402), 656–666. https://doi.org/10.1016/S0140-6736(23)00918-2

Rains, L. S., & al. (2019). Variations in patterns of involuntary hospitalisation and in legal frameworks: An international comparative study. *The Lancet, 6*(5), 403–417. https://doi.org/10.1016/S2215-0366(19)30090-2
Robinson v. *California*, 370 U.S. 660 (1962).
Rose, N. (1985). Unreasonable rights: Mental illness and the limits of the law. *Journal of Law & Society, 12*, 199–218. https://doi.org/10.2307/1409967
Rossero, E. (2023). Care in a Time of crisis. In *An ethnography of coercive practices in Italian acute mental health provision*. Palgrave Macmillan. https://doi.org/10.1007/978-3-031-34418-3
Rusch, L., & Banner, F. (2024). Homeless group representation in Detroit's problem-solving court. *Law & Social Inquiry, 49*(1), 278–307. https://doi.org/10.1017/lsi.2022.68
Salam, Z., Odenigbo, O., Newbold, B., Wahoush, O., & Schwartz, L. (2022). Systemic and individual factors that shape mental health service usage among visible minority immigrants and refugees in Canada: A scoping review. *Administration and Policy in Mental Health and Mental Health Services Research, 49*(4), 552–574. https://doi.org/10.1007/s10488-021-01183-x
Samson, C. (1994). The three faces of privatisation. *Sociology, 28*(1), 79–97. https://doi.org/10.1177/0038038594028001006
Samson, C. (2020). *The colonialism of human rights: Ongoing hypocrisies of western liberalism.* Wiley.
Schölin, L., Borschmann, R., & Chopra, A. (2024). Temporal patterns and individual characteristics of compulsory treatment orders for mental disorders in Scotland from 2007 to 2020. BJPsych Open, 10(6), e204. doi:https://doi.org/10.1192/bjo.2024.751.
Schram, S. F. (2018). Neoliberalizing the welfare state: Marketizing social policy/disciplining clients. In D. Cahill, M. Cooper, M. Konings, & D. Primrose (Eds.), *The SAGE handbook of neoliberalism* (pp. 308–322). Sage. https://doi.org/10.4135/9781526416001
Series, L. (2022). *Deprivation of Liberty in the Shadows of the Institution.* Bristol University Press.
Steele, L. (2020). *Disability, Criminal Justice and Law: reconsidering court diversion.* Routledge.
Studer, N. S. (2015). The hidden patients: North African women in French colonial psychiatry. Böhlau. doi:https://doi.org/10.7788/9783412502874.
Wexler, D. (1990). *Therapeutic Jurisprudence: The Law as a Therapeutic Agent.* Carolina Academic Press.

Wexler, D. B. (1992). Justice, mental health, and therapeutic jurisprudence. *Cleveland State Law Review, 40*(3), 517–526.
Wexler, D. B. (2008). Two decades of therapeutic jurisprudence. *Touro Law Review, 24*, 17–30.
Wexler, D. B. (2021). Creating a therapeutic justice culture. *SAL Prac, 20.*
White House. (2025, July 24). *Ending crime and Disorder on America's Streets*. Executive Orders. https://www.whitehouse.gov/presidential-actions/2025/07/ending-crime-and-disorder-on-americas-streets/ (accessed August 9, 2025).
Winick, B. J. (1997). The jurisprudence of therapeutic jurisprudence. *Psychology, Public Policy and Law, 3*(1), 184–206. https://psycnet.apa.org/doi/10.1037/1076-8971.3.1.184
Winick, B. J. (2003). Problem solving courts: Therapeutic jurisprudence in practice. *Fordham Law Review, 30*(3), 1055–1103. https://ir.lawnet.fordham.edu/ulj/vol30/iss3/14
Winkler, P., Barrett, B., McCrone, P., Csémy, L., Janouskova, M., & Höschl, C. (2016). Deinstitutionalised patients, homelessness and imprisonment: Systematic review. *The British Journal of Psychiatry, 208*(5), 421–428. https://doi.org/10.1192/bjp.bp.114.161943
Wipond, R. (2023). *Your consent is not required: The rise in psychiatric detentions, forced treatment, and abusive guardianships*. BenBella.
World Health Organization. (2008). The global burden of disease: 2004 update. *Report*.
World Health Organization (2016, April 13). *Out of the shadows: making mental health a global priority.* Speech transcription. https://www.who.int/director-general/speeches/detail/out-of-the-shadows-making-mental-health-a-global-priority (accessed August 9, 2025).
Zingone, F., Secchettin, E., Marsilio, I., Valiante, F., Zorzetto, V., Cataudella, G., D'Odorico, A., & Canova, C. (2021). Clinical features and psychological impact of celiac disease at diagnosis. *Digestive and Liver Disease, 53*, 1565–1570. https://doi.org/10.1016/j.dld.2021.05.016

2

The "Mental Health Crisis," a Political Issue

> In the days of the insane asylum, the nature of psychiatry was clear: the madhouse was a snake pit and snake pits could be found only in insane asylums. Today, the nature of psychiatry is unclear: "snake pits" are everywhere, from the kindergarten to the hospice.—Thomas Szasz, 2007: 11–12

Mental health is everywhere.[1] In political media and social discourse; in workplaces, schools, and universities; in families and neighborhoods—everyone talks about mental health and has an opinion about it. Mental health is a "state of well-being" (WHO, 2001) and a human right (WHO, 2024), but also an individual responsibility, a burden—and, today, a "crisis."

The increasingly common use of the term "mental health," in society as well as in scientific context, is a relatively new development and a

[1] In reference to Otto F. Wahl in the first chapter of the *Book Media Madness: Public Images of Mental Illness*, "Madness, Madness Everywhere."

E. Bernheim, *Therapeutic (In)justice and the Shadow Carceral State*, The Politics of Mental Health and Illness, https://doi.org/10.1007/978-3-032-16186-4_2

move away from terms such as madness[2] or mental illness. This semantic shift was intended to put an end to stigmatization and labeling (Fusar-Poli et al., 2020). It acknowledges that mental health "enables people to cope with the stresses of life, realize their abilities, learn well and work well, and contribute to their community" (WHO, 2001). Mental health thus refers to a spectrum of situations and problems ranging from personal development and burnout to psychosis and depression. The notion of mental health is as much about having a healthy home, eating a balanced diet and getting a good night's sleep as it is about psychology and psychiatry (Fusar-Poli et al., 2020).

Despite or perhaps because of its indeterminacy (Harbush, 2022), the notion of mental health has not altered the normative dimension associated with mental disorder, quite the contrary. By creating a scale of lifestyle that characterizes "good" or "normal" mental health—managing stress, learning, working, fulfilling oneself, contributing to the community—the notion defines both the goals to be achieved and the behaviors, habits, and preferences that are unhealthy. People with no mental health problems function well in society, fulfilling their potential; others have mental health issues of varying degrees of severity ranging from mental health problems to mental disorders, depending on their level of social functioning.

The concept of social functionality, at the heart of the notion of mental health, establishes a passageway between the actual "mental health crisis" and psychiatry (Harbush, 2022). By implying that not functioning in an increasingly unequal society is abnormal, the notion of mental health has encouraged the pathologization and the psychiatrization of a growing number of social issues (Beeker et al., 2021; Frances, 2013; Mills, 2015). The distress caused by poverty, job insecurity, discrimination and domination may thus appear to be a mental disorder that psychiatry can solve (Mills, 2015).

The notion of mental health also conceals the political dimension of psychiatric knowledge developed within asylums, at the expense of marginalized (Foucault, 1989, 2006; Porter, 1987) and colonized people

[2] Although it is no longer commonly used, the term "Mad" has been utilized by psychiatric patient liberation movements for several decades and by the current of research and activism Mad Studies (Starkman, 2012; Menzie et al., 2012).

(Fanon, 1986; Studer, 2016). Mental health is conceptualized as an individual issue, stripped of its intimate links with social, cultural, economic, and political structures (Parker, 1997). Psychiatry is Western-centric (Mills, 2014). Class, gender, and race biases are present and documented in psychiatric diagnoses (Ali et al., 2010; Garb, 2021; Metzl, 2009). There is a disparity in psychiatric services, particularly in terms of the treatments offered, with black, Indigenous, and recent immigrant people, as well as people living in poverty, less likely to be offered psychotherapy, and more likely to be offered medication, to seek help in emergency and to undergo coercion (Barnett et al., 2019; Eswaran et al., 2023; King, 2019; Moloney et al., 2022; Ogilvie & Kisely, 2022; Salam et al., 2022; Tran et al., 2019; Wong et al., 2019). A significantly higher proportion of women than men undergo psychiatric treatment, including antidepressants and, in the case of older women, electroconvulsive therapy (Bernheim et al., 2025; Kirk et al., 2017). An estimated 80% of people who have mental illnesses reside in low-and middle-income countries (WHO, 2008).

A Fabricated Crisis

Neoliberalism has been described as a "new colonialism" (Orelus & Chomsky, 2014), a "class-based project" (Davidson, 2018), an "economic experiment" (Beattie, 2019). It is an ideology based on competitive individualism, where acquisition and possession constitute success and justify increased political power, and systemic issues are "silenced" (Lyon-Callo, 2008). Being successful demonstrates an ability to make use of opportunities, to be "agile," and to make the right choices (Inda, 2023). According to this competitive worldview, hard-working, bright, original individuals stand out from the crowd. They deserve the power associated with their wealth, given that wealth is a testament to their exceptional character or personality. Neoliberal society "valorizes a hierarchical and highly unequal set of social relations while claiming to offer individuals from all backgrounds an equal chance to compete for elite status" (Gilbert, 2013: 11). Yet, opportunities are not equally distributed between genders, races, and social classes, with a high number of choices between attractive alternatives afforded to people from privileged backgrounds. In contrast, there are far fewer choices for those who lack economic, social, cultural, and gender capital. Within the worldview that defines the problem of inequality in terms of "character," "personality" or choices, the erasure of social classes and the privileges associated with them—both in political and public discourse as well as in academic studies—has the effect of justifying and legitimizing precariousness as a consequence of individual failure (Lawler, 2018). According to neoliberalism, inequality would generate more productivity, as the less affluent aspire to the lifestyle of the wealthy (Beattie, 2019). However, for about forty years, inequalities have increased in almost all countries, including those where social policies are most developed, which means that today's global inequalities are "close to early twentieth century levels, at the peak of Western imperialism" (Chancel et al., 2022: 11), with the value of inheritance outweighing that of work in the fortunes of the "one percent." According to the economist Thomas Picketty (2014: 22), "[n]ow as in the past, [...] inequalities of wealth exist primarily within age cohorts, and inherited wealth comes close to being as decisive at the beginning of the twenty-first century as it was in the age of Balzac's *Père Goriot*."

Because neoliberalism is "harmful to most of the population" (Orelus & Chomsky, 2014: 67), it could be imposed only through economic and political strategies. In *The Shock Doctrine* (2007), Naomi Klein explains that the neoliberal project can only be implemented in a context of crisis—real or perceived, fabricated or genuine. She shows how, since the 1980s, market manipulation, terrorism, and natural disasters have led to a succession of shock moments, during which profound changes in state structures and transnational power relationships have taken place.

> Almost all states, from those newly minted after the collapse of the Soviet Union to old-style social democracies and welfare states such as New Zealand and Sweden, have embraced, sometimes voluntarily and in other instances in response to coercive pressures, some version of neoliberal theory and adjusted at least some policies and practices accordingly. Post-apartheid South Africa quickly embraced neoliberalism, and

> even contemporary China, as we shall see, appears to be headed in this direction. Furthermore, the advocates of the neoliberal way now occupy positions of considerable influence in education (the universities and many 'think tanks'), in the media, in corporate boardrooms and financial institutions, in key state institutions (treasury departments, the central banks), and also in those international institutions such as the International Monetary Fund (IMF), the World Bank, and the World Trade Organization (WTO) that regulate global finance and trade. Neoliberalism has, in short, become hegemonic as a mode of discourse. It has pervasive effects on ways of thought to the point where it has become incorporated into the common-sense way many of us interpret, live in, and understand the world. (Harvey, 2007: 3)

Officially, neoliberalism advocates for "a minimal role for the state" (Veitch, 2016), with free market and private property being the best ways to ensure equality and with public institutions not able to intervene effectively in economic and social matters. Driven by autonomous, rational, and strategic individuals, the market would be self-regulating, and any constraint on individuals' freedom of choice would be harmful. In the neoliberal culture, the "free market" is an ideal to be achieved. It is the foundation and the condition of freedom, which shapes the actual policies and public life (Carrier, 2020). However, a reduction in the size of neoliberal states has not been observed, quite the contrary: the neoliberal state is crafted by policies and laws, not by the free market (Beattie, 2019). It is with the power of the state that the neoliberal agenda is realized, through privatization, marketization of social policies, and financialization (Davies, 2018; Gilbert, 2013; Samson, 1994), as well as through public safety and judicial institutions—police, courts, prisons—which are essential to protect property rights (Harvey, 2006). According to David Harvey (2007, 2010), the structure of the neoliberal state is designed to enable a minority to appropriate collective assets, what he calls "accumulation by dispossession." This accumulation by dispossession, and the resulting dramatic increase in inequalities, operates through a transformation of power relationships on a transnational scale. Until the 1970s, the countries of the North imposed their will on the countries of the South via colonial policies. The governments of Reagan and Thatcher initiated a change, with the dominant classes of the North and South forming alliances against the dominated classes of the North and South (Orelus & Chomsky, 2014). The role of states has been central in the development of neoliberalism through representation of the interests of the wealthy classes in international financial institutions, initiatives such as the Davos summit, support provided by Northern states for the ruling classes of the South, promotion by international agencies of international alliances based on free-market rhetoric, and other mechanisms such as international law (Navarro, 2007).

Yet, neoliberal ideology is not about convincing people that the free market works. Rather, "it is to console us that the sense of insecurity, of perpetual competition and individual isolation produced by neoliberal government is natural, because 'that's what life is really like'" (Gilbert, 2013: 15). The establishment of a system of meanings that appears natural—individualism, competitiveness, inequalities, successive crises—whose effects are accepted as legitimate imposes a way of thinking associated with fear and survival, which is fertile for the "shift to neoliberal hegemony" (Huber, 2016). This system of meanings, concealing social classes and power relationships, is the breeding ground for slow violence, described by Rory Kramer and Brianna Remster (2022: 44) who refer to Geoff Ward as "the 'more attritional, dispersed, and hidden' racial and class-based harms inflicted by the state." Structural by nature, the slow violence of discrimination, dispossession, neglect, and abandonment, accumulates to create devastating consequences that are difficult to attribute to specific individuals or decisions.

While the neoliberal state has drained financial resources away from its social mission—social housing construction and rent control, welfare, education, health services, and social services—social crises have multiplied. The housing crisis, homelessness crisis, opioid crisis, and mental health crisis have not only been provoked but were foreseen and predicted by many advocates, academics, and civil society actors. Through policing, disciplining and punishing (Brown, 2006; Davies, 2018; Lyon-Callo, 2008; Wacquant, 2010), neoliberal policies directly target the people who suffer from these crises, constructing them as "others" (Springer, 2016), or "surplus" population (Adler-Bolton & Vierkant, 2022). The opposition between "ordinary" people and the "others," between those who still manage to get by and those who are portrayed as unwilling to "self-empower" creates three classes of citizens: (1) those, few in number, who benefit directly from neoliberalism, (2) those who manage to survive ("ordinary" people), and (3) "the others," who have grown increasingly numerous. In the neoliberal state, not everyone is subject to the same requirements and standards: "while it embraces *laissez-faire* at the top, releasing restraints on capital and expanding the life chances of the holders of economic and cultural capital, it is anything but *laissez-faire* at the bottom" (Wacquant, 2010: 216). The mission of public institutions—police, courts, prisons, but also child welfare services, health care, and social services—is redefined to serve disciplinary objectives through responsibility and empowerment (Lyon-Callo, 2008; Schram, 2018). The organization of these institutions into a "continuum" allows for hybridization between their missions and the formation of a coherent structure of control and discipline (Stuart, 2016).

Extreme situations, which normalize compassion fatigue, have become daily occurrences for ordinary people living under neoliberal conditions: food insecurity for families and children, social isolation of the elderly, disabled people experiencing homelessness, homeless people forced to camp in the heat or cold, high proportion of suicides in Indigenous communities and migrants dying by the hundreds at sea. With the neoliberal culture transforming our relationship with social solidarity, adherence to the ideas of individualism, competitiveness, and responsibility has diminished empathy and support for supportive social measures (Adam et al., 2019). The "others" appear more as threats to economic stability, safety and public morality than as people in need of social support—which makes it seem acceptable to deny them services (Lincoln, 2006), to intervene against them with force and authority, or to make them disappear, by moving them to another location, locking them up or even eliminating them. In Ontario, Canada, a survey on mental health and addiction conducted in 2024 showed that nearly 80% of Ontarians would like to see greater investment in services, especially for crisis intervention, but also that 67% of respondents support a reform to "allow families and physicians to provide mental health and addiction treatment to involuntary patients" (Campaign Research, 2024). The previous year, a quarter of respondents to a Canada-wide survey said they strongly (11%) or moderately agree (16%) with seeking medical assistance in dying for people living in poverty or homelessness (Research Co, 2023). The complicity—and the direct participation—of ordinary people is an essential component in the implementation of the violence of neoliberal policies:

> Fantasy and reality collide under neoliberalization, and our involvement in this process allows for the normative entrenchment of violence against the marginalized, the dispossessed, the poor, the downtrodden, the homeless, the unemployed, the disaffected, and the "Other." Yet this necropolitics of violence is not the conclusion of neoliberalism's violent fantasy; rather, it is its genesis. (Springer, 2016: 159)

The concept of mental health fits strongly into the neoliberal agenda. Because neoliberalism is based on personal self-realization, psychology appears as "the scientific source of techniques for forming individuals who would exemplify neoliberal selfways" (Adams et al., 2019: 10) and as a data source supporting the neoliberal project. Today's psychology and psychiatry adhere to neoliberal culture through the concepts of functionality, responsibility, and empowerment. According to Micha Frazer-Carroll (2023: 33), who is writing based on both research and personal experience:

> [C]ure is framed as a clear and steady path, as long as we are willing to try going to health services, taking our medication, paying for therapy, practising self-care, taking up mindfulness, eating better, getting regular exercise, having an active social life—or anything else on the expanding list of practices that are promised to help us recover. While many of these things may make people feel better, an exclusive focus on these individual actions overlooks the fact that they don't work for everyone; and the road to "recovery" is rocky, complex or even impossible for many of us in our current conditions. It frames ongoing distress as a personal failure to self-discipline or seek out appropriate services, rather than acknowledging the structural conditions that also dictate our lives. This approach aligns perfectly with neoliberal ideology, which emphasizes free-market competition, decreased state spending, and increased personal responsibility.

In addition to being subjugated and instrumentalized by neoliberal culture, mental health has been subject to neoliberal policies under the leadership of the World Bank since the 1980s. For the World Bank, health is a marketable commodity, and private-sector players, including pharmaceutical companies, are regarded as credible and effective partners in the delivery of care and services. Health care for people marginalized or living in poverty is helpful for increasing their "human capital," their productivity and thus their economic growth. Given the conditionality of its loans, the World Bank has several levers for imposing health policies on countries, especially in low- and middle-income countries (Laurell & Arellano, 1996). The Bank conducts numerous studies on health in many countries and has developed strategic documents on the subject. The World Bank is therefore a major producer and disseminator of knowledge in the healthcare field (Mehta, 2001). There has been widespread criticism of the World Bank's colonial orientations and of the consequences of its policies in the global South. This criticism addresses problems such as mismatch with local health realities and priorities (Kalkan & Madi, 2022; Risal, 2014), unavailability of healthcare and deterioration of the population's state of health resulting from privatization (Marriot, 2023; Ruger, 2005), "medical exploitation" through clinical trials (Kim et al., 2017), and the promotion of Western thinking and practices to the detriment of traditional and Indigenous knowledge (Kwete et al., 2022; McCoy et al., 2023). Despite growing awareness of these problems, the approach advocated by the World Bank enjoys broad consensus among global North countries, international organizations such as the World Health Organization (WHO) and the Organisation for Economic Co-operation and Development (OECD), as well as numerous non-governmental organizations (Anbazhagan & Surekha, 2016). This consensus could be the result of changes in practice, as the Bank has been promoting the inclusion of beneficiary countries and citizens in the process of policymaking for over a decade, with inclusionary practices proving more effective than top-down ones (Sondarjee, 2021).

In 2016, the World Bank held a major international conference on the theme of "Out of the shadows: making mental health a global development priority" (Mnookin, 2016). Featuring the event on its website, the Bank stated that mental health problems "impose an enormous burden on society, accounting for almost one in three years lived with disability globally." In addition to the physical health problems they cause, mental health problems constitute a "significant economic burden." Identifying depression and anxiety as major issues, the World Bank encourages investments that "will provide a strong return on investment, with scale-up leading to good returns in restored productivity as well as improved health." At the conference, WHO (2016) representatives stated that the cost of depression and anxiety worldwide amounts to one trillion dollars every year and that every dollar spent on treatment "brings about a return of four dollars in improved health and the ability to work. That is an excellent return on investment." The WHO stated that the problem was the "gap" between the need for mental health treatment and access to it. In so doing, it promoted the "Mental Health Gap Action program," a project the Organization had been developing since 2008. Targeting primarily the countries of the global South, the program defines "Global Mental Health" according to the biomedical model of Western psychiatry, ignoring the many scientific controversies related to the low scientific validity of psychiatric diagnoses (Cosci et al., 2024; Frances, 2013; Karter & Kamens, 2019; Moncrieff et al., 2024; Paris, 2023) and treatments (Burke, 2023; Freedland & Zorumski, 2023; Moncrieff et al., 2024; Tajika et al., 2023; Verhoeven et al., 2023), whether pharmacological (Gøtzsche, 2017; Tajika et al., 2023), electroconvulsive (Read et al., 2023; Yoldi-Negrette et al., 2022; National Institute for Health and Care Excellence, 2009), or digital (Adams, 2024; Cosgrove et al., 2020), particularly for depression and anxiety (Verhoeven et al., 2023; Winter et al., 2022). It also ignores the influence of the pharmaceutical industry on the training of psychiatrists, clinical trials, scientific publications and prescription (Doshi, 2024; Fernando, 2014; Frances, 2013; Oostrom, 2024); the lack of consideration for political, historical, and social contexts, as well as of the experiential knowledge of the people concerned (Guy et al., 2020; Porter, 2013; Rose & Kalathil, 2019; Russo, 2023); and the Western-centric and colonial approach of psychiatry and psychology (Limenih, 2024; Malott et al., 2023; Rose & Kalathil, 2019; Tomičić & Gjorgjioska, 2024).

In response to criticism, the WHO currently suggests a rights-based approach (WHO, 2024; WHO & Office of the High Commissioner for Human Rights, 2023; Patel et al., 2023).[3] According to Lisa Cosgrove and Justin M. Karter (2018: 672), reconceptualizing Global Mental Health as a human rights issue "cannot change its economic grounding, and, concomitantly, the reduction of the human to the biological. The casting of [Global Mental Health] as a human rights issue occurs simultaneously with an effacement of human beings as social and political." It is apparent that rights are at least as closely tied to neoliberalism as psychiatry and psychology are. On an epistemological level, law and rights promote individualism, freedom, and responsibility, and are detached from structural, social, and political issues while claiming universality and equality. Rights are central to establishing the neoliberal political project—on the one hand, they protect private property, contracts, and economic development; on the other hand, in social matters, they absolve states of social and political responsibility, particularly regarding resource allocation, by placing on individuals the responsibility to know their rights and pursue legal action (Grewal & Purdy, 2014; Moyn, 2014). Human beings have never had as many rights as they have had since the advent of neoliberalism 40 years ago.

Since the beginning of the twenty-first century, rights have not translated into specific concrete advances for marginalized social groups (Adler-Bolton & Vierkant, 2022). The examples are numerous: while rights historically directly supported colonialism, by granting settlers rights over indigenous territories, the current recognition of Indigenous peoples' rights does little to prevent the ongoing land grabbing and extractive activities on their territories (Samson, 2020); in the context of increasing homelessness, homeless rights ombudsperson offices have been created with no structural mandate to get people off the streets; the recognition of rights for people in mental health does not prevent the resurgence and dramatic increase in the use of coercion against them (Bernheim, 2022; Lee & Cohen, 2020; Lebenbaum et al., 2018; Rains

[3] A study documenting the responses of medical and psychiatric organizations showed great resistance to this proposal, based on two arguments: "Binary positions and contesting articulations of good mental health care" and "Rejecting the UN reports in defence of Psychiatry" (Oute & McPherson, 2024: 479).

et al., 2019; Wipond, 2023). According to Lucy Series (2022: 84), "social care detention is anchored in the right to liberty [... and] international human rights law." A study conducted between 2008 and 2017 in 23 countries, all signatories to the *Convention on the Rights of Persons with Disabilities* (CRPD), demonstrates an increase in the prevalence of involuntary admission in most of these countries (Rains et al., 2019). This observation leads the authors to say that there is "no clear association between legislation and rates of involuntary hospitalization" (Rains et al., 2019: 415). In Finland, a fifteen-year study demonstrated that legislative changes aimed at reducing the use of seclusion and restraints had not changed the risk faced by patients of being secluded or restrained, and that the duration of seclusion periods had increased over that period. The authors concluded that the fact that the law focused on individuals' right to self-determination, without formally prohibiting the use of seclusion and restraints or providing training to care staff, had not led to the necessary cultural change (Keski-Valkama et al., 2007). Phil Brown asserts that from the reforms of the mental health laws in the 1960s, rights have been "coopted" by governments and mental health professionals "in order to achieve outcomes favorable to them" (Brown, 1981: 532).

It is in this context that the World Bank and the World Health Organization talk about a "mental health crisis." According to studies, the mental health crisis has been rapidly growing in all social spheres such as education (Evans et al., 2018), workplaces (Taubman & Parikh, 2023), and intimate and family life, affecting everyone, from children (Centers for Disease Control & Prevention, 2020) to the elderly persons (Lenze, 2015). Especially since the COVID-19 pandemic, the mental health crisis has been described as "global" (Patel et al., 2023), "threatening" (Czulada et al., 2022), and a public-health issue (Health, 2020). Neoliberal policies are explicitly identified as a trigger for this crisis. Olivier De Schutter, the Special Rapporteur on extreme poverty and human rights (2024: 3), states that "the focus on increasing material consumption and on competition threatens mental health." For him, the mental health crisis originates from growing social inequalities. It has long been known that poverty generates negative emotions and associated stress affecting mental health (Beatty, 2019). The lack of accessible health and social services and lack of professionals due to decades of austerity policies by neoliberal states are "often identified as the core reasons" for the crisis (Patel et al., 2023: 656). In addition to the lack of services, their inadequacy is also a concern. Mental health services tend to be narrow, segmented, and organized around psychiatric diagnoses and acute phases, ignoring people's experiences and preferences, as well as their day-to-day needs, including basic needs (housing, food, etc.), and thus exacerbating distress (Patel et al., 2023; Stewart, 2019).

The existence of a mental health crisis is disputed, or at least controversial, in scientific literature (Malla & Gold, 2024). Some epidemiological studies conclude that the prevalence of mental health problems has remained relatively unchanged (Richter et al., 2019), while others conclude that they have been increasing (Fan et al., 2025; OECD, 2023). Given the scientific controversies related to psychiatric diagnoses and treatment, these findings raise several questions: is the increase the result of misdiagnosis, particularly in the case of diagnoses made for anxiety or distress related to ordinary life events (Ormel et al., 2022) or neoliberal policies (Stewart, 2019)? As psychiatrist Allen Frances (2013: 85) states, is the increase due to the use of "a method that is inherently flawed and systematically biased in the direction of overreporting?" Or is the increase linked to destigmatization, reflecting the psychiatrization of society (Beeker et al., 2021; Frances, 2013), or a way of disciplining "the other" (Lyon-Callo, 2008; Willse, 2010)?

Regardless of whether or not mental health problems are on the rise, the increase in the use of psychiatric services and medication is very real. In 2023, roughly 25% of American adults accessed mental health treatment, with 16% receiving psychotropic medication, while among adolescents aged 12–17, approximately one-third utilized mental health services and 13% were prescribed medication (Substance Abuse & Mental Health Services Administration, 2023). Canadian figures are similar (Stephenson, 2023). Worldwide, sales of psychotropic medications rose by 4.08% per year between 2008 and 2019, to 123,61 daily doses per 1,000 inhabitants (Brauer et al., 2021) despite the adverse effects and associated risks (Brisnik et al., 2024; Cosci et al., 2024; Desaunay et al., 2024; Ray et al., 2024).

First and foremost, the "mental health crisis" is real: it exists at least through its political instrumentalization. Mental health is increasingly invoked in political, public and media narrative to explain homelessness, violent behavior, distress in the workplace, failure at school, and so on—and to justify increasingly repressive policies. Despite the declared desire to destigmatize, mental health is very strongly associated with risk of violence in current public discourse.

Mental Health Risks and Moral Panic

Studies show that mental health is represented in the media of the global North as "one of the important issues of our time" (Ohlsson, 2018: 31), without differentiating between mental health and mental disorder (Malla & Gold, 2024), and without mentioning scientific controversies. As Otto Wahl (1995: 14) says, "words have power. They have the power to hurt or soothe, to honor or insult, to inform or disinform. [...] A common complaint of mental health advocates about mass medias is that psychiatric labels are often used incorrectly and serve to misinform and confuse viewers and readers." In addition to inaccuracies and dehumanizing language (Wahl, 1995), the media, often echoing political narratives, tends to draw links between mental health and the risk of violence (Ohlsson, 2018) or criminality (Olstead, 2002). Taking up the discourse on "others" (Olstead, 2002), the media contributes to spreading the ordinary prejudices associated with sanism—treating people with a psychiatric diagnosis as "inferior, childlike, incompetent, violent, or dangerous" (Gosselin, 2022: 294)—and fueling "moral panic" (Applebaum, 2003). In the past few years, the tendency of media coverage and political debates about mass killings and incidents of violence to report that the perpetrators have mental disorder—even if these reports are unfounded—may have contributed to public perception of the risk of violence related to mental health (Steiger et al., 2022; Whitley et al., 2017). Even if not supported by evidence-based data (Ahonen et al., 2019; Ghiasi et al., 2022), the public perception of mental health risk and support for coercion have been increasing continually since the fifties (Pescosolido et al., 2019; Steiger et al., 2022).

Indeed, recent studies have demonstrated that the main risk factors for violence associated with mental disorders (Whiting et al., 2021), particularly psychoses, are criminal history and substance abuse (Lagerberg et al., 2025), the same as those for the risk of criminal behavior and recidivism without mental disorders (Goodley et al., 2022).

The association between risk and mental health is far from new. According to Michel Foucault (2006), risk, from the start, has been inseparable from the epistemology and practice of the psychiatric discipline:

> At the turn of the nineteenth century, psychiatry became an autonomous discipline and assumed such prestige precisely because it had been able to develop within the framework of a medical discipline conceived of as a reaction to the dangers inherent in the social body. The alienists of the period may well have had endless discussions about the organic or psychic origin of mental illnesses; they may well have proposed physical or psychic therapies. Nonetheless, through all their differences, they were all conscious that they were treating a social "danger," either because insanity seemed to them to be linked to living conditions (overpopulation, overcrowding, urban life, alcoholism, debauchery), or because it was perceived as a source of danger for oneself, for others, for one's contemporaries, and also for one's descendants through heredity. Nineteenth-century psychiatry was a medical science as much for the societal body as for the individual soul. (Foucault et al., 1978: 7)

Mental health risk discourse incorporates not only the condition's supposed inherent dangers but also the constructed notion of patients' incapacity to recognize their condition, accept its risks, and make rational decisions—concepts framed as denial, "lack of insight" or "anosognosia" (Rossero, 2023). These two attributes of mental health—risk and incapacity—make it an unpredictable condition, and it is in this unpredictability that the political roots of psychiatric intervention lie (Castel, 1991; Keller, 2001, 2019; Rose, 1996).

The concept of risk is highly imprecise. Risk is made up of insecurities and hazards that are possible, but that cannot necessarily be accurately or reliably predicted. It is inherent to neoliberal societies, which are constantly at risk of crisis, whether financial, ecological, or social (Beck,

1992). With a significant proportion of economic activities dedicated to risk prediction, monitoring, and control (Lupton, 2013), risks are lucrative markets (Inda, 2023; Rigakos, 2002). Among these markets, the public safety risk market has been flourishing. In Canada, between 2010 and 2021 and in constant dollars, budgets allocated to police services in 19 of the 20 largest cities increased between 7.8 and 54.8% with no correlation or impact on crime rates (Seabrook et al., 2023). During the same period, the budget allocated to the correctional system increased by 26% (Statistics Canada, 2024).

Mental health risk is described by Nikolas Rose (1996: 349) as "posed by the individuals themselves when they cannot adequately manage their life within the community, and the risk these individuals pose to the community on account of their failure to govern themselves." Unlike danger, which must be established by facts, risk is the interrelationship of multiple imprecise factors that are not necessarily dangerous when considered individually, but that make the occurrence of unwanted behaviors more or less likely (Castel, 1991; Ward, 2016). Imprecision and unpredictability related to the notion of risk make it an essentially normative judgment with little connection with psychological processes (Ward, 2016).

Empirical observation of psychiatric assessment practices shows that men's, especially younger and racialized men's, presumed risk is associated to violence (Barnett et al., 2019; Ogilvie & Kisely, 2022; Wong et al., 2019), while women's presumed risk is, on the contrary, associated to their inherent vulnerability (Burstow, 2015; Chunn & Menzies, 1998). Studies also demonstrate that risk and capacity assessment scales structurally target marginalized and non-white people (Foltz et al., 2025; Fazel et al., 2022; Garett, 2023; Sreenivasan et al., 2022), including Indigenous people (Choate & Lindstrom, 2017; Muir et al., 2023; Olver et al., 2024), thus constituting tools of discrimination and colonial governance (Choate & Lindstrom, 2017; Muir et al., 2023).

According to Swanson et al. (2015: 371), "[p]sychiatrists' predictions of which patients would be violent, based on their clinical assessments in the emergency setting, turned out to be only slightly more accurate than flipping a coin." The poor reliability of risk predictions has prompted legal practitioners and researchers to recommend eliminating risk considerations from judicial detention decisions, particularly due to the potential for imposing unnecessarily prolonged detentions that violate individual rights (Fazel et al., 2012; Reyes, 2017). However, risk predictions have made possible preventive deprivations of liberty, designed to mitigate mental health risk, from the very first laws on involuntary commitment around 200 years ago and still in force today (Bernheim, 2020). The power to involuntarily admit and involuntarily treat outside the criminal justice and child welfare systems is unique to psychiatry. The rights to liberty and consent to treatment are inalienable and fundamental, and their exercise can only be restricted in exceptional cases—it is thus accepted that refusal of treatment leading to death must be respected. On the one hand, the exercise of the right to liberty can be limited by criminal law as a punishment following a due-process trial and must be proportional to the offense committed. The right to liberty protects personal autonomy so that individuals can make intrinsically private choices without interference from the state, including the right to commit suicide. On the other hand, the exercise of the right to consent to treatment can be limited only in urgent situations, such as those where life is threatened. Otherwise, the right to consent to treatment protects the autonomy to make decisions about one's own body for reasons of preference or belief—even if these preferences or beliefs run counter to professional advice.

Criminal and civil legislation in mental health provides for unique exceptions based on mental health risk, incapacity, or need for treatment. These exceptions allow for involuntary commitment, detention, conditional release, involuntary treatment, and the use of seclusion rooms and restraints against the will of individuals based on a psychiatric diagnosis. Historically, the management of mental health risk using coercion has been possible by virtue of the *parens patriae* competence of the state, under which the state, as a "good father of the family," protects public safety and acts as a guardian for incapable citizens. With international movements for the recognition of rights, this competence has been called into question, as have coercive psychiatric practices (Curtis, 1976). The legislative reforms that took place after the 1970s implemented more rigid procedures, including judicial ones in several jurisdictions, but did not shift "the political economy of oppression" (Adler-Bolton &

Vierkant, 2022). During those years, the courts recognized the rights to dignity, equality, non-discrimination, and protection against unusual, inhumane, and degrading treatment for people involuntary committed (Brown, 1981). However, they have also recognized that imposing involuntary treatment and hospitalization for reasons of mental health or addiction does not constitute punishment and may be constitutional (Robinson v. California, 1962; Wexler, 1972). At the international level, the United Nations adopted the *Principles for the protection of persons with mental illness and the improvement of mental health care* in 1991 and the *Convention on the Rights of Persons with Disabilitie* (CRPD) in 2006. These international instruments recognize the rights to freedom and to consent to treatments in mental health but also contain exceptions such as involuntary admission and involuntary treatment "in conformity with the law," with the requirement that "the existence of a disability shall in no case justify a deprivation of liberty" (CRPD, art. 14 b). Although these instruments advocate for human rights, they do not denounce the sanism conveyed by the concepts of risk and incapacity in mental health legislations. According to Michael L. Perlin (1992, 2013), the legal system makes several assumptions about mental health and thus participates through its narrative and practices in the construction of an "other." For Perlin, in the legal system, people with psychiatric diagnosis,

> are invariably more dangerous than persons without mental illness, and such dangerousness is easily and accurately identified by experts; that for a person in treatment for mental illness to decline to take prescribed antipsychotic medication is an excellent predictor of (1) future dangerousness and (2) need for involuntary institutionalization; that people with mental illness should be segregated in large, distant institutions because their presence threatens the economic and social stability of residential communities (Perlin, 2013: 878).

In addition to being rooted in scientifically unfounded prejudices, the legal concepts of mental health risk and incapacity have the combined effect of legitimizing the use of coercion, of invalidating the opinions and experience of people in mental health and of contributing to the hegemony and authority of psychiatric knowledge (Foucault, 2006; Foucault et al., 1978). Mental health risk and incapacity not only legitimize and require coercive intervention for the sake of public safety but also protect the "best interests" of the persons incapable of making "appropriate" decisions (Rossero, 2023). In the process, people's experiences and knowledge are disqualified, both because they are presumed to be dishonest, unreliable, threatening or unpredictable, and because others know better than they do what would work for them (Legghio, 2012). This epistemic violence against people in mental health especially affects survivors of coercive psychiatry for whom the use of coercion constitutes a confirmation bias affecting their overall experience (Scrutton, 2017), in addition to being a major trauma (Aragonés-Calleja & Sánchez-Martínez, 2024; Munt & Littlechild, 2024).

Psychiatric knowledge has its roots in asylums, through the observation and classification of inmate behaviors into normal and deviant (Foucault, 2003a, 2003b, 2006). In Europe, the fifteenth century's "great lockup" as described by Foucault (1989), served first to keep out of sight people, be they homeless, mad, orphaned, etc., whose presence disturbs others. With the separation of the insane from other troublesome people from the early nineteenth century, and the political recognition of the knowledge on madness (Foucault et al., 1978; Rose, 2017) as well as of the expertise in the control of deviance, psychiatrists have been entrusted with "considerable power" (Fernando, 2010: 57). Psychiatry experienced significant growth starting from the mid-1800s, with the proliferation of asylums in Europe and North America, and the rapid increase in the number of inmates incarcerated for long periods of time (Wright, 1997)—sometimes at the request of their families. As a result of industrialization, families were less able to take care of their family members, especially those with low productivity, in need of care, or who did not comply with social norms (Krasnick Warsh, 1988).

This period was also the golden age of colonialism and slavery (Fernando, 2014) and asylums became places where the colonized peoples' knowledge was extracted for the benefit of the colonists (Fanon, 1963). In the European colonies, alongside military and police institutions, "psychiatry allied itself closely with civilizing missions as it assembled knowledge about 'indigenous psychologies' that facilitated rule" (Keller, 2001: 297), providing scientific justifications for racist policies (Deacon, 1996; Keller, 2001'; Studer, 2016) and sidelining political opponents (Fanon, 1986; Swartz, 2010). In some cases, Indigenous people were transported to European asylums; in other cases, private asylums were developed by colonial investors and managed as a business; and in yet other cases, the colonizers themselves opened and managed asylums in their colonies (Keller, 2001). In North America, although data is patchy, asylum seems to have been used as a tool for assimilating Indigenous peoples (Menzie & Palys, 2006; Ness, 2016). In European colonies in the global South, as well as in North America, Indigenous people died in large numbers in asylums (Keller, 2001; Menzie & Palys, 2006).

Under the influence of Darwinism, asylums were constructed with the idea that "biology, rather than culture, shaped mentality" (Keller, 2019: 126); madness was therefore regarded as innate (Grob, 1998; Shorter, 1997). The writings of psychiatrists and psychologists published at the time differentiate between normal and pathological behavior (Foucault, 2003a, 2006), between masculine and feminine roles (Hirshbein, 2010), and between "civilized" and "barbaric" races (Fernando, 2010: 61). The belief in the biological inferiority of certain groups based on their class, race, and gender has led to classist, racist, sexist, segregationist, and eugenic practices within the asylums (Chesler, 2018; Deacon, 1996; Fernando, 2010, 2014; Hirshbein, 2010; Keller, 2001, 2019; Swartz, 2010) that mirrored society at large. Inmates were treated differently according to their social class (Deacon, 1996). Whites and non-whites were segregated and treated differently:

> On the one hand, the recuperative potential of non-Africans was seen to be dependent on the elimination of "Africa" from the treatment environment as this was seen as largely responsible for their disorder. And on the other hand, the superiority of the colonists could only be maintained if their insane were kept apart from the African insane (Deacon, 1996: 295).

Men considered too feminine and women too masculine were targeted to be reformed by hormonal treatments (Hirshbein, 2010). Women, especially Indigenous and racialized women, were detained for not performing their traditional roles, and subjected to sterilization (Hirshbein, 2010; Krasnick Warsh, 1988; Ness, 2016; Stahnisch & Kurbegović, 2020). In addition to confinement, inmates were subject to experimentation with treatments such as electroconvulsive therapy, sleep cures, depatterning, psychic driving, or lobotomy, a practice that has continued over time, with psychiatrists collaborating, for example, in the German Nazi program (Dudley & Gale, 2002; Lindert et al., 2012), the Soviet program in the USSR (Luty, 2014; Van Voren, 2025) or the CIA's "MKUltra Mind Control Project" (Torbay, 2023).

Psychiatric knowledge can hardly be detached from the historical coercive and political context of its development. The first psychiatric nosographies were developed by observing people confined to closed institutions and subjected to experimentation (Foucault, 1989), in some cases against a backdrop of great political violence. Psychiatrists came from the elite; they focused on diagnosing and treating marginalized, poor, racialized, and colonized people. The political dimensions of these practices are multiple, but they are intrinsically linked to coercion: it is to carry out acts of a political nature that the power of coercion has been delegated to psychiatry—psychiatry implementing the *parens patriae* competence of the state—whereas the very exercise of coercion constitutes a political act by virtue of its exceptional nature. The participation of psychiatrists in the drafting of the first legislations on involuntary commitment shows the closeness of psychiatrists to the political powers since the middle of the nineteenth century (Foucault et al., 1978; Scull, 1989). Yet, the association of law and psychiatry depersonalizes and depoliticizes coercion and its use (Adler-Bolton & Vierkant, 2022), transforming it into care. The framework of legal procedures and standardized evaluations justifies the use of coercion, concealing the contexts of implementation and the people concerned. This is what Eleonora Rossero (2023) observed in the ethnographic research of two mental health centers in Italy. With care-associated terminology, arguments invoking procedures and protocols, and the inclusion of coercion as an aspect of the therapeutic relationship, coercion is emptied of its political meaning and erased.

Has the transformation of practices in the twentieth century, through the closure of asylums, deinstitutionalization, the development of medication, the recovery approach and the change in vocabulary from madness to mental health, changed the political vocation of psychiatry? It seems that the political mission of psychiatry has evolved as society has been striving toward neoliberalism, but that its specificity—risk management, treatment, coercion— has simply changed form. Risk management is still at the heart of psychiatric practices, but the nature of the risks it has to deal with has changed: "the subjects of psychiatry are no longer unified by their institutional confinement, and the visibility which confinement conferred upon them, but by the fact that they are unable to manage themselves prudently in the matrix of encounters outside the asylum" (Rose, 1996: 14). Managing mental health risk outside the asylum requires a psychiatric presence in the community, as well as collaboration between organizations dealing with social services and mental health, with the aim of supporting "recovery." Recovery does not have a clear definition, but it is based on individual responsibility, empowerment, and engagement. It occurs repeatedly in the documents of the World Bank and the WHO and is at the heart of mental health policies in an ever-growing number of countries, with medication and treatment compliance as an essential part. Although recovery relies on the participation of the individuals, particularly through their right to consent, an increasing number of studies conclude that recovery is a means of controlling, disciplining, and coercing (Cohen, 2025; Johansson & Holmes, 2024; McWade, 2016; Poole, 2011). In many jurisdictions, recovery policies have been accompanied by legal devices allowing forced treatment in the community, thus blurring the boundaries between hospital, clinic, and community, and between what is voluntary and what is coerced—expanding in practice the scope of coercion (Ben-Moshe, 2020). Yet law and rights offer little concrete guidance when it comes to assessing what constitutes coercion, as they do not consider the experiences of the people subjected to it (Szmukler, 2008). Psychiatrists Goerges Szmukler and Paul S. Appelbaum (2008: 234) suggest that "treatment pressures" fall on a spectrum composed of the "persuasion, interpersonal leverage, inducements, threats and compulsory treatment (in the community or as an inpatient)." To formal and informal coercion is added violence or abuses of power documented by studies, which occur as much in hospital settings as in the community, such as verbal abuse, or the systematic ignoring of questions or requests for assistance (Munt & Littlechild, 2024).

Prevention, Police, and Justice

Psychiatry is not alone in managing mental health risk and the mental health crisis. In the wake of the neoliberalization of public policy, health, and social services have been reorganized into a "continuum of care," with recovery as the goal. First introduced by the United States Clinton administration in the early 1990s, the continuum of care in social matters seeks to offer long-term solutions by integrating a multitude of services so that people do not fall into "service gaps." Along the continuum, enrollment in medium- to long-term therapies and services is seen as the way to bring about real change, for both the individual and society, while managing risk. The continuum of care has profoundly altered the philosophy of many public and private institutions, including community organizations and shelters that previously offered their services without conditions. Accessing services on the continuum implies a commitment to some form of therapy, be it in the form of attending appointments with professionals, taking medication, or abstaining from drugs or alcohol. Engaging and retaining people in the continuum of care presents many challenges (Stuart, 2016), in particular due to scarcity of services and social support, which are often determined according to the stages of recovery rather than according to what people want.

The police play a central role in the continuum of care in mental health. On the one hand, in the absence of easily accessible health or social services, police officers are generally considered to be the "default first responders" (Marcus & Stergiopoulos, 2022), even to the point of being described as "front-line mental health workers" (Mclean et al., 2010). Police are also directly tasked by policymakers with dealing with social issues, including mental health. Under the guise of crime fighting and law enforcement, police appear "as the 'solution' to mental health, substance use disorder, or homelessness through demands for public order 'crackdowns'" (Koziarski & Huey, 2021: 272), which contributes to making the "mental health crisis" a risk-management issue. On the other hand, the police, and community police, in particular, have been actively seeking closer ties with citizens and partnerships with other institutions such as hospitals, shelters and community groups (Ouellet et al., 2021). Because of its physical proximity to communities and its use of the repressive tools of criminal law, the police can encourage people to engage in therapy, sometimes at the request of partnering organizations (Stuart, 2016). The deployment of specialized police mental health teams, staffed by social workers or nurses and police officers, testifies to this increasingly important therapeutic role of the police. According to studies, up to 50% of calls to police services concern mental health (Lamanna et al., 2017; Puntis et al., 2018; Watson & Wood, 2017), and mental health interventions account for 20% of police officers' working time (Langton et al., 2021).

Justice is also a powerful lever for engaging people in therapy. In recent decades, in the wake of the recognition of mental health rights, the involvement of the courts in mental health has developed, be it through court diversion programs, new mandates for existing court, or the creation of tribunals dedicated to mental health.

Despite the existence of therapeutic police and justice for several decades, only little research has demonstrated effectiveness or has focused on the perspective of the people subject to it (Collins, 2020, 2023; Furness et al., 2017; Puntis et al., 2018; Steele, 2020). Criticisms of therapeutic police and justice on the continuum of care include the use of informal coercion to force consent to treatment; the sharing of personal information between different organizations; an increased level of surveillance and control, exceeding legal requirements and involving many institutions; and social and racial profiling associated with the indeterminacy of the mental health category (Frederick et al., 2018; Steele, 2020). Indeed, as part of a study conducted in Montreal, Canada, about police intervention in mental health, police officers described the people targeted by these interventions as "autistic," "schizophrenic," "incapable," "psychopaths," "nymphomaniacs," "maniacs," "suicidal," or "intellectually disabled," as well as "homeless," "isolated," "elderly,"

"Indigenous," or "Inuit" persons (Ouellet et al., 2021). During focus groups, police officers have also stated that in recent years, the "mental health" category has been replaced in their practices by "vulnerable," which would be less stigmatizing. Yet, the crisis they describe is rather the structural neglect and abandonment—and thus the vulnerabilization—of an increasingly large portion of the population, than mental health issues. Police officers said that "before," they had "mental health or homelessness situations;" today, they face people living with intellectual disabilities, experiencing homelessness and sometimes intoxicated, or involved in sex work activities—complex situations for which they have no expertise and no preparation. They explained having to make calls for medical follow-ups, to intercede with hospital services to have them conduct evaluations, or to buy bread and milk for people unable to leave their homes. They recounted having no choice but to bring individuals into the judicial system with the objective that they receive services they are otherwise unable to obtain—a well-documented reality (Pariseau-Legault et al., 2025). Under neoliberal governance, solidarity appears to operate more through coercion rather than reciprocal support.

References

Adams, G., Estrada-Villalta, S., Sullivan, D., & Markus, H. R. (2019). The psychology of neoliberalism and the neoliberalism of psychology. *Journal of Social Issues, 75*(1), 189–216. https://doi.org/10.1111/josi.12305

Adams, J. (2024). Examining ethical and social implications of digital mental health technologies through expert interviews and sociotechnical systems theory. *Digital Society, 3*(2), 24. https://doi.org/10.1007/s44206-024-00110-5

Adler-Bolton, B., & Vierkant, A. (2022). *Health communism.* Verso Books.

Ahonen, L., Loeber, R., & Brent, D. A. (2019). The association between serious mental health problems and violence: Some common assumptions and misconceptions. *Trauma, Violence & Abuse, 20*(5), 613–625. https://doi.org/10.1177/1524838017726423

Ali, A., Caplan, J., & Fagnant, R. (2010). Gender stereotypes in diagnostic criteria. In J. C. Chrisler, & D. R. McCreary (Eds.), *Handbook of gender research in psychology: Volume 2: Gender research in social and applied psychology* (pp. 91–109). Springer Nature.

Anbazhagan, S., & Surekha, A. (2016). Role of non-governmental organizations in global health. *International Journal of Community Medicine and Public Health, 3*(1), 1–22. https://doi.org/10.18203/2394-6040.ijcmph20151544

Applebaum, S. (2003). Dangerous persons, moral panic, and the uses of psychiatry. *Psychiatric Services, 54*(4), 441–442. https://doi.org/10.1176/appi.ps.54.4.441

Aragonés-Calleja, M., & Sánchez-Martínez, V. (2024). Evidence synthesis on coercion in mental health: An umbrella review. *International Journal of Mental Health Nursing, 33*(2), 259–280. https://doi.org/10.1111/inm.13248

Barnett, P. et al. (2019). Ethnic variations in compulsory detention under the Mental Health Act: A systematic review and meta-analysis of international data. *The Lancet, 6*(4), 305–317.https://doi.org/10.1016/S2215-0366(19)30027-6

Beattie, P. (2019). The road to psychopathology: Neoliberalism and the human mind. *Journal of Social Issues, 75*(1), 89–112. https://doi.org/10.1111/josi.12304

Beck, U. (1992). *Risk society*. Sage.

Beeker, T., Mills, C., Bhugra, D., te Meerman, S., Thoma, S., Heinze, M., & von Peter, S. (2021). Psychiatrization of society: A conceptual framework and call for transdisciplinary research. *Frontiers in Psychiatry, 12*, Article 645556. https://doi.org/10.3389/fpsyt.2021.645556

Bernheim, E., Ferron-Parayre, A., & Gauthier-Boiteau, D. (2025). To consent and to refuse electroconvulsive therapy: A study of consent documents and court orders in the province of quebec. *Canada. Ethical Human Psychology & Psychiatry, 27*(1), 25–45. https://doi.org/10.1891/EHPP-2024-0011

Bernheim, E. (2022). The triumph of the "therapeutic" in Quebec Courts: Mental health, behavioral reform and the decline of rights. *Windsor Yearbook on Access to Justice, 38*, 125–147. https://doi.org/10.22329/wyaj.v38.7779

Bernheim, E. (2020). Justice, power and intersectionality: Beyond Psychiatry, the social issue in question. In M.-A. Jacob, & A. Kirkland (Eds.), *Research handbook on law, medicine and society* (pp. 386–402). Edward Elgar Publishing. https://doi.org/10.4337/9781786437983.00034

Ben-Moshe, L. (2020). *Decarcerating disability: Deinstitutionalization and prison abolition*. University of Minnesota Press.

Bly, N. (1991). *Ten days in a mad house (first published in 1887)*. Munro, Publisher.

Boyd, J., & Kerr, T. (2016). Policing "Vancouver's mental health crisis:" A critical discourse analysis. *Critical Public Health, 26*(4), 418–433. https://doi.org/10.1080/09581596.2015.1007923

Brauer, R., Alfageh, B., Blais, J. E., Chan, E. W., Chui, C. S., Hayes, J. F., & Wong, I. C. (2021). Psychotropic medicine consumption in 65 countries and regions, 2008–19: A longitudinal study. *The Lancet Psychiatry, 8*(12), 1071–1082. https://doi.org/10.1016/S2215-0366(21)00292-3

Brisnik, V., Rottenkolber, M., Vukas, J., Schechner, M., Lukaschek, K., Jung-Sievers, C., & Dreischulte, T. (2024). Potential deprescribing indications for antidepressants between 2012 and 2019: Repeated cross-sectional analysis in two Scottish health boards. *BMC Medicine, 22*(1), 378. https://doi.org/10.1186/s12916-024-03584-9

Brown, P. (1981). The mental patients' rights movement and mental health institutional change. *International Journal of Health Services, 11*(4), 523–540. https://doi.org/10.2190/CU8G-D0RJ-YY54-UC3F

Brown, W. (2006). American nightmare: Neoliberalism, neoconservatism, and de-democratization. *Political Theory, 34*(6), 690–714. https://doi.org/10.1177/0090591706293016

Burke, M. J. (2023). A fundamental change is needed for appraising placebo responses in psychiatry. *Lancet Psychiatry, 10*(5), 316–317. https://doi.org/10.1016/S2215-0366(23)00068-8

Burstow, B. (2015). *Psychiatry and the business of madness: An ethical and epistemological accounting*. Palgrave Macmillan.

Campaign Research. (2024, August 1). *Mental health and addictions - Public opinion research*. Report. https://www.campaignresearch.com/single-post/mental-health-and-addictions-public-opinion-research (accessed August 9, 2025).

Carrier, J. G. (Ed.). (2020). *Meanings of the market: The free market in Western culture*. Routledge.

Castel, R. (1991). From dangerous to risk. In G. Burchell, C. Gordon, & Miller, P. (Eds.), *The Foucault effect: Studies in governmentality* (pp. 281–298). University of Chicago Press.

Centers for Disease Control and Prevention. (2020). *Youth risk behavior survey: Data summary and trends report 2009- 2019*. Report. https://www.cdc.gov/yrbs/dstr/pdf/YRBSDataSummaryTrendsReport2019-508.pdf (accessed August 9, 2025).

Chancel, L., Piketty, T., Saez, E., & Zucman, G. et al. (2022). *World Inequality Report 2022*. https://wir2022.wid.world/www-site/uploads/2023/03/D_FINAL_WIL_RIM_RAPPORT_2303.pdf (accessed August 9, 2025).

Chesler, P. (2018). *Women and madness*. Chicago Review Press.

Choate, P., & Lindstrom, G. (2017). Parenting capacity assessment as a colonial strategy. *Canadian Family Law Quarterly, 37*(1), 41–60.

Chunn, D. E., & Menzies, R. (1998). Out of mind, out of law: The regulation of criminally insane women inside British Columbia's public mental hospitals, 1888–1973. *Canadian Journal Women and the Law, 10*(2), 241–279.

Cohen, C. I. (2025). Neorecovery: A critical analysis of the relationship between neoliberalism and the recovery movement. *Community Mental Health Journal, 61*(2), 248–253. https://doi.org/10.1007/s10597-024-01275-6

Collins, E. (2023). Problem-solving courts and the outcome oversight gap. *University of Missouri-Kansas City Law Review, 92*(3), 533–554.

Collins, E. R. (2020). The problem of problem-solving courts. *University of California Davis Law Review, 54*, 1573–1630.

Convention on the Rights of Persons with Disabilities, A/RES/61/106, 12 December 2006.

Cosci, F., Chouinard, V. A., & Chouinard, G. (2024). Selective serotonin reuptake inhibitor and serotonin-noradrenaline reuptake inhibitor withdrawal changes DSM presentation of mental disorders: Results from the diagnostic clinical interview for drug withdrawal. *Psychotherapy and Psychosomatics, 93*(5), 340–345. https://doi.org/10.1159/000540031

Cosgrove, L., Karter, J. M., Morrill, Z., & McGinley, M. (2020). Psychology and surveillance capitalism: The risk of pushing mental health apps during the COVID-19 pandemic. *Journal of Humanistic Psychology, 60*(5), 611–625. https://doi.org/10.1177/0022167820937498

Cosgrove, L., & Karter, J. M. (2018). The poison in the cure: Neoliberalism and contemporary movements in mental health. *Theory & Psychology, 28*(5), 669–683. https://doi.org/10.1177/0959354318796307

George, B., & Curtis, G. B. (1976). The checkered career of parens patriae: The state as parent or tyrant? *DePaul Law Review, 25*(4), 895–917.

Czulada, L., Kover, K. M., Gracias, G., Kumar, K.-N., Desai, S., Stawicki, S. P., Costello, K., & Erickson-Parsons, L. (2022). Toxic stress affecting families and children during the covid-19 pandemic: A global mental health crisis and an emerging international health security threat. In S. P. Stawicki, R. Izurieta, M. S. Firstenberg, & S. C. Galwankar (Eds.), Vol. 3, *Contemporary developments and perspectives in international health security*. IntechOpen. https://doi.org/10.5772/intechopen.104991

Davidson, N. (2018). Neoliberalism as a class-based project. In D. Cahill, M. Cooper, M., Konings, & D. Primrose (Eds.), *The Sage handbook of neoliberalism* (pp. 55–68). Sage. https://doi.org/10.4135/9781526416001

Davies, W. (2018). The neoliberal state: Power against "Politics." In D. Cahill, M. Cooper, M. Konings, & D. Primrose (Eds.), *The Sage handbook of neoliberalism* (pp. 273–288). Sage. https://doi.org/10.4135/9781526416001

Deacon, H. J. (1996). Madness, race and moral treatment: Robben Island Lunatic Asylum, Cape Colony, 1846–1890. *History of Psychiatry, 7*(26), 287–297. https://doi.org/10.1177/0957154X9600702606

Desaunay, P., Eslier, M., Alexandre, J., Dreyfus, M., Chrétien, B., & Guénolé, F. (2024). Antidepressants and fetal death: A systematic review and disproportionality analysis in the WHO Safety Database (VigiBase®). *Psychiatry Research, 339*, Article 116048. https://doi.org/10.1016/j.psychres.2024.116048

De Schutter, O. (2024, July 16). *Report of the Rapporteur on extreme poverty and human rights, The burnout economy: Poverty and mental health*. A/79/162.

Doshi, P. (2024). Revolving doors: Board memberships, hedge funds, and the FDA chiefs responsible for regulating industry. *bmj, 385*, q975. https://doi.org/10.1136/bmj.q975

Dudley, M., & Gale, F. (2002). Psychiatrists as a moral community? Psychiatry under the Nazis and its contemporary relevance. *Australian & New Zealand Journal of Psychiatry, 36*(5), 585–594. https://doi.org/10.1046/j.1440-1614.2002.01072.x

Eswaran, V., Molina, M. F., Hwong, A. R., Dillon, D. G., Alvarez, L., Allen, I. E., & Wang, R. C. (2023). Racial disparities in emergency department physical restraint use: A systematic review and meta-analysis. *JAMA internal medicine, 183*(11), 1229–1237. https://doi.org/10.1001/jamainternmed.2023.4832

Evans, T., Bira, L., Gastelum, J. B., Weiss, L. T., & Vanderford, N. L. (2018). Evidence for a mental health crisis in graduate education. *Nature Biotechnology, 36*(3), 282–284. https://doi.org/10.1038/nbt.4089

Fan, Y., Fan, A., Yang, Z., & Fan, D. (2025). Global burden of mental disorders in 204 countries and territories, 1990–2021: Results from the global burden of disease study 2021. *BMC Psychiatry, 25*(1), 486. https://doi.org/10.1186/s12888-025-06932-y

Fanon, F. (1986). *Black skin, white masks (first published in 1952)*. Pluto Press.
Fanon, F. (1963). *The wretched of the earth*. Grove Weidenfeld.
Fazel, S., Sariaslan, A., & Fanshawe, T. (2022). Towards a more evidence-based risk assessment for people in the criminal justice system: The case of OxRec in the Netherlands. *European Journal on Criminal Policy and Research, 28*(3), 397–406. https://doi.org/10.1007/s10610-022-09520-y
Fazel, S., Singh, J. P., Doll, H., & Grann, M. (2012). Use of risk assessment instruments to predict violence and antisocial behaviour in 73 samples involving 24 827 people: Systematic review and meta-analysis. *BMJ, 345*, Article e4692. https://doi.org/10.1136/bmj.e4692
Fernando, S. (2010). *Mental health, race and culture*. Bloomsbury Publishing.
Fernando, S. (2014). *Mental Health Worldwide—Culture, Globalization and Development*. Londres: Palgrave Macmillan.
Foltz, D., Badolato, G. M., Schultz, T. R., Patel, S. J., Payne, A. S., Morrison, S., Boyle, M., & Goyal, M. K. (2025). Behavioral health flag use by race and ethnicity in a pediatric emergency department. *JAMA Network Open, 8*(5), e259502. https://doi.org/10.1001/jamanetworkopen.2025.9502
Foucault, M. (2006). *Psychiatric power: Lectures at the Collège de France, 1973–1974*. Picador.
Foucault, M. (2003a). *Abnormal: Lectures at the College de France 1974–1975*. Verso.
Foucault, M. (2003b). *The Birth of the clinic*. Routledge.
Foucault, M. (1989). *Madness in civilization: A history of insanity in the age of reason*. Routledge.
Foucault, M., Baudot, A., & Couchman, J. (1978). About the concept of the "dangerous individual" in 19th-century legal psychiatry. *International Journal of Law and Psychiatry, 1*(1), 1–18. https://doi.org/10.1016/0160-2527(78)90020-1
Frances, A. (2013). *Saving Normal: An insider's revolt against out-of-control psychiatric diagnosis, DSM-5, big pharma, and the medicalization of ordinary life*. William Morrow & Co.
Frazer-Carroll, M. (2023). *Mad world: The politics of mental health*. Pluto Press.
Frederick, T., O'Connor, C., & Koziarski, J. (2018). Police interactions with people perceived to have a mental health problem: A critical review of frames, terminology, and definitions. *Victims & Offenders, 13*(8), 1037–1054. https://doi.org/10.1080/15564886.2018.1512024
Freedland, K. E., & Zorumski, C. F. (2023). Success rates in psychiatry. *JAMA Psychiatry, 80*(5), 407–408. https://doi.org/10.1001/jamapsychiatry.2023.0056

Furness T., Maguire T., Brown S. et B. McKenna. (2017). Perceptions of Procedural Justice and Coercion during Community-Based Mental Health Crisis: A Comparison Study among Stand-Alone Police Response and Co-Responding Police and Mental Health Clinician Response. Policing: *A Journal of Policy and Practice*, 11(4): 400–409. https://doi.org/10.1093/police/paw047

Fusar-Poli, P., Salazar de Pablo, G., De Micheli, A., Nieman, D. H., Correll, C. U., Vedel Kessing, L., Pfennig, A., Bechdolf, A., Borgwardt, S., Arango, C., & van Amelsvoort, T. (2020). What is good mental health? A scoping review. *European Neuropsychopharmacology, 31*, 33–46. https://doi.org/10.1016/j.euroneuro.2019.12.105

Garb, H. N. (2021). Race bias and gender bias in the diagnosis of psychological disorders. *Clinical Psychology Review, 90*, Article 102087. https://doi.org/10.1016/j.cpr.2021.102087

Garett, W. S., et al. (2023). Racial disparities in psychiatric decisional capacity consultations. *Psychiatric Services, 74*(1), 10–16. https://doi.org/10.1176/appi.ps.202100685

Ghiasi, N., Azhar, Y. & Singh, J. (2022). *Psychiatric illness and criminality*. StatPearls Publishing.

Gilbert, J. (2013). What kind of thing is "neoliberalism"? *New Formations, 80*(80), 7–22. https://doi.org/10.3898/nEWF.80/81.IntroductIon.2013

Goffman, E. (1961). *Asylums: Essays on the social situation of mental patients and other inmates*. Anchor.

Goodley, G., Pearson, D., & Morris, P. (2022). Predictors of recidivism following release from custody: A meta-analysis. *Psychology, Crime & Law, 28*(7), 703–729. https://doi.org/10.1080/1068316X.2021.1962866

Gosselin, A. (2022). Responding to sanist microaggressions with acts of epistemic resistance. *Hypatia, 37*(2), 293–314. https://doi.org/10.1017/hyp.2022.9

Gøtzsche, C. (2017). Psychopharmacology is not evidence-based medicine. In J. Davies (Ed.), *The sedated society: The causes and harms of our psychiatric drug epidemic* (pp. 23–49). Palgrave Macmillan. https://doi.org/10.1007/978-3-319-44911-1_2

Grewal, D. S., & Purdy, J. (2014). Introduction: Law and neoliberalism. *Law and Contemporary Problems, 77*(1), 1–23.

Grob, G. N. (1998). Psychiatry's holy grail: The search for the mechanisms of mental diseases. *Bulletin of the History of Medicine, 72*(2), 189–219.

Guy, A., Brown, M., Lewis, S., & Horowitz, M. (2020). The "patient voice:" patients who experience antidepressant withdrawal symptoms are often dismissed, or misdiagnosed with relapse, or a new medical condition. *Therapeutic Advances in Psychopharmacology, 10*, 2045125320967183. https://doi.org/10.1177/2045125320967183

Harbusch, M. (Ed.). (2022). *Troubled persons industries: The expansion of psychiatric categories beyond psychiatry*. Palgrave Macmillan. https://doi.org/10.1007/978-3-030-83745-7

Harvey, D. (2010). The right to the city: from capital surplus to accumulation by dispossession. In S. Banerjee-Guha (Eds.), *Accumulation by dispossession: Transformative cities in the new global order* (pp. 17–32). Sage Publication. https://doi.org/10.4135/9788132105923.n2

Harvey, D. (2007). *A brief history of neoliberalism*. Oxford University Press. https://doi.org/10.1093/oso/9780199283262.001.0001

Harvey, D. (2006). Neo-liberalism as creative destruction. *Geografiska Annaler: Series B, Human Geography, 88*(2), 145–158. https://doi.org/10.1111/j.0435-3684.2006.00211.x

Health, T. L. P. (2020). COVID-19: From a PHEIC to a public mental health crisis? *The Lancet. Public Health, 5*(8), Article e414. https://doi.org/10.1016/S2468-2667(20)30165-1

Hirshbein, L. (2010). Sex and gender in psychiatry: A view from history. *Journal of Medical Humanities, 31*, 155–170. https://doi.org/10.1007/s10912-010-9105-5

Huber, M. (2016). Neoliberal energies: Crisis, governance and Hegemony. In S. Springer, K. Birch, & J. MacLeavy (Eds.), *The handbook of neoliberalism* (pp. 493–502). Routledge.

Inda, J. X. (2023). Diminishing life: Racialized medicine, neoliberalism, and precarity in the United States. In *Handbook on governmentality* (pp. 287–303). Edward Elgar Publishing. https://doi.org/10.4337/9781839108662.00026

Johansson, J. A., & Holmes, D. (2024). "Recovery" in mental health services, now and then: A poststructuralist examination of the despotic State machine's effects. *Nursing Inquiry, 31*(1), Article e12558. https://doi.org/10.1111/nin.12558

Kalkan, E., & Madi, J. M. (2022). The mismatch between the cameroonian health realities and the international policies of the world health organization: A post-colonial analysis. In N. Iyit, B. Hastaoglu Ozbek, & A. Toptas (Eds.), *Current research in social, human and administrative sciences* (pp. 1–16). Gece Kitapligi.

Karter, J. M., & Kamens, S. R. (2019). Toward conceptual competence in psychiatric diagnosis: An ecological model for critiques of the DSM. In

S. Steingard (Ed.), *Critical psychiatry: Controversies and clinical implications* (pp. 17–69). Springer Nature. https://doi.org/10.1007/978-3-030-02732-2_2

Keller, R. C. (2019). *Colonial madness: Psychiatry in French North Africa.* University of Chicago Press.

Keller, R. (2001). Madness and colonization: Psychiatry in the British and French empires, 1800–1962. *Journal of Social History, 35*(2), 295–326.

Keski-Valkama, A., Sailas, E., Eronen, M., Koivisto, A. M., Lönnqvist, J., & Kaltiala-Heino, R. (2007). A 15-year national follow-up: Legislation is not enough to reduce the use of seclusion and restraint. *Social Psychiatry and Psychiatric Epidemiology, 42*(9), 747–752. https://doi.org/10.1007/s00127-007-0219-7

Knight, S., Jarvis, E., Ryder, A., Lashley, M., & Rousseau, C. (2022). Ethnoracial differences in coercive referral and intervention among patients with first- episode psychosis. *Psychiatric Services, 73*(1), 2–8. https://doi.org/10.1176/appi.ps.202000715

Kim, J. U., Oleribe, O., Njie, R., & Taylor-Robinson, S. D. (2017). A time for new north–south relationships in global health. *International Journal of General Medicine,* 401–408. https://doi.org/10.2147/IJGM.S146475

King, C. (2019). Race, mental health, and the research gap. *The Lancet Psychiatry, 6*(5), 367–368.

Kirk, S. A., Gomery, T., & Cohen, D. (2017). *Mad science: Psychiatric coercion, diagnosis, and drugs*. Routledge.

Klein, N. (2007). *The shock doctrine*. Penguin Random House.

Koziarski, J., & Huey, L. (2021). #Defund or #Re-Fund? Re-examining Bayley's blueprint for police reform. *International Journal of Comparative and Applied Criminal Justice, 45*(3), 269–284. https://doi.org/10.1080/01924036.2021.1907604

Kramer, R., & Remster, B. (2022). The slow violence of contemporary policing. *Annual Review of Criminology, 5*(1), 43–66. https://doi.org/10.1146/annurev-criminol-030321-041307

Krasnick Warsh, C. (1988). The first Mrs. Rochester: Wrongful confinement, social redundancy, and commitment to the private asylum, 1883–1923. *Historical Papers, 23*(1), 145–167.

Kwete, X., Tang, K., Chen, L., Ren, R., Chen, Q., Wu, Z., Cai, Y., & Li, H. (2022). Decolonizing global health: What should be the target of this movement and where does it lead us? *Global Health Research and Policy, 7*(1), 3. https://doi.org/10.1186/s41256-022-00237-3

Lagerberg, T., Lambe, S., Paulino, A., Yu, R., & Fazel, S. (2025). Systematic review of risk factors for violence in psychosis: 10-year update. *The British Journal of Psychiatry, 226*(2), 100–107. https://doi.org/10.1192/bjp.2024.120

Lamanna, D., & Shapiro, G. K. et al. (2017). Co-responding police–mental health programmes: Service user experiences and outcomes in a large urban centre. *International Journal of Mental Health Nursing, 27*(2), 891–900. https://doi.org/10.1111/inm.12384

Langton, S., Bannister, J., Ellison, M., Haleem, M. S., & Krzemieniewska-Nandwani, K. (2021). Policing and mental ill-health: Using big data to assess the scale and severity of, and the frontline resources committed to, mental ill-health-related calls-for-service. *Policing: A Journal of Policy and Practice, 15*(3), 1963–1976. https://doi.org/10.1093/police/paab035

Laurell, A. C., & Arellano, O. L. (1996). Market commodities and poor relief: The World Bank proposal for health. *International Journal of Health Services, 26*(1), 1–18. https://doi.org/10.2190/PBX9-N89E-4QFE-046V

Lawler, S. (2018). Social mobility talk: Class-making in neo-liberal times. In S. Lawler, & G. Payne (Eds.), *Social mobility for the 21st century: Everyone a winner?* (pp. 118–132). Routledge. https://doi.org/10.4324/9781351996808

Lebenbaum, M., Chiu, M., Vigod, S., & Kurdyak, P. (2018). Prevalence and predictors of involuntary psychiatric hospital admissions in Ontario, Canada: a population-based linked administrative database study. *British Journal of Psychiatry Open, 4*(2), 31–38. https://doi.org/10.1192/bjo.2017.4

Lee, G., & David Cohen, D. (2020). Incidences of involuntary psychiatric detentions in 25 U.S. States. *Psychiatric Services, 72*(1), 61–68. https://doi.org/10.1176/appi.ps.201900477

Leggio, M. (2012). A denial of being: Psychiatrization as epistemic violence. In B. A. LeFrançois, R. Menzies, & G. Reaume (Eds.), *Mad matters: A critical reader in Canadian mad studies* (pp. 122–129). Canadian Scholars.

Lenze, E. J. (2015). Solving the geriatric mental health crisis in the 21st century. *JAMA psychiatry, 72*(10), 967–968. https://doi.org/10.1001/jamapsychiatry.2015.1306

Limenih, G., MacDougall, A., Smith, M. W. J., & Nouvet, E. (2024). "Impaired in life:" Analyzing people's accounts of depression in Ethiopia-Implications for a cultural-eco social approach to global mental health. *International Journal of Social Psychiatry, 71*(1), 78–89. https://doi.org/10.1177/00207640241280620

Lindert, J., Stein, Y., Guggenheim, H., Jaakkola, J. J., & Strous, R. D. (2012). How ethics failed—the role of psychiatrists and physicians in Nazi programs from exclusion to extermination, 1933–1945. *Public Health Reviews, 34*, 1–26. https://doi.org/10.1007/BF03391660

Lincoln, A. (2006). Psychiatric emergency room decision-making, social control and the "undeserving sick." *Sociology of Health & Illness, 28*(1), 54–75. https://doi.org/10.1111/j.1467-9566.2006.00482.x

Lupton, D. (2013). *Risk*. Routledge.

Luty, J. (2014). Psychiatry and the dark side: Eugenics, Nazi and Soviet psychiatry. *Advances in psychiatric treatment*, *20*(1), 52–60. https://doi.org/10.1192/apt.bp.112.010330

Lyon-Callo, V. (2008). *Inequality, poverty, and neoliberal governance: Activist ethnography in the homeless sheltering industry*. University of Toronto Press.

Malla, A., & Gold, I. (2024). Public discourse on mental health: A critical view. *Journal of Psychiatry and Neuroscience, 49*(2), E126–E131. https://doi.org/10.1503/jpn.230161

Menzie, R., Lefrançois, B., & Reaume, G. (2012). Introducing Mad Studies. In B. A. LeFrançois, R. Menzies, & G. Reaume (Eds.), *Mad matters: A critical reader in Canadian mad studies* (pp. 1–22). Canadian Scholars.

Malott, K. M., Barraclough, S., & Yee, T. (2023). Towards decolonizing diagnosis: A critical review and suggested alternatives. *International Journal for the Advancement of Counselling, 45*(1), 1–17. https://doi.org/10.1007/s10447-022-09501-0

Marcus, N., & Stergiopoulos, V. (2022). Re-examining mental health crisis intervention: A rapid review comparing outcomes across police, co-responder and non-police models. *Health & Social Care in the Community, 30*, 1665–1679. https://doi.org/10.1111/hsc.13731

Marriot A. (2023). *Sick development. how rich-country government and World Bank funding to for-profit private hospitals causes harm, and why it should be stopped*. Oxfam International. https://doi.org/10.21201/2023.621529

Mehta, L. (2001). Commentary: the World Bank and its emerging knowledge empire. *Human Organization, 60*(2), 189–196. https://doi.org/10.17730/humo.60.2.cl4dw5yv0gv7867c

McCoy, D., Kapilashrami, A., Kumar, R., Rhule, E., & Khosla, R. (2023). Developing an agenda for the decolonization of global health. *Bulletin of the World Health Organization, 102*(2), 130–136. https://doi.org/10.2471/BLT.23.289949

Mclean, N., & Marshall, L. A. (2010). A front line police perspective of mental health issues and services. *Criminal Behaviour and Mental Health, 20*(1), 62–71. https://doi.org/10.1002/cbm.756

McWade, B. (2016). Recovery-as-policy as a form of neoliberal state making. *Intersectionalities: A Global Journal of Social Work Analysis, Research, Polity, and Practice*, *5*(3), 62–81. https://doi.org/10.48336/IJXSRN4104

Menzies, R., & Palys, T. (2006). Turbulent spirits: Aboriginal patients in the British Columbia psychiatric system, 1879–1950. In J. E. Moran & D. Wright (Eds.), *Mental health and Canadian society: Historical perspectives* (pp. 149–175). McGill-Queen's University Press.

Metzl, J. M. (2009). *The protest psychosis: How Schizophrenia became a Black disease*. Beacon Press.

Mills, C. (2014). *Decolonizing global mental health: The psychiatrization of the majority world*. Routledge.

Mills, C. (2015). The psychiatrization of poverty: Rethinking the mental health-poverty nexus. *Social and Personality Pschology Compass, 9*(5), 213–222. https://doi.org/10.1111/spc3.12168

Mnookin, S. (2016, April 1). *Out of the shadows: making mental health a global development priority.* Report 105052. World Bank Group. http://documents.worldbank.org/curated/en/270131468187759113 (accessed August 9, 2025).

Munt, C., & Littlechild, B. (2024). The lived experience of coercion. In N. Hallett, R. Whittington, D. Richter, & E. Eneje (Eds.), *Coercion and violence in mental health settings: Causes, consequences, management* (pp. 3–25). Springer Nature. https://doi.org/10.1007/978-3-031-61224-4_1

Muir, N., Viljoen, J. L. & Sheperd, S. (2023). Violence risk assessment tools and indigenous peoples: Colonialism as an underlying cause of risk ratings on the SAVRY. *International Journal of Forensic Mental Health, 22*(4), 289–301. https://doi.org/10.1080/14999013.2023.2178554

Moloney, N., et al. (2022). Homelessness amongst psychiatric In-patients: A cross-sectional study in the Mid-West of Ireland. *Irish Journal of Medical Science, 191*(1), 321–326. https://doi.org/10.1007/s11845-021-02546-x

Moncrieff, J., Cooper, R. E., Stockmann, T., Amendola, S., Hengartner, M. P., & Horowitz, M. A. (2024). Difficult lives explain depression better than broken brains. *Molecular Psychiatry, 29*(1), 206–209. https://doi.org/10.1038/s41380-024-02462-3

Moyn, S. (2014). A powerless companion: Human rights in the age of neoliberalism. *Law and Contemporary Problems, 77*(4), 147–169. https://www.jstor.org/stable/24244651

National Institute for Health and Care Excellence. (2009). *Guidance on the use of electroconvulsive therapy*. First published in 2003, last update in 2009. https://www.nice.org.uk/guidance/ta59 (accessed August 9, 2025).
Navarro, V. (2007). Neoliberalism as a class ideology; or the political causes of the growth of inequalities. *International Journal of Health Services, 37*(1), 47–62. https://doi.org/10.2190/AP65-X154-4513-R520
Ness, M. (2016). *Federal Indian policy, psychiatric care, assimilation and the Hiawatha Asylum for Insane Indians* (Publication No. 10131557). [Master dissertation, University of South Dakota]. ProQuest Dissertations & Theses Global. https://www.proquest.com/dissertations-theses/federal-indian-policy-psychiatric-care/docview/1819295648/se-2?accountid=14701
Ogilvie, J. M., & Kisely, S. (2022). Examining the health and criminal justice characteristics for young people on compulsory community treatment orders: An Australian birth cohort and data linkage study. *International Journal of Law and Psychiatry, 83*, Article 101813. https://doi.org/10.1016/j.ijlp.2022.101813
Ohlsson, R. (2018). Public discourse on mental health and psychiatry: Representations in Swedish newspapers. *Health, 22*(3), 298–314. https://doi.org/10.1177/1363459317693405
Olstead, R. (2002). Contesting the text: Canadian media depictions of the conflation of mental illness and criminality. *Sociology of Health & Illness, 24*(5), 621–643. https://doi.org/10.1111/1467-9566.00311
Olver, M. E., Stockdale, K. C., Helmus, L. M., Woods, P., Termeer, J., & Prince, J. (2024). Too risky to use, or too risky not to? Lessons learned from over 30 years of research on forensic risk assessment with Indigenous persons. *Psychological Bulletin, 150*(5), 487–553. https://psycnet.apa.org/doi.org/10.1037/bul0000414
Oostrom, T. (2024). Funding of clinical trials and reported drug efficacy. *Journal of Political Economy, 132*(10), 3298–3333. https://doi.org/10.1086/730383
Orelus, W., & Chomsky, N. (2014). Neoliberalism: The rich over the poor: Noam Chomsky and Pierre Orelus in dialogue. *Counterpoints, 458*, 65–76. http://www.jstor.org/stable/42982198
Organisation for Economic Co-operation and Development. (2023). *Health at a Glance 2023: OECD indicators*. OECD Publisher. https://doi.org/10.1787/c7a518c0-en
Ormel, J., Hollon, S. D., Kessler, R. C., Cuijpers, P., & Monroe, S. M. (2022). More treatment but no less depression: The treatment-prevalence paradox.

Clinical Psychology Review, 91, Article 102111. https://doi.org/10.1016/j.cpr.2021.102111
Ouellet, G., Bernheim, E., & Morin, D. (2021). VU pour vulnérable : La police thérapeutique à l'assaut des problèmes sociaux. *Champ Pénal, 22*, 1–24. https://doi.org/10.4000/champpenal.12988
Oute, J., & McPherson, S. (2024). Conflict and antagonism within global psychiatry: A discourse analysis of organisational responses to the UN reports on rights-based approaches in mental health. *Sociology of Health & Illness, 46*(3), 473–494. https://doi.org/10.1111/1467-9566.13717
Paris, J. (2023). *Fads and fallacies in psychiatry*. Cambridge University Press.
Pariseau-Legault, P., Pelosse, D., Bernheim, E., Goulet, M. H., Ouellet, G., Labrecque-Lebeau, L., & Holmes, D. (2025). When psychiatric services become a waiting room: Situational analysis of involuntary commitment and treatment as experienced by patients and nurses. *Clinical Nursing Research, 34*(3–4), 168–178. https://doi.org/10.1177/10547738251321067
Parker, I. (1997). *Psychoanalytic culture: Psychoanalytic discourse in Western society*. Sage Publications.
Patel, V., Saxena, S., Lund, C., Kohrt, B., Kieling, C., Sunkel, C., et al. (2023). Transforming mental health systems globally: Principles and policy recommendations. *The Lancet, 402*(10402), 656–666. https://doi.org/10.1016/S0140-6736(23)00918-2
Perlin, M. L. (2013). Sanism and the law. Virtual Mentor. *American Medical Association Journal of Ethics, 15*(10), 878–885.
Perlin, M. L. (1992). *On Sanism. Smulaw Review, 46*(2), 373–407.
Pescosolido, B. A., Manago, B., & Monahan, J. (2019). Evolving public views on the likelihood of violence from people with mental illness: Stigma and its consequences. *Health Affairs, 38*(10), 1735–1743. https://doi.org/10.1377/hlthaff.2019.00702
Picketty, T. (2014). *Capital in the twenty-first century*. The Belknap Press of Harvard University Press.
Poole, J. (2011). *Behind the rhetoric: A critical analysis of recovery discourses in Ontario*. Fernwood.
Porter, D. (2013). Establishing normative validity for scientific psychiatric nosology: The significance of integrating patient perspectives. In J. Paris & J. Phillips (Eds.), *Making the DSM-5: Concepts and controversies* (pp. 63–74). Springer. https://doi.org/10.1007/978-1-4614-6504-1_5
Porter R. (1987). *A social history of madness: stories of the insane*. Weidenfeld and Nicolson.

Principles for the protection of persons with mental illness and the improvement of mental health care, A/RES/46/119, 17 December 1991.

Puntis, S., Perfect, D., Kirubarajan, A., Bolton, S., Davies, F., Hayes, A., Harris, E., & Molodynski, A. (2018). A systematic review of co-responder models of police mental health "street" triage. *BMC Psychiatry, 18*(1), 256. https://doi.org/10.1186/s12888-018-1836-2

Rains, L. S. et al. (2019). Variations in patterns of involuntary hospitalisation and in legal frameworks: An international comparative study. *The Lancet, 6*(5), 403–417. https://doi.org/10.1016/S2215-0366(19)30090-2

Ray, W. A., Fuchs, D. C., Olfson, M., Patrick, S. W., Stein, C. M., Murray, K. T., Daugherty, M. S., & Cooper, W. O. (2024). Antipsychotic medications and mortality in children and young adults. *JAMA psychiatry, 81*(3), 260–269. https://doi.org/10.1001/jamapsychiatry.2023.4573

Read, J., Morrison, L., & Harrop, C. (2023). An independent audit of electro-convulsive therapy patient information leaflets in Northern Ireland. *Scotland and Wales. Psychology & Psychotherapy, 96*(4), 885–901. https://doi.org/10.1111/papt.12481

Research Co. (2023, May 5). *Most Canadians back status quo on medical assistance in dying.* Report. https://researchco.ca/wp-content/uploads/2023/05/Tables_MAiD_CAN_05May2023.pdf (accessed August 9, 2025).

Reyes, M. (2017). Danger! The defendant is "Disturbed". risks of using psychiatric assessments to predict future dangerousness. *Connecticut Public Interest Law Journal, 17*, 141–168.

Richter, D., Wall, A., Bruen, A., & Whittington, R. (2019). Is the global prevalence rate of adult mental illness increasing? Systematic review and meta-analysis. *Acta Psychiatrica Scandinavica, 140*(5), 393–407. https://doi.org/10.1111/acps.13083

Rigakos, G. (2002). *The new parapolice: Risk markets and commodified social control*. University of Toronto Press.

Risal, S. (2014). Mismatch between NGO services and beneficiaries' priorities: Examining contextual realities. *Development in Practice, 24*(7), 883–896. https://doi.org/10.1080/09614524.2014.950190

Robinson v. California, 370 U.S. 660 (1962).

Rose, D., & Kalathil, J. (2019). Power, privilege and knowledge: The untenable promise of co-production in mental "health." *Frontiers in Sociology, 4*, 57. https://doi.org/10.3389/fsoc.2019.00057

Rose, N. (1996). Psychiatry as political science: Advanced liberalism and the administration of risk. *History of the Human Sciences, 9*(2), 1–23. https://doi.org/10.1177/095269519600900201

Rose, S. (2017). *No right to be idle: The invention of disability, 1840–1930s*. University of North Carolina Press.
Ross, C. A. (2006). *The C.I.A. Doctors: Human rights violations by American Psychiatrists*. Greenleaf Book Group.
Rossero, E. (2023). *Care in a time of crisis. An ethnography of coercive practices in Italian acute mental health provision*. Palgrave Macmillan. https://doi.org/10.1007/978-3-031-34418-3
Rosenhan, D. L. (1973). On being sane in insane place. *Science, 179*(4070), 250–258. https://doi.org/10.1126/science.179.4070.250
Ruger, J. P. (2005). The changing role of the World Bank in global health. *American Journal of Public Health, 95*(1), 60–70. https://doi.org/10.2105/AJPH.2004.042002
Russo, J. (2023). Psychiatrization, assertions of epistemic justice, and the question of agency. *Frontiers in Sociology, 8*, 1092298. https://doi.org/10.3389/fsoc.2023.1092298
Salam, Z., Odenigbo, O., Newbold, B., Wahoush, O., & Schwartz, L. (2022). Systemic and individual factors that shape mental health service usage among visible minority immigrants and refugees in Canada: A scoping review. *Administration and Policy in Mental Health and Mental Health Services Research, 49*(4), 552–574. https://doi.org/10.1007/s10488-021-01183-x
Samson, C. (2020). *The colonialism of human rights: Ongoing hypocrisies of western liberalism*. Wiley.
Samson, C. (1994). The three faces of privatisation. *Sociology, 28*(1), 79–97. https://doi.org/10.1177/0038038594028001006
Seabrook, M. S., Luscombe, A., Balian, N., Lofters, A., Matheson, F. I., O'Neill, B. G., Owusu-Bempah, A., Persaud, N., & Pinto, A. D. (2023). Police funding and crime rates in 20 of Canada's largest municipalities: A longitudinal study. *Canadian Public Policy, 49*(4), 383–398. https://doi.org/10.3138/cpp.2022-050
Series, L. (2022). *Deprivation of liberty in the shadows of the institution*. Bristol University Press.
Shorter, E. (1997). *A history of psychiatry: From the era of asylum to the age of Prozac*. Wiley.
Schram, S. F. (2018). Neoliberalizing the welfare state: Marketizing social policy/disciplining clients. In D. Cahill, M. Cooper, M. Konings, & D. Primrose (Eds.), *The Sage handbook of neoliberalism* (pp. 308–322). Sage. https://doi.org/10.4135/9781526416001

Scrutton, A. P. (2017). Epistemic injustice and mental illness. In I. J. Kidd, J. Medina, & G. Pohlhaus (Eds.), *The Routledge handbook of epistemic injustice* (pp. 347–355). Routledge.

Scull, A. (1989). *Social order/mental disorder: Anglo-American psychiatry in historical perspective*. University of California Press.

Sreenivasan, S., DiCiro, M., Rokop, J., & Weinberger, L. E. (2022). Addressing systemic bias in violence risk assessment. *Journal of the American Academy of Psychiatry and the Law, 50*(4), 626–35. https://doi.org/10.29158/JAAPL.220031-21

Sondarjee, M. (2021). Collective learning at the boundaries of communities of practice: Inclusive policymaking at the world bank. *Global Society, 35*(3), 307–326. https://doi.org/10.1080/13600826.2020.1835833

Stahnisch, F. W., & Kurbegović, E. (Eds.). (2020). *Psychiatry and the legacies of eugenics: historical studies of Alberta and beyond*. Athabasca University Press. https://doi.org/10.15215/aupress/9781771992657.01

Starkman, M. (2012). The movement. In B. A. LeFrançois, R. Menzies, & G. Reaume (Eds.), *Mad matters: A critical reader in Canadian mad studies* (pp. 27–37). Canadian Scholars.

Statistics Canada. (2024). *Operating expenditures for adult correctional services*. Data. https://www150.statcan.gc.ca/t1/tbl1/en/tv.action?pid=3510001301&request_locale=en (accessed August 9, 2025).

Steele, L. (2020). Disability. *Criminal Justice and Law : Reconsidering Court Diversion. Routledge.* https://doi.org/10.4324/9781351240338

Stephenson, E. (2023, September 22). *Mental disorders and access to mental health care.* Report. Statistics Canada. https://www150.statcan.gc.ca/n1/pub/75-006-x/2023001/article/00011-eng.htm (accessed August 9, 2025).

Substance Abuse and Mental Health Services Administration. (2023). *Key Substance Use and Mental Health Indicators in the United States: Results from the 2023 National Survey on Drug Use and Health.* HHS Publication No. PEP24–07–021, NSDUH Series H-59. https://www.samhsa.gov/data/report/2023-nsduh-annual-national-report (accessed August 9, 2025).

Szmukler, G. (2008). Treatment pressures, coercion and compulsion in mental health care. *Journal of Mental Health, 17*(3), 229–231. https://doi.org/10.1080/09638230802156731

Szmukler, G., & Appelbaum, S. (2008). Treatment pressures, leverage, coercion, and compulsion in mental health care. *Journal of Mental Health, 17*(3), 233–244. https://doi.org/10.1080/09638230802052203

Springer, S. (2016). The violence of neoliberalism. In S. Springer, K. Birch, J. MacLeavy (Eds.), *The handbook of neoliberalism* (pp. 153–163), Routledge. https://doi.org/10.4324/9781315730660

Steiger, S., Moeller, J., Sowislo, J. F., Lieb, R., Lang, U. E., & Huber, C. G. (2022). Approval of coercion in psychiatry in public perception and the role of stigmatization. *Frontiers in Psychiatry, 12*, Article 819573. https://doi.org/10.3389/fpsyt.2021.819573

Stewart, M. (2019). Preventable harm: Creating a mental health crisis. *Journal of Public Mental Health, 18*(4), 224–230. https://doi.org/10.1108/JPMH-07-2019-0070

Stuart, F. (2016). *Down out, and under arrest: Policing and everyday life in skid row*. University of Chicago Press.

Studer, N. S. (2016). The hidden patients: North African women in French Colonial psychiatry. *Böhlau*. https://doi.org/10.7788/9783412502874

Swanson, J. W., McGinty, E. E., Fazel, S., & Mays, V. M. (2015). Mental illness and reduction of gun violence and suicide: Bringing epidemiologic research to policy. *Annals of Epidemiology, 25*(5), 366–376. https://doi.org/10.1016/j.annepidem.2014.03.004

Swartz, S. (2010). The regulation of British colonial lunatic asylums and the origins of colonial psychiatry, 1860–1864. *History of Psychology, 13*(2), 160–177. https://psycnet.apa.org/doi.org/10.1037/a0019223

Szasz, T. (2007). *Coercion as cure: A critical history of psychiatry*. Routledge.

Tajika, A., Furukawa, T. A., Shinohara, K., Kikuchi, S., Toyomoto, R., Furukawa, Y., et al. (2023). Blinding successfulness in antipsychotic trials of acute treatment for schizophrenia: A systematic review. *BMJ Ment Health, 26*(1), Article e300654. https://doi.org/10.1136/bmjment-2023-300654

Taubman, D. S., & Parikh, S. V. (2023). Understanding and addressing mental health disorders: A workplace imperative. *Current Psychiatry Reports, 25*(10), 455–463. https://doi.org/10.1007/s11920-023-01443-7

Tomičić, A., & Gjorgjioska, M. A. (2024). Epistemic inequality in the digital era: Unpacking biases in digital mental health. *Theory & Psychology, 34*(6), 777–797. https://doi.org/10.1177/09593543241279131

Torbay, J. (2023). The work of Donald Ewen Cameron: From psychic driving to MK Ultra. *History of Psychiatry, 34*(3), 320–330. https://doi.org/10.1177/0957154X231163763

Tran, D. Q., Ryder, A. G., & Jarvis, E. (2019). Reported immigration and medical coercion among immigrants referred to a cultural consultation service. *Transcultural Psychiatry, 56*(5), 807–826. https://doi.org/10.1177/1363461519847811

Veitch, K. (2016). Law, social policy, and the neoliberal state. *Neoliberal legality* (pp. 89–103). Routledge.

Van Voren, R. (2025). Abuse of psychiatry for political purposes in the USSR: A case-study and personal account of the efforts to bring them to an end. In H. Helmchen, N. Sartorius, & J. Gather (Eds.), *Ethics in psychiatry: European contributions* (pp. 659–677). Springer. https://doi.org/10.1007/978-94-024-2274-0_36

Verhoeven, J. E., Han, L. K., Lever-van Milligen, B. A., Hu, M. X., Révész, D., Hoogendoorn, A. W., et al. (2023). Antidepressants or running therapy: Comparing effects on mental and physical health in patients with depression and anxiety disorders. *Journal of Affective Disorders, 329*, 19–29. https://doi.org/10.1016/j.jad.2023.02.064

Wacquant, L. (2010). Crafting the Neoliberal state: Workfare, Prisonfare, and social insecurity. *Sociological Forum, 25*, 197–220. https://www.jstor.org/stable/40783391

Wahl, O. F. (1995). *Media madness: Public images of mental illness*. Rutgers University Press.

Ward, T. (2016). Dynamic risk factors: Scientific kinds or predictive constructs. *Psychology, Crime & Law, 22*(1–2), 2–16. https://doi.org/10.1080/1068316X.2015.1109094

Watson, A. C., & Wood, J. D. (2017). Everyday police work during mental health encounters: A study of call resolutions in Chicago and their implications for diversion. *Behavioral Sciences & the Law, 35*(5–6), 442–455. https://doi.org/10.1002/bsl.2324

Wexler, D. (1972). Therapeutic justice. *Minnesota Law Review, 57*, 289–338.

Whitley, R., Wang, J., Carmichael, V., & Wellen, R. (2017). Newspaper articles related to the not criminally responsible on account of mental disorder (NCRMD) designation: A comparative analysis. *The Canadian Journal of Psychiatry, 62*(1), 697–701. https://doi.org/10.1177/0706743717720688

Whiting, D., Lichtenstein, P., & Fazel, S. (2021). Violence and mental disorders: A structured review of associations by individual diagnoses, risk factors, and risk assessment. *Lancet Psychiatry, 8*, 150–161. https://doi.org/10.1016/S2215-0366(20)30262-5

Willse, C. (2010). Neo-liberal biopolitics and the invention of chronic homelessness. *Economy and Society, 39*(2), 155–184. https://doi.org/10.1080/03085141003620139

Winter, N. R., Leenings, R., & Ernsting, J., et al. (2022). Quantifying deviations of brain structure and function in major depressive disorder across neuroimaging modalities. *JAMA Psychiatry, 79*(9), 879–888. https://doi.org/10.1001/jamapsychiatry.2022.1780

Wipond, R. (2023). *Your consent is not required: The rise in psychiatric detentions, forced treatment, and abusive guardianships.* BenBella.

Wong, A. H., Taylor, R. A., Ray, J. M., & Bernstein, S. L. (2019). Physical restraint use in adult patients presenting to a general emergency department. *Annals of Emergency Medicine, 73*(2), 183–192. https://doi.org/10.1016/j.annemergmed.2018.06.020

World Health Organization. (2024). *Mental health: Promoting and protecting human rights.* https://www.who.int/news-room/questions-and-answers/item/mental-health-promoting-and-protecting-human-rights

WHO & Office of the High Commissioner for Human Rights. (2023). *Mental health, human rights and legislation: guidance and practice.* https://iris.who.int/bitstream/handle/10665/373126/9789240080737-eng.pdf

World Health Organization. (2016, April 13). *Out of the shadows: making mental health a global priority.* Speech transcription. https://www.who.int/director-general/speeches/detail/out-of-the-shadows-making-mental-health-a-global-priority (accessed August 9, 2025).

World Health Organization. (2008). *The Global Burden of Disease: 2004 Update.* Report.

World Health Organization. (2001). *Strengthening mental health promotion.* Report.

Wright, D. (1997). Getting out of the asylum: Understanding the confinement of the insane in the nineteenth century. *Social History of Medicine, 10*(1), 137–155. https://doi.org/10.1093/shm/10.1.137

Yoldi-Negrette, M., Gill, L. M., Olivares, S., Lauzière, A., Désilets, M., & Tourjan, S. V. (2022). The effect of continuation and maintenance electroconvulsive therapy on cognition: A systematic review of the literature and meta-analysis. *Journal of Affective Disorders, 1*(316), 148–160. https://doi.org/10.1016/j.jad.2022.08.005

3

The Promise of Therapeutic Justice

> A question, then, for proponents is: why not take a more radical standpoint? One answer might be that it is not the remit of therapeutic jurisprudence to challenge law, only to find better or more "therapeutic" ways to the support the status quo's law and order regimen. Another answer might be that therapeutic jurisprudence is acutely aware of its tenuous tenure; it wants to keep its seat at the table and therefore cannot afford to "rock the boat" too much.—Amanda Wilson (2023: 324)

The "mental health crisis" comes on the heels of political discourse, starting in the 1970s, that attributed several social problems to deinstitutionalization[1] (Winkler et al., 2016). These include homelessness and

[1] Deinstitutionalization is defined by a 1977 U.S. General Accounting Office as "the process of (1) preventing both unnecessary admission to and retention in institutions; (2) finding and developing appropriate alternatives in the community for housing, treatment, training, education, and rehabilitation of persons who do not need to be in institutions; and (3) improving conditions, care, and treatment for those who need to have institutional care" (Segal, 2013). Deinstitutionalization has targeted people with mental disorders and people with disabilities, youth, adults, and elderly persons incarcerated in asylums and in the child welfare system.

E. Bernheim, *Therapeutic (In)justice and the Shadow Carceral State*, The Politics of Mental Health and Illness, https://doi.org/10.1007/978-3-032-16186-4_3

extreme poverty; revolving doors, whereby people constantly return to the institutions; and an increase in crime and incarceration rates.

However, studies on mental health and deinstitutionalization suggest a much more nuanced reality. Deinstitutionalization is the result of a combination of circumstances, such as the advancement of knowledge about the negative effects of institutionalization and about alternative medical and psychological care and treatments, the rising costs of institutionalization and the development of less expensive alternatives and public services, as well as the struggle for the rights of institutionalized people. According to Steven P. Segal (2013), deinstitutionalization has been the fruit of a rare political "momentum:"

> Conservatives supported deinstitutionalization, viewing it as a means to reduce institutional censuses, use cheaper institutional placements, and limit government spending. Liberals and progressives championed civil rights protections and humane community care. The only opposition came from employee unions affected by job decreases resulting from institutional closures.

Yet, deinstitutionalization has been nothing more than "transinstitutionalization," i.e. moving people from one institution to another without reducing the number of individuals institutionalized. US studies show major changes in the number of people institutionalized in the various institutions—asylums, prisons, group homes, nursing homes, child welfare system—and a notable transfer from asylums to prisons and group homes or nursing homes, with the total number of institutionalized people remaining unchanged or almost unchanged over time (Adler-Bolton & Vierkant, 2022; Harcourt, 2006; Mowbray et al., 2002). This observation disproves the frequently made assumption that poverty, revolving doors, and criminalization stem from a lack of investment or poor planning of deinstitutionalization. It suggests, on the contrary, that deinstitutionalization was a political shift in the way marginalized social groups were managed rather than a mass discharge from carceral institutions and did not modify fundamentally state coercive practices.

In the wake of transinstitutionalization, the presence of defendants with mental health or addiction problems in the criminal justice system has been the subject of debate. Not only was it acknowledged that the rights of these defendants were inherently violated through criminalization and by the criminal procedure, but the justice system itself appeared helpless and inadequate to manage these challenges. Without calling police and judicial practices into question, the idea that criminal justice can play a different social role—a therapeutic one—has been gaining ground.

The Therapeutic Jurisprudence Doctrine

The idea that justice can be therapeutic has its origins in the debate about the constitutional rights of defendants living with mental disorders or addictions (Wexler, 1972). In *Robinson v. California* in 1962, the Supreme Court of the United States was inspired by the British approach developed forty years earlier that involved the government and the police collaborating with the medical community to respond to drug trafficking. From this perspective, addiction problems are treated as health issues, not criminal-justice issues (Schur, 1961). The court asserts that "in the light of contemporary human knowledge, a law which made a criminal offense of such a disease would doubtless be universally thought to be an infliction of cruel and unusual punishment" (370 U.S 660, 1962: 666). However, in his concurrent opinion, Justice Douglas explains why it is cruel and unusual "to treat as a criminal a person who is a drug addict" (370 U.S 660, 1962: 668):

> The addict is a sick person. He may, of course, be confined for treatment or for the protection of society. Cruel and unusual punishment results not from confinement, but from convicting the addict of a crime. The purpose of [confinement] is not to cure, but to penalize. (370 U.S 660, 1962: 676)

In other words, it is unconstitutional to punish a person suffering from addiction or illness, but it is constitutional to involuntarily confine them for treatment purposes. Criminal justice—punitive and retributive—is therefore inadequate when it comes to addiction or mental health

(Winick, 2003). For Justice Douglas, a curative model of justice was needed.

David Wexler, a law professor in Tucson, Arizona, did not view this paradigm shift favorably. In "Therapeutic Justice" (1972), they identified several slippery slopes in the idea that involuntary treatment could become a judicial measure substituting for sentencing. For them, the "elasticity" of the notions of "mental illness" and "danger," "coupled with a pressure to intervene and treat whenever that appears possible, enables the therapeutic state to coerce conformity in many instances where coercion is not essential for social protection" (1972: 294). At the time, Wexler's fears were shared by several scholars who pointed out an increase in surveillance and control of marginalized social groups within the therapeutic approach, sometimes far beyond what the law prescribed or allowed (Katz, 1969; Rieff, 1966). In line with Michel Foucault's (2008, 2015) theories on bio-power and governmentality, according to which the state disciplines and controls its citizens by various regulatory means, the therapeutic approach requires from individuals to "exchange rights for welfare" (Garland, 1981: 43) "without offering any appreciable clinical benefit" (Eastman, 1995: 1082). While this period was an era of judicial recognition of the right to consent to treatment (Faden & Beauchamp, 1986)—as a means of adjusting the balance of power between physicians and patients—it also saw increasing emphasis on and development of the medical paradigm as the basis of the therapeutic state (Leifer, 1990; Nolan, 1998; Polsky, 1991; Szasz, 1984). However, in the wake of transinstitutionalization, the right to consent to care, and therefore to refuse it, has been considered by some psychiatrists as a cause of the state's abandonment of the most disadvantaged individuals. The deterioration of mental health resulting from refusal of care has appeared as a violation of the right to health, dignity, and life. In this regard, some psychiatrists have argued that their patients have a right to treatment, which would protect them from the consequences of their own decisions and authorize psychiatrists to protect their "best interests" (Birnbaum, 1960). Yet, for Wexler,

> the state may not know what is in fact "best" for the individual, it may not have the ability to improve his lot even if it properly understands

his best interest, and, perhaps most important, it offends one's dignity to have the state meddling in his personal affairs. (Wexler, 1972: 324)

In the decades that followed, Wexler studied the relationship between law and psychiatry from the point of view of therapeutic effects (1975, 1981, 1988)—the positive or negative consequences of law and its administration on "psychological well-being" (Wexler, 2021: 3). Focusing on involuntary commitment, they concluded that legal provisions can produce anti-therapeutic effects, and that interdisciplinary collaboration in the design of law can improve both justice and therapeutic objectives, even though psychiatrists have participated in drafting mental health laws since the first laws in the nineteenth century (Foucault et al., 1978; Scull, 1989). Based on these observations, they wrote their doctrine in *Therapeutic Jurisprudence: The Law as a Therapeutic Agent* (1990), a book that would revolutionize their career and the practice of mental health law. According to therapeutic jurisprudence, "[l]egal decision making should consider not only economic factors, public safety, and the protection of patients' rights; it should also take into account the therapeutic implications of a rule and its alternatives" (Wexler & Winick, 1991: 982).

Going against the grain of therapeutic justice, which is paternalistic and poses a threat to rights, therapeutic jurisprudence adheres to the principle of individual autonomy "on the basis that self-determination is therapeutically advantageous" (Winick, 1997: 191). On the one hand, therapeutic jurisprudence is based on respect for people's decisions concerning their health and treatment (Winick, 1994). On the other hand, the main premise of therapeutic jurisprudence is the idea that if people can express themselves and feel validated by a court, it will increase compliance with judicial decisions and treatments (Winick, 1994, 1999). This compliance could be further enhanced by "behavioral contracts" designed "to increase motivation and psychological functioning" (Winick, 1997: 194). Generally used in clinical contexts and based on positive reinforcement, the behavioral contract establishes measurable goals to be achieved and involves individuals making commitments to the court in exchange for rewards, or penalties in the event of failure (Winick, 2003). For Wexler, behavioral contracts are a means of increasing the therapeutic potential of the judicial process:

> Therapeutic jurisprudence would suggest that trial judges shaping conditional release orders might increase compliance with such orders if a patient/defendant were asked to embody the conditional release plan in a behavioral contract, and if the hearing were used as a forum for the patient/defendant to make a "public" commitment to comply—a commitment made in the presence of the judge and agreed-upon family members. Such a procedure would tap therapeutic potential without offending our notions of justice. (Wexler, 1992: 519)

The philosophical orientation of therapeutic jurisprudence, focusing on individual responsibility and choice, and the words used by the authors David Wexler and Bruce Winick—motivation, behavior, and compliance—reflect a strong ideological affinity with neoliberalism. Thus, the therapeutic jurisprudence doctrine does not consider any of the structural, historical or political issues that affect people judicialized in mental health, such as precarious work and living conditions, or systemic sexism or racism (Kerrigan, 2020; Wilson, 2023); instead, it promotes an individualized judicial process. It fully embraces the recovery approach, promoting treatment regardless of the many scientific controversies surrounding the psychiatric discipline, risk, and capacity assessment tools, as well as treatment. And it does not call into question criminalization and judicialization in mental health, or police practices, despite the revolving doors that tend to constantly bring the same people back in courts. On the contrary, therapeutic jurisprudence relies on the judicial process to change individual behavior while bringing about social transformation driven by the idea that "[l]egal rules and the way they are applied are social forces" (Winick, 2003: 1062). To achieve this social transformation, therapeutic jurisprudence aims to transform the legal system (Perlin, 1993), and more specifically the role of the courts, to make it capable of managing social problems, such as homelessness and poverty (Winick, 2003).

"Court diversion"—criminal courts processes established to deal with specific problems such as mental health, substance abuse, homelessness, veteran issues or prostitution—"utilize a designated judicial, legal, and treatment team to divert individuals from the criminal justice system into community-based treatment in lieu of traditional case processing and sentencing" (Castellano, 2011: 958). Initially developed in parallel with therapeutic jurisprudence, court diversion—also called "problem-solving courts" or "wellness courts"—has become the way in which the doctrine of therapeutic jurisprudence has been typically implemented (Nolan, 2003). Originating in the United States, the development of court diversion programs has spread to several common-law jurisdictions—England, Ireland, Scotland, Australia, New Zealand, and Canada. The operation of these courts varies enormously due to a high degree of discretion enjoyed by judges in the judicial process (Castellano, 2011; Collins, 2020), and also because the notion of therapy is "intentionally vague" (Winick, 1997: 192), meaning that a wide variety of social or medical interventions can constitute therapy. The indeterminacy of the notion of therapy within therapeutic jurisprudence is said to be explained in terms of "honoring" people's wishes (Winick, 1997: 192), a surprising choice when we recall that the indeterminacy of notions in therapeutic justice had been identified by Wexler as a slippery slope that could negatively affect rights.

Court diversion is presented as a "second chance" or an "alternative" for people who have often had repeated contact with the justice system (Lane, 2002; MacDonald et al., 2022). According to Linda Steele (2020), these specific court programs share five characteristics: they (1) target defendants on the basis of a more or less clearly established medical diagnosis or condition; (2) facilitate access to services; (3) use legal considerations different from those governing conventional criminal judicial processes, notably criminal responsibility; (4) involve coercion; and (5) involve collaboration between police, justice, health, and social services, as well as community groups. Embodying the continuum of care and stepping out of their usual role as neutral arbiters, the courts coordinate legal and social services, connect defendants to various therapeutic providers, and monitor and control their therapeutic progress. This operation involves the collection and use of defendants' personal information, as well as the sharing of this information between the various actors on the continuum of care (Lane, 2002; Nolan, 2003; Steele, 2020). These characteristics of court diversion programs recall and resonate with the statements police officers in Montreal, Canada, which I reported at the end of the preceding chapter, when they affirmed that judicialization is a lever for them to seek services for people who are otherwise neglected and abandoned.

Court diversion has been developed locally by judges or teams of legal professionals, based on the specific contexts of different jurisdictions, as well as on their preferences (Collins, 2023). Enrollment in therapy leads to the suspension of charges while therapy is ongoing, and then the charges are dropped or reduced if therapy is successful. Successful completion of the therapeutic objectives is essential to benefit from the reduction or dropping of charges; failure of the therapy, on the other hand, results in the defendants going through the traditional criminal trial. The objectives vary greatly from one court diversion program to another, whether in terms of the requirements for successful completion, the sanctions for non-compliance, or the outcome after successful completion of the therapy.

Studies have shown that court diversion is a long way from the promises of therapeutic jurisprudence. Admission to a program depends primarily on the selection of legal actors who enjoy great discretion; yet, beyond the legal criteria, judges' opinions vary as to the importance of issues involved (Macdonald et al., 2024). Studies show that being Indigenous, under 45 or having substance-induced psychosis are factors that make defendants less likely to be diverted despite eligibility (Macdonald et al., 2023; Marr et al., 2024). Diverted defendants participate in programs under the threat of trial or incarceration and have little say in the direction of the judicial process (MacDonald et al., 2022). They must defer to legal, social work or health professionals when it comes to problem identification, objectives, and therapy choices. In the process, defendants must disclose information about their personal lives, which exposes them to demands that go beyond the medical dimension of their lives (Epperson et al., 2022; Steele, 2020). Amanda Wilson (2023) shows, for example, that Indigenous defendants may be required by the court to distance themselves from their families, which are often perceived as dysfunctional by judicial actors. The objectives of the judicial process and the means of achieving them are determined by the judicial actors, leaving little opportunity for defendants to express their preferences and exercise self-determination (Epperson et al., 2022; MacDonald et al., 2022). Court diversion programs have shown little inclination to take cultural differences into account, imposing Western thinking and mental health practices, and perpetuating the colonial practices characteristic of the criminal justice system (Steele, 2020; Wilson, 2023), including in former colonies (Kerrigan, 2020).

The informal, flexible, and collaborative procedure typical of court diversion can create situations that might violate the traditional procedural safeguards of the criminal trials and the right to due process (Nolan, 2020; Steele, 2020); defendants must admit to the facts or plead guilty even though the evidence has not been uncovered; judges intervene during hearings to encourage defendants or make "judgement calls" (Lane, 2002: 961); judges monitor the progress of defendants through "extensive communication" with community-based programs: "the court informs the treatment programs of each defendant's compliance conditions, and the programs keep the court informed as to defendants' progress" (Lane, 2002: 967); the duration and intensity of monitoring and control exercised by the court is often out of proportion to the offense allegedly committed, in terms of both duration and intensity.

In addition to raising questions about the quality and validity of the consent of defendants when they enroll in court diversion programs, the particular procedure calls into question the ability of counsels to play their role of defense and of the judges to make independent and impartial decisions at the time of admission of facts or guilty plea, as well as afterwards (Lane, 2002; Nolan, 1998). What is more, the offenses involved are usually minor, and are often linked to poor living conditions, addiction, or homelessness. While many North American cities have specific court diversion programs for different social problems, studies show that the same people tend to appear before these courts, and that they may "be subjected to criminal punishment processes for longer than they would have been if they had opted not to enroll in the first place" (Collins, 2023: 552).

But do court diversion programs work? Curiously, the efficacy of court diversion programs is generally assessed in terms of reduction of recidivism and cost, rather than the therapeutic benefit for the defendants.

Support for court diversion, therefore, focuses on the programs' ability to manage risk and reduce costs, rather than on improving the health or living conditions of the defendants. The success rate is relatively low, with about half of the defendants "incarcerated after trying—and failing—at the treatment program" (Collins, 2023: 552). Indigenous defendants have difficulty meeting their therapy objectives due to the discord with their values and beliefs, and the process exposes them and their families to the risk of intervention by the criminal justice or child welfare systems (Wilson, 2023). Failure is considered a systemic aberration and attributed to the defendants, instead of to the model itself (Collins, 2020). Although court diversion program, especially drug courts, has been the subject of numerous empirical studies over the past two decades, "the mechanisms through which problem-solving courts reduce recidivism and support rehabilitation are unclear" (Rusch & Banner, 2024). The question of who is included and who is excluded is often absent from analyses; data are mixed, showing at best a modest reduction in recidivism; various methodological flaws affect several studies, and several problem-solving court models have not been evaluated (Collins, 2023). Anecdotes and personal stories, as well as the impressions or opinions of court diversion practitioners (Collins, 2020), are often used to demonstrate efficacy (Slate, 2003).

In the absence of adequate and available health and social services, the criminal justice system has increasingly been seen as the "gateway to services" (Shdaimah & McGarry, 2018). The police and the courts are therefore increasingly seen as key players in social and mental health intervention, sometimes at the request of family or community members (Rusch & Banner, 2024). However, research has not shown that court diversion programs connect defendants to health or social services any better than well-funded public services do. Studies show, on the contrary, that the practices of care and social professionals—particularly nurses and social workers—on a continuum of care including police, criminal courts and prisons, are complicated by the fact that they must deal with demanding requirements that are in tension with the values of their own profession (Franke & Shdaimah, 2022; Nyvoll, 2025; Rasmussen & Suslovic, 2025; Sasso et al., 2018). In other words, the priorities and values emanating from institutions charged with surveillance, social control and individual responsibility infuse the entire continuum of care (Shdaimah & McGarry, 2018).

Despite the absence of tangible proof of efficacy, court diversion programs are most often presented as an "evidence-based approach to criminal justice reform" (Collins, 2020: 1585; Nolan, 2009). Two reasons for the popularity of court diversion include the belief that it is less repressive than regular criminal courts and that it can bring about change in people (Ouellet et al., 2021). Judges tend to be "'true believers' who saw [court diversion] as a panacea, a revolutionary innovation that promised to radically transform or 'reinvent' the [...] criminal justice system" (Nolan, 2020: 646), producing structural social changes (Collins, 2023). Frustrated by the limits of their traditional role, some judges have become personally involved in the local development of court diversion programs, and also in leading a movement to extend therapeutic jurisprudence. According to Erin R. Collins (2020: 1601),

> many judges who preside over [court diversion programs] have a professional self-interest in sustaining and expanding the [court diversion programs] court empire. These personal interests provide an independent reason, apart from the public interest, that judges may seek to entrench the [court diversion] model.

Although it in no way challenges the status quo in criminal justice, which entails the overcriminalization of marginalized people and coercion, therapeutic jurisprudence is a cultural shift consistent with neoliberalism suggesting—in contrast to decades of research—that criminal justice can serve a positive function. Yet therapeutic jurisprudence is not limited to criminal justice. Early in the development of the theory, Wexler (2008) identified five main areas for the development of therapeutic jurisprudence: (1) legal education, (2) moving from theory to practice, (3) interdisciplinary collaboration, (4) international dimensions, and (5) expansion across the legal spectrum. The goal of reforming the law and its practice in all legal fields has taken shape in the "normative agenda [that has] drive[n] therapeutic jurisprudence research" since its inception (Winick, 1997: 188). And the plan worked. The exponential number of publications on therapeutic jurisprudence in all areas of law and the creation of the International Society of Therapeutic Jurisprudence in 2017 indicate the current importance of the doctrine.

The Problem of Rights

Therapeutic jurisprudence is ultimately what justice is in a neoliberal society (Nolan, 2003): rooted in the conviction that social problems are due to individuals and can be resolved through responsibility and empowerment. It is based on the premise that mental health problems cause and explain behaviors and situations, to the exclusion of structural causes, whether economic, political, or social (Collins, 2020; Nolan, 1998). Not only are these premises not supported by data; they also construct an "other" imbued with common prejudices associated with sanism such as risk and incapacity, as well as assume the necessity of police, judicial, and therapeutic interventions including by coercion if necessary (Gosselin, 2022; Perlin, 1992, 2013). Yet therapeutic jurisprudence conceals coercion through various mechanisms such as the use of terminology associated with therapy, and therefore with best interests, the application of procedures that would guarantee the necessity of therapeutic measures, and relational anchoring more akin to the helping relationship than to the judicial process (Rossero, 2023).

The therapeutic jurisprudence doctrine, as well as movements to judicialize involuntary commitment and treatment, is the result of the commitment and work of rights advocates. At the international level, the *Convention on the Rights of People with Disabilities* (CRPD, 2006) is the product of two decades of activism. CRPD innovatively included people with mental health experience in its drafting process, whereas they had previously been systematically excluded, including in the drafting of the *Principles for the protection of persons with mental illness and the improvement of mental health care* (1991) (Kanter, 2014). The CRPD asserts that states "shall closely consult with and actively involve persons with disabilities, including children with disabilities" in the development and implementation of legislation and policies that affect them (article 4 (3)). The CRPD also represents a shift from a strictly medical model of disability to a social model that recognizes the structural and social dimensions of discrimination, in particular the fact that most disabled people live in poverty. In addition to recognizing the right to protection against discrimination, the convention affirms several rights, including the right to live in a community, to freedom, to equality, to free and informed consent, and to protection against torture or cruel, inhumane or degrading treatment or punishment, including medical experimentation without consent. The CRPD stipulates that people living with a disability enjoy legal capacity, and that states must implement measures to support the exercise of legal capacity, as well as safeguards to prevent abuse.

Nevertheless, the CRPD has not achieved unanimity. Its elaboration has highlighted opposing and irreconcilable visions of mental health, between complete abolition of mental health laws and coercion, and an approach based on risk management and protection of incapacitated individuals (Wilson, 2022). Thus, and as mentioned in Chapter 2, the CRPD affirms that deprivation of liberty is possible in accordance with the law and without discrimination. It makes no mention of the criminal justice system, or of the use of seclusion rooms, restraints, or controversial practices such as electroconvulsive therapy.

International law recognizes and assumes the legitimacy of criminal, civil, and administrative justice, just as it assumes that rights are not absolute. In mental health, this rationale prevents the questioning of coercive practices, believing, on the contrary, that the conformity of decisions to restrict rights with mental health legislation is a guarantee against arbitrariness (Steele, 2020). However, there is no consensus on this interpretation of international law, echoing the debate that took place in the wake of the CRPD's development. The "Geneva impasse" reflects the fact that, over time, United Nation bodies and officials have taken contradictory positions on the compliance of coercive practices with human rights standards—some asserting that coercion is consistent with human rights, and others taking an abolitionist stance (Martin & Gurbai, 2019; Wilson, 2022). The CRPD requires states to enact "appropriate legislative, administrative and other measures for the implementation of the rights recognized in the present Convention" (article 4(1)a). This provision is open-ended enough to allow legislators to do their work, regardless of where they stand in relation to the Geneva impasse. In practice, the abolition of coercion appears to be an unrealistic objective in the view of most individuals working toward its reduction, and a rights-based approach is generally advocated for (Birkeland et al., 2024; Szmuler, 2025). Over the past thirty years, mental health laws were amended in most of the global North jurisdictions; none have effectively abolished coercion—including in places where alternatives to psychiatric hospitalization are actively implemented and promoted, such as in Trieste, Italy (Wilson, 2022)—and the involvement of experienced people in legislative processes remains quite rare (Joffe & Lattanzio, 2024; Löve, 2023).

In several countries, reducing the use of coercion in psychiatry has been a goal expressly pursued for decades (Whittington et al., 2023). Research shows that structural changes can reduce the use of coercion in psychiatric settings (Gooding et al., 2020). For example, physically reorganizing care units, enhancing of the therapeutic relationship and making restraint equipment less readily available are measures that can reduce the use of seclusion rooms and restraints (Torrents & Björkdahl, 2024). Access to social and crisis services in the community can help avoid involuntary commitments (Molyneaux et al., 2019). Acting on the social determinants of health, notably housing, reduces mental health problems in general (Patel et al., 2023). These measures require an investment of financial and material resources that is inconsistent with neoliberal policies and that has not been done in most of the countries of the global North, which have opted instead for legislative changes. Mental health legislations generally ensure procedural rights and remedies for people subject to coercive practices in psychiatry. For example, the use of seclusion rooms and restraints without consent must be limited to emergency risk-management situations, and not for reasons of understaffing or discipline; in civil matters, the decisions of involuntary commitment or treatment have been entrusted to or can be reviewed by a court or an administrative tribunal; in criminal cases, defendants found not criminally responsible on account of mental disorder or unfit to stand trial can no longer be detained indefinitely, and their situation must be reviewed periodically. However, legislative changes without policy changes are ineffective. Involuntary admissions have been on the rise for over a decade (Bernheim, 2022; Lebenbaum et al., 2018; Lee & Cohen, 2021; Rains et al., 2019; Wipond, 2023), as has involuntary treatment in community (Kisely et al., 2024; Light, 2019; Schölin et al., 2024; Wipond, 2023). Defendants found not criminally responsible on account of mental disorder are detained on average three times longer than those convicted of the same offenses (Martin, 2019; Perlin, 2017). Violations of substantive and procedural rights in the application of mental health laws—failure to meet time limits, to provide information and to obtain a consent; difficulty accessing legal services; the deference of courts to expert opinions and courts exceeding their jurisdiction—have been documented in both psychiatric and judicial environments in many jurisdictions for decades (Appelbaum, 1997; Bernheim, 2022; Brooks, 2010; Case, 2016; Doll, 2016; Hiday, 1977, 1988, 1990; Thom & Nakarada-Kordic, 2014). The remedies available under mental health legislation have been rarely used (Appelbaum, 1997; Bernheim, 2022). These finding suggest that legislative changes have served more to redefine the political and symbolic landscape than to produce tangible outcomes for people concerned (Adler-Bolton & Vierkant, 2022).

This interpretation is supported by the emergence and integration of new coercive practices into legislation in several jurisdictions since the turn of the century and since the elaboration of the CRPD. To the risk that has been present in legislation for decades, criteria have been added over time, such as the need for treatment or the incapacity to make decisions, particularly treatment decisions, to justify involuntary commitment and treatment (Appelbaum, 1997). The addition of these criteria does not alter the sanism present in the legal system (Perlin, 1992, 2013), while it significantly extends the scope of mental health legislation. Transinstitutionalization and policies to rationalize public spending have led to a search for effective, less costly alternatives to hospitalization (Gerbasi et al., 2000). Involuntary commitment and treatment in the community have become increasingly common measures. These measures make it possible to impose hospitalization and treatment on people in their living environment. The modalities and criteria differ from country to country, but in many jurisdictions, people are placed in situations where they can be admitted involuntarily in hospital or treated involuntarily at home. In Ontario, Canada, for example, community treatment orders are granted with the consent of individuals who, should they refuse treatment within the community, may be subjected to involuntary commitment. Mental health laws have therefore continued to permit formal coercion—detention, involuntary admission, and involuntary treatment—but have also legitimized informal coercion as a threat or bargain to gain "consent" to involuntary treatment. As with court diversion programs, involuntary treatment in the community modifies the legal notion of consent, which must be both informed and free. Freedom of consent requires that it be free of all pressure, influence, or coercion, including informal ones. However, it seems to be accepted that a consent obtained in a context where refusal has consequences for freedom—trial and potential detention for court diversion, involuntary admission for involuntary treatment in the community—is considered valid in a mental health context.

The issue of consent has been at the heart of the ongoing battle for mental health rights. In line with the Geneva impasse, there are two opposing interpretations on the topic. First is the strict application of the principles of consent to care, ensuring that a refusal of psychiatric treatment must be respected regardless of the consequences. Second is the contradiction I explained in the beginning of this chapter between these principles and the "right to treatment," which would stem from the denial or the "lack of insight." This last interpretation implicitly considers the incapacity and need for protection of people with mental health issues, who would not be able to make "good decisions" according to their "best interest." However, the "best interest" is determined from a clinical perspective, without considering factors such as lived experience, beliefs, and preferences, as well as power imbalances that are likely to influence consent (Brosnan & Flynn, 2017). Although the question of the capacity to make good decisions concerns all areas of medicine (Schneider, 2006), it manifests itself differently in psychiatry. According to psychiatrist Paul S. Appelbaum (2007: 1835) "the assignment of diagnostic categories may be confused with the determination of capacity." Research shows that the profile of people considered incapable to consent to treatment varies according to the assessment tools used (Curley et al.,

2022), and that these tools particularly target marginalized and racialized people (Garett et al, 2023). Interpreting the question of consent in psychiatry from the angle of best interest gives rise to different practices in physical medicine and psychiatry and results in epistemic violence and discrimination (Leggio, 2012; Russo, 2023; Scrutton, 2017;). This is what psychiatrist Silvana Galderisi and colleagues explain in an article entitled "Ethical challenges in contemporary psychiatry: an overview and an appraisal of possible strategies and research needs:"

> In jurisdictions with well-developed laws governing non-consensual treatment in general medicine, it is only when a person lacks the decision-making capacity to consent to a treatment that the possibility of non-consensual treatment enters the frame. There is usually a further requirement: treatment must be in the person's "best interests." It is accepted that patients with "physical" disorders, if they have decision-making capacity, can make treatment refusals even when this may carry grave consequences.
> For a person with a "mental disorder" who rejects treatment, conventional mental health law does not demand that special regard be given to the person's decision-making ability, as it is usually done for people with "physical" diseases—for example, the ability to understand important information about the illness and reasons for the proposed treatment; to appreciate the relevance of that information to one's predicament; and to use or reason with that information in the light of one's values or personal life goals. Nor does the question arise of how the proposed treatment is purported to be in the person's "best interests." The perspective is essentially the clinician's, not the service user's one. The unfair discrimination towards those with a "mental disorder" is thus clear. (Galderisi et al., 2024: 367)

These differing interpretations of consent in mental health consistently bring us back to the "considerable power" historically delegated to psychiatry (Fernando, 2010: 57), discussed in the preceding chapter. The fact that psychiatrists can detain a person because of the risk they would represent justifies in itself the possibility of overriding their consent to treatment. Otherwise, the psychiatric hospital would be little more than a prison, and psychiatry little more than a public safety institution (Katz, 1969).

Beyond the need to protect people with mental health conditions, involuntary treatment has been more recently justified as "compassion" toward people who would be vulnerable. Because involuntary treatment has "a negative social intonation" (Halam, 2024), it is becoming increasingly common to see it replaced by "compassionate treatment," whether in political, public, or legal discourse. The rhetoric of compassion, which crosses the entire continuum of care, is a perfect example of the therapeuticization referred to by Eleonora Rossero (2023), in that it conceals coercion behind benevolence and empathy. Not only would involuntary treatment be compassionate, but so would the courts, inspired by therapeutic jurisprudence (Hueston, 2020; Perlin, 2023).

The example of California legislation is particularly telling. The 2022 *Community Assistance, Recovery and Empowerment (CARE) Court Program Act* created "a compassionate civil court process" (Government of California, 2025) for people with a diagnosis of schizophrenia or psychosis spectrum disorders "who are experiencing or are at risk of homelessness, criminal justice involvement, hospitalization, or conservatorship" (CARE Act, Sect. 1). The program is presented as a "paradigm shift" (Government of California, 2025) and has as its goal to get people out of homelessness by enrolling them in therapy and providing them with housing. The innovation here lies in the fact that to enter the program, which is presented as a court diversion like the programs in criminal matters discussed above, individuals are not required to have charges against them. In the CARE court program, diversion is not only about criminal convictions and imprisonment, but also about certification for intensive treatment or conservatorship, which are provided for in the *Lanterman-Petris-Short Act* (LPS Act). Adopted in 1967, the provisions of the LPS Act explicitly aim to "end the inappropriate, indefinite, and involuntary commitment of persons with mental health disorders, developmental disabilities, and chronic alcoholism, and to eliminate legal disabilities" (Section 5001 (a)).

Until the CARE Act, there were two paths to involuntarily treat someone for mental health in California—both of which are still in place. The first concerns people who, because of a mental health issue, are "a danger to others, or to themselves, or gravely disabled," who lack capacity to consent and who can be treated involuntarily for up to fourteen days (renewable) (LPS Act, Section 5150). The second concerns people "gravely disabled as a result of a mental-health disorder or impairment by chronic alcoholism" for whom the court appoints a legal representative with the aim of "providing individualized treatment, supervision, and placement" (LPS Act, Sections 5350, 5350.1). Whereas intensive treatment certification was considered by some to be too restrictive (Boldt, 2017) and conservatorship too paternalistic (Olmedo, 2023), the CARE Act has created a forced treatment regime that explicitly targets social conditions.

To be admitted to the CARE program, six criteria must be met: (1) being 18 years of age or older; (2) experiencing a severe mental illness and having a diagnosis of schizophrenia spectrum or other psychotic disorder; (3) not being stabilized with an ongoing voluntary treatment; (4) having a deteriorating condition and being "unlikely to survive safely in the community without supervision" or risk of "relapse or deterioration that would be likely to result in grave disability or serious harm to the person or others;" (5) participating in the program would be the least restrictive alternative to ensure recovery and stability; and (6) benefits are probable (CARE Act, Section 5972). The CARE Act is redundant with several existing provisions: it was already possible to intervene with persons presenting a danger via the provisions of the LPS Act—but then it was only possible to keep them for 72 hours (which could turn into certification for intensive treatment), and they retained their civil rights; the LPS Act already provided for recourse to the least restrictive setting. Also, the LPS Act already allowed involuntary treatment, but under much stricter conditions, the CARE Act imposing a limit of one year, renewable once.

The CARE program is quite clearly part of a therapeutic jurisprudence approach, taking the logic of court diversion a step further by including civil justice. In so doing, the program avoids the procedural rigidity associated with the LPS Act and gives greater discretion and power to the court. The five characteristics of court diversion programs developed by Linda Steele (2020) work with a few adjustments in the case of CARE: (1) target defendants on the basis of a medical diagnosis and a social condition; (2) facilitate access to services; (3) use legal considerations different from those governing criminal or civil judicial processes; (4) involve coercion; and (5) involve collaboration between police, justice, health, and social services, as well as community groups. Just like court diversion programs in criminal matters, the CARE program is also built on assumption about causality between mental health problems and homelessness; it facilitates access to housing, but only in exchange for enrollment in therapy; it requires people to succeed in the program by committing to a recovery path. California is the US state with the highest number of homeless people, the largest increase in the number of homeless people in the last decade, and housing that is particularly unaffordable. Yet, the "mental health crisis," rather than these factors, is at the center of the political narrative on homelessness and has been invoked to justify the development of new legal frameworks (Carroll, 2024; Pickett, 2023).

Although that approach is controversial (Camejo et al., 2024; Carroll, 2024; Wu, 2023), many jurisdictions took a "compassionate approach to homelessness" in recent years. These initiatives constitute in practice a legal fast-track to facilitate involuntary admission and treatment of homeless people. While access to services is often lengthy and difficult in North America (Canadian Institute for health Information, 2024; National Council for Mental Wellbeing, 2025)—especially for the people who struggle the most with poverty—with individuals often unable to obtain the services they voluntarily seek, governments have been announcing massive investments in coercion, notably through the construction of new detention facilities. The examples are numerous. Since 2022, in New York, the "Mental Health Involuntary Removals program" has allowed health professionals and police officers to take into custody, for evaluation purposes, homeless individuals who appear to have mental disorders and who seem unable to meet their basic needs, "even when there is no recent dangerous act" (Office of Mental Health of New York, 2022). In May 2025, a budget of nearly 200 million US dollars has been announced, including to open 100 new psychiatric beds, as well as legislative changes aimed at strengthening mental health laws so that "compassionate care" can be offered to those who need it most are expected to follow (New York State, 2025). In July 2025, the US federal administration, claiming to take "a new approach," aims to combat urban insecurity due to "endemic vagrancy, disorderly behavior, sudden confrontations, and violent attacks" by "restoring civil commitment." In addition to strengthening the prohibition of drug use, camping, loitering, and squatting, the administration intends to "shift homeless individuals into long-term institutional settings for humane treatment." Funding for "implementation of maximally flexible civil commitment, institutional treatment, and 'step-down' treatment standards that allow for the appropriate commitment and treatment of individuals with mental illness who pose a danger to others or are living on the streets and cannot care for themselves" will be available (White House, 2025). In Canada, debates have been taking place in several provinces around addiction and mental health crises. Involuntary treatments are available nationwide, but many politicians have been calling for or announcing imminent legislative changes, and they have been supported by several civil society groups. The province of Alberta was the first to move forward with the *Compassionate Intervention Act*, which provides for the involuntary assessment and treatment of individuals who are likely to cause harm to themselves or others due to their addiction. A budget of 180 million dollars has been released for the construction of two Compassionate Intervention Centers, totaling 300 beds (Government of Alberta, 2025). In the preceding year, the provinces of British Columbia, Saskatchewan, Manitoba, and Quebec have variously legislated or promulgated policies that liberalize the admissions criteria and procedural safeguards surrounding involuntary hospitalization and coerced care, or broadening their scope. The Canadian Conservative Party leader reiterated on multiple occasions during the 2025 federal election campaign that he would implement "compassionate intervention" that would allow for the involuntary treatment of 50,000 people (Conservative Party of Canada, 2025), and replace homeless encampment by treatment centres (Zimonjic, 2025).

The question that arises at that point is about the effectiveness of coercion to address crises in mental health, addiction, and homelessness. A major challenge in assessing effectiveness is the diverse objectives pursued by coercion—be it therapy, control, or reducing the revolving-doors effect. While many of the supporters of coercion assert that the benefits are therapeutic, the criteria of risk or danger, present in one form or another in all legislation, as well as the role of the police suggest that it is primarily a matter of controlling behavior or protecting public safety. Therapeutic benefits have not been clearly established—significant variations in methods make the evaluation of their effectiveness unreliable (Belayneh et al., 2024; Giacco et al., 2018)—with studies giving at best mixed results (Corderoy et al., 2024; Giacco et al., 2018; Iudici et al., 2022; Kisely et al., 2024). Some of the beneficial effects documented in a few studies, such as stabilization of symptoms and improvement in general condition, are mitigated by dissatisfaction, loss of trust and a decline in the quality of the therapeutic relationship (Corderoy et al., 2024; Rugkåsa, 2016). In many cases, coercive practices, in particular community involuntary treatment, do not seem to succeed in encouraging greater adherence to treatment, in preventing some people from stopping treatments as soon as they are no longer forced to, in preventing readmissions, or in reducing the length of hospital stays or the revolving-doors effect (Barnett et al., 2019; Corderoy et al., 2024; Kisely et al., 2024). In a study on involuntary admission, researchers found that certain individuals fall within a "gray area:" they would be admitted by some psychiatrists, but not by others. Their admission therefore depends more on psychiatrists' "judgment calls" than on their actual situation. In the case of these people, due to the earning and housing losses associated with involuntary admission, it doubles their probability of dying by suicide or being charged with a violent crime within three months of their admission (Emanuel et al., 2025).

Healthcare providers report positive effects of coercion on safety, whether for the individuals themselves or for third parties. They generally affirm that coercion is necessary in certain circumstances, even if imposing or forcing treatment, even informally, creates a dissonance with their role of providing care. The people subject to coercion express more nuanced views: some report feeling safe in a moment of crisis, but many nevertheless report on the contrary losing control over their own bodies. The traumatic effects of coercion are known and documented, including feeling powerless, unheard, unimportant, and dehumanized (Aragonés-Calleja & Sánchez-Martínez, 2024; Oaks, 2011; Pariseau-Legault et al., 2025). People who have experienced violence and trauma may suffer re-traumatization through coercive practices, particularly seclusion and restraint, which worsens their mental health. For many, fear of new coercion and the loss of trust means they hide how they feel and refuse to seek help when they need it. There is thus a major discrepancy between the opinions of people with lived experience who want to be listened to and to be connected, and those of professionals and often families who see coercion as being in people's best interests in certain circumstances.

Overall, the use of coercion does not appear to be bearing fruit. Mental health, addiction, and homelessness crises continue to worsen despite the increased use of involuntary commitment and treatment. Most importantly, abusive ideas and practices that were thought to have been banned are reemerging. The targeting of the poorest and most marginalized individuals, the calls for the reopening of asylums (Sisti et al., 2015) or for rehabilitation in "wellness farms" (Love, 2025), and the development of a lucrative private market for coercion—through insurance or by entrusting the management of facilities to private companies (Friends of Medicare, 2025; Morehead, 2024; Wipond, 2023)—are "new" only in their invocation of compassion. Their choice to ignore recent research findings demonstrates their ideological grounding.

The "Shadow Carceral State"

Historically, criminal law exercised a social control function associated with economic policies (Becker, 1963; Black, 1983; Foucault, 1995; Galanter, 1983). For over six centuries, wandering and begging have been criminalized. People living in poverty were locked up to punish them for their alleged laziness, to keep them out of sight of the privileged classes for whom begging and precariousness were morally inadmissible, and to encourage economic activity, as the presence of poor people in a neighborhood might scare off potential customers (Englander, 1998; Simon, 1991).

In the wake of the recognition of universal rights following the Second World War, these repressive penal practices became the subject of a body of case law that became transformative. In several countries, targeting people living in poverty or homelessness by criminalizing wandering and begging was declared unconstitutional (Simon, 1991). Studies show, however, that although penal practices have become more sophisticated, they have only minimally changed. Following the "broken windows" theory—according to which disorder and incivility in a neighborhood are signs of risk for deviant and criminal behaviors, the theory formed the foundation for the development of community policing and foot patrol officers in the early 1980s (Wilson & Kelling, 1982)—targeting people living in poverty became justified by safety arguments associated with risk and disturbance. It has been established that the revolving-door phenomenon within the criminal justice system is the result of social and racial profiling carried out by police services against marginalized groups (Mofette & Bruckert, 2023), particularly people experiencing homelessness (Kauppi & Pallard, 2016), members of the 2SLGBTQIA+ community (Daum, 2019; Girardi, 2023), racialized and Indigenous individuals (Comack, 2012; Wilson, 2023), or those considered "vulnerable" (Ouellet et al., 2021). Judicial practices, particularly regarding release conditions and the routinization of criminal procedures have the effect of bringing the same people back in courts (Sylvestre et al., 2015, 2020). Alongside traditional criminal justice, court diversion allows extensive monitoring and surveillance in community.

Driven by neoliberal reforms, civil and administrative justice—meant to arbitrate or protect—has been used for punitive and control practices similar to those of the criminal justice system. Integrated into the continuum of care alongside the criminal courts, civil and administrative courts oversee responsibility and empowerment through the application of rules that manage social programs and public services. With public services and social programs having become less generous and often conditional, judicial and administrative activity has been redirected toward controlling access and conditions, thus multiplying opportunities for sanctions. For Karine Beckett and Naomi Murakawa (2012), civil and administrative courts constitute a "shadow carceral state," which they describe as follows:

> In legal terms, the shadow carceral state often makes use of *legally liminal authority*, in which expansion of punitive power occurs through the blending of civil, administrative, and criminal legal authority. In institutional terms, the shadow carceral state includes institutional annexation of

> sites and actors beyond what is legally recognized as part of the criminal justice system: immigration and family courts, civil detention facilities, and even county clerks' offices. Although these institutions are not officially recognized as "penal," they have nonetheless acquired the capacity to impose punitive sanctions—including detention—even in the absence of criminal conviction. The shadow carceral state also operates in opaque, entangling ways, ensnaring an ever-larger share of the population through civil injunctions, legal financial obligations, and violations of administrative law. Over time, these seemingly small incursions compound the heightened surveillance that comes with institutional enmeshment, longer (if not technically "criminal") rap sheets, and inescapable debt.

Today, all North American jurisdictions have a network of mental health courtrooms on a spectrum between the carceral state—criminal courts—and the shadow carceral state—civil courts, and administrative tribunals. Integrated into the continuum of care, these courts and tribunals are an integral part of the "healthcare to prison pipeline" (Campbell, 2023: 46), alongside social, police, and health services. However, the data on their activities are incomplete, as few states systematically collect public data on psychiatric coercion, particularly on involuntary treatments in the community and on the use of seclusion rooms, and as the activity of these tribunals is inseparable from other institutions on the continuum of care. Few studies also focus on the experiences and opinions of individuals facing civil and administrative tribunals, as well as on the daily activity of judicial hearings. This absence of data conceals an entire dimension of the state's surveillance and control as it unfolds through therapeutic justice.

References

Adler-Bolton, B., & Vierkant, A. (2022). *Health communism*. Verso Books.

Appelbaum, P. S. (1997). Almost a revolution: An international perspective on the law of involuntary commitment. *Journal of the American Academy of Psychiatry and the Law Online, 25*(2), 135–147.

Appelbaum, P. S. (2007). Assessment of patients' competence to consent to treatment. *New England Journal of Medicine, 357*(18), 1834–1840. https://doi.org/10.1056/NEJMcp07404

Aragonés-Calleja, M., & Sánchez-Martínez, V. (2024). Evidence synthesis on coercion in mental health: An umbrella review. *International Journal of Mental Health Nursing, 33*(2), 259–280. https://doi.org/10.1111/inm.13248

Barnett, P., Mackay, E., Matthews, H., Gate, R., Greenwood, H., Ariyo, K., Bhui, K., Halvorsrud, K., Pilling, S., & Smith, S. (2019). Ethnic variations in compulsory detention under the Mental Health Act: A systematic review and meta-analysis of international data. *The Lancet, 6*(4), 305–317. https://doi.org/10.1016/S2215-0366(19)30027-6

Becker, H. (1963). *Outsiders, studies in the sociology of deviance*. Free Press of Glencoe.

Beckett, K., & Murakawa, N. (2012). Mapping the shadow carceral state: Toward an institutionally capacious approach to punishment. *Theoretical Criminology, 16*(2), 221–244. https://doi.org/10.1177/1362480612442113

Belayneh, Z., Chavulak, J., Lee, D. C. A., Petrakis, M., & Haines, T. P. (2024). Methodological issues in measuring restrictive care practices (Mechanical/physical restraint, chemical restraint and seclusion) in adult mental health inpatient units: A systematic review of recent literature. *Journal of Clinical Nursing, 34*(5), 1629–1647. https://doi.org/10.1111/jocn.17588

Bernheim, E. (2022). The triumph of the "therapeutic" in Quebec Courts: Mental health, behavioral reform and the decline of rights. *Windsor Yearbook on Access to Justice, 38*, 125–147. https://doi.org/10.22329/wyaj.v38.7779

Birkeland, S., Steinert, T., Whittington, R., & Gildberg, F. A. (2024). Abolition of coercion in mental health services–A European survey of feasibility. *International Journal of Law and Psychiatry, 94*, Article 101992. https://doi.org/10.1016/j.ijlp.2024.101992

Birnbaum, M. (1960). The right to treatment. *American Bar Association Journal, 46*, 499–505.

Black, D. (1983). Crime as social control. *American Sociological Review, 48*(1), 34–45. https://doi.org/10.2307/2095143

Boldt, R. C. (2017). Emergency detention and involuntary hospitalization: Assessing the front end of the civil commitment process. *Drexel Law Review, 10*, 1–68.

Brooks, W. (2010). The tail still wags the dog: The pervasive and inappropriate influence by the psychiatric profession on the civil commitment process. *North Dakota Law Review, 86*, 259–320.

Brosnan, L., & Flynn, E. (2017). Freedom to negotiate: Proposal extricating capacity from consent. *International Journal of Law in Context, 13*(1), 58–76. https://doi.org/10.1017/S1744552316000471

Camejo, D. A., Bido-Medina, R. O., Koh, K. A., & Keuroghlian, A. S. (2024). Reconsidering the city of New York directive on mental health involuntary removals. *Harvard Review of Psychiatry, 32*(6), 218–227. https://doi.org/10.1097/HRP.0000000000000412

Campbell, T. (2023). Involuntary civil commitment as mass incarceration. *National Lawyers Guild Review, 79*(1), 32–46.

Canadian Institute for Health Information. (2024, March 21). *Canadians report increasing need for mental health care alongside barriers to access*. https://www.cihi.ca/en/canadians-report-increasing-need-for-mental-health-care-alongside-barriers-to-access. Accessed August 10, 2025.

Carroll, M. M. (2024). *Consumers' Lived Experience of Santa Barbara, California's Mental Health Services: A Portraiture Study* (Publication No. 31564763) [Doctoral dissertation, Pacifica Graduate Institute]. ProQuest Dissertations & Theses Global. https://www.proquest.com/dissertations-theses/consumers-lived-experience-santa-barbara/docview/3112455497/se-2?accountid=14701

Case, P. (2016). Dangerous liaisons? Psychiatry and law in the court of protection—Expert discourses of "insight" (and "compliance"). *Medical Law Review, 24*(3), 360–378. https://doi.org/10.1093/medlaw/fww027

Castellano, U. (2011). Problem-solving courts: Theory and practice. *Sociology Compass, 5*(11), 957–967. https://doi.org/10.1111/j.1751-9020.2011.00422.x

Collins, E. (2023). Problem-solving courts and the outcome oversight gap. *University of Missouri-Kansas City Law Review, 92*, 533–554.

Collins, E. R. (2020). The problem of problem-solving courts. *University of California Davis Law Review, 54*, 1573–1630.

Comack, E. (2012). *Racialized policing: Aboriginal people's encounters with the police*. Winnipeg Fernwood Publishing.

Community Assistance, Recovery and Empowerment Court Program Act, SB 1388.

Compassionate Intervention Act, SA 2025, c C 21.5.

Conservative Party of Canada. (2025). *Polievre Promises "Compassionate intervention: To help people struggling with severe addiction*. https://www.conservative.ca/poilievre-promises-compassionate-intervention-to-help-people-struggling-with-severe-addiction/. Accessed August 10, 2025.

Convention on the Rights of Persons with Disabilities, A/RES/61/106, 12 December 2006.

Corderoy, A., Kisely, S., Zirnsak, T., & Ryan, C. J. (2024). The benefits and harms of inpatient involuntary psychiatric treatment: A scoping review. *Psychiatry, Psychology and Law, 32*(5), 734–781. https://doi.org/10.1080/13218719.2024.2346734

Curley, A., Watson, C., & Kelly, B. D. (2022). Capacity to consent to treatment in psychiatry inpatients–A systematic review. *International Journal of Psychiatry in Clinical Practice, 26*(3), 303–315. https://doi.org/10.1080/13651501.2021.2017461

Daum, C. W. (2019). *Violence against and policing of LGBTQ communities: A historical perspective*. In S. J. Rickard (Ed.), *Oxford research encyclopedia of politics*. Oxford University Press. https://doi.org/10.1093/acrefore/9780190228637.013.1221

Doll, A. (2016). Lawyering for the "mad": Social organization and legal representation for involuntary-admission cases in Poland. In B. Burstow (Ed.), *Psychiatry interrogated: An institutional ethnography anthology* (pp. 183–202). https://doi.org/10.1007/978-3-319-41174-3_10

Eastman, N. (1995). Anti-therapeutic community mental health law: Rules cannot substitute for resources. *British Medical Journal, 310*(6987), 1081–1082. https://doi.org/10.1136/bmj.310.6987.1081

Emanuel, N., Welle, P., & Bolotnyy, V. (2025, July). A danger to self and others: Health and criminal consequences of involuntary hospitalization. *Federal Reserve Bank of New York Staff Report*, 1158. https://doi.org/10.59576/sr.1158

Englander, D. (1998). *Poverty and poor law reform in nineteenth-century Britain, 1834–1914*. Routledge.

Epperson, M. W., Sarantakos, S. P., Suslovic, B. J., Thompson, J. G., & Self, J. J. (2022). "You feed and water a rose bush and eventually it blossoms": Constructions of self-transformation among mental health court defendants. *International Journal of Law and Psychiatry, 85*, Article 101839. https://doi.org/10.1016/j.ijlp.2022.101839

Faden, R. R., & Beauchamp, T. L. (1986). *A history and theory of informed consent*. Oxford University Press.

Fernando, S. (2010). *Mental health, race and culture*. Bloomsbury Publishing.

Foucault, M. (1995). *Discipline and punish: The birth of the prison*. Random House.

Foucault, M. (2008). *The birth of biopolitics: Lectures at the Collège de France, 1978–1979*. Palgrave Macmillan.

Foucault, M. (2015). *The punitive society: Lectures at the Collège de France, 1972–1973*. Palgrave Macmillan.

Foucault, M., Baudot, A., & Couchman, J. (1978). About the concept of the "dangerous individual" in 19th-century legal psychiatry. *International Journal of Law and Psychiatry, 1*(1), 1–18. https://doi.org/10.1016/0160-2527(78)90020-1

Franke, N. D., & Shdaimah, C. (2022). "I have different goals than you, we can't be a team:" Navigating the tensions of a courtroom workgroup in a prostitution diversion program. *Ethics and Social Welfare, 16*(2), 193–205. https://doi.org/10.1080/17496535.2022.2069544

Friends of Medicare. (2025, February, 25). *There is nothing compassionate about the Government's addictions care plan*. https://www.friendsofmedicare.org/nothing_compassionate_addictions_plan. Accessed August 10, 2025.

Galanter, M. (1983). Making law for the oppressed. *The Other Side, 3*(2), 7–15.

Galderisi, S., Appelbaum, P. S., Gill, N., Gooding, P., Herrman, H., Melillo, A., Myrick, K., Pathare, S., Savage, M. K., Szmukler, G., & Torous, J. (2024). Ethical challenges in contemporary psychiatry: An overview and an appraisal of possible strategies and research needs. *World Psychiatry, 23*(3), 364–386. https://doi.org/10.1002/wps.21230

Garett, W. S. et al. (2023). Racial Disparities in Psychiatric Decisional Capacity Consultations. *Psychiatric Services*, 74(1), 10–16. https://doi.org/10.1176/appi.ps.202100685

Garland, D. (1981). The birth of the welfare sanction. *British Journal of Law and Society, 8*, 29–46.

Gerbasi, J. B., Bonnie, R. J., & Binder, R. L. (2000). Resource document on mandatory outpatient treatment. *The Journal of the American Academy of Psychiatry and the Law, 28*(2), 127–144.

Giacco, D., Conneely, M., Masoud, T., Burn, E., & Priebe, S. (2018). Interventions for involuntary psychiatric inpatients: A systematic review. *European Psychiatry, 54*, 41–50. https://doi.org/10.1016/j.eurpsy.2018.07.005

Girardi, R. (2023). "It's easy to mistrust police when they keep on killing us:" A queer exploration of police violence and LGBTQ+ victimization. *Journal of Gender Studies, 31*(7), 852–862. https://doi.org/10.1080/09589236.2021.1979481

Gooding, P., McSherry, B., & Roper, C. (2020). Preventing and reducing 'coercion' in mental health services: An international scoping review of English-language studies. *Acta Psychiatrica Scandinavica, 142*(1), 27–39. https://doi.org/10.1111/acps.13152

Gosselin, A. (2022). Responding to sanist microaggressions with acts of epistemic resistance. *Hypatia, 37*(2), 293–314. https://doi.org/10.1017/hyp.2022.9

Government of Alberta. (2025, May). *Providing life-saving treatment for substance abuse and addiction.* https://www.alberta.ca/providing-life-saving-treatment-for-substance-abuse-and-addiction. Accessed August 10, 2025.

Government of California. (2025). *Community Assistance, Recovery and Empowerment Act.* https://www.chhs.ca.gov/care-act/. Accessed August 10, 2025.

Halam, H. (2024, September 26). Party leaders of different stripes seem to agree on involuntary addiction treatment. The Canadian Press. *Global News.* https://globalnews.ca/news/10776206/bc-nb-election-campaign-involuntary-care-drug-addictions/. Accessed August 10, 2025.

Hiday, V. A. (1977). Reformed commitment procedures: An empirical study in the courtroom. *Law & Society Review, 11*(4), 651–666. https://doi.org/10.2307/3053176

Hiday, V. A. (1988). Civil commitment: A review of empirical research. *Behavioral Science and the Law, 6*(1), 15–43. https://doi.org/10.1002/bsl.2370060104

Hiday, V. A. (1990). Dangerousness of civil commitment candidates: A six-month follow-up. *Law and Human Behaviour, 14*(6), 551–567. https://doi.org/10.1007/BF010144881

Harcourt, B. E. (2006). From the asylum to the prison: Rethinking the incarceration revolution. *Texas Law Review, 84*(7), 1751–1786.

Hueston, J. H. (2020). The compassionate court: Reforming the justice system inside and outside. *American Judges Association, Court Review, 57*(2), 100–118.

Iudici, A., Girolimetto, R., Bacioccola, E., Faccio, E., & Turchi, G. (2022). Implications of involuntary psychiatric admission: Health, social, and clinical effects on patients. *The Journal of Nervous and Mental Disease, 210*(4), 290–311. https://doi.org/10.1097/NMD.0000000000001448

Joffe, K., & Lattanzio, R. (2024). Law-making within a critical disability rights framework. In M. H. Rioux, A. Buettgen, E. Zubrow, & J. Viera (Eds.), *Handbook of disability: Critical thought and social change in a globalizing world* (pp. 1349–1367). Springer Nature.

Kanter, A. S. (2014). *The development of disability rights under international law: From charity to human rights.* Routledge.

Katz, J. (1969). The right to treatment—An enchanting legal fiction? *University of Chicago Law Review, 36*(4), 755–785.

Kauppi, C., & Pallard, H. P. (2016). Social profiling, homelessness, and policing in Canada. *The International Journal of Interdisciplinary Civic and Political Studies, 11*(4), 13–26. https://doi.org/10.18848/2327-0047/CGP/v11i04/13-26

Kerrigan, D. (2020). Therapeutic jurisprudence in Trinidad and Tobago: Legitimacy, inclusion, and the neo-colonialism of procedural justice. In D. Nehring, O. J. Madsen, E. Cabanas, C. Mills, & D. Kerrigan (Eds.), *The Routledge international handbook of global therapeutic cultures* (pp. 446–458). Routledge. https://doi.org/10.4324/9780429024764

Kisely, S., Zirnsak, T., Maylea, C., Bull, C., & Brophy, L. (2024). Latest findings highlight the continuing uncertainty over the utility of compulsory psychiatric treatment in the community. *Bjpsych Open, 10*(5), Article e133. https://doi.org/10.1192/bjo.2024.718

Lane, E. (2002). Due process and problem-solving courts. *Fordham Urban Law Journal, 30*, 955–1026.

Lanterman-Petris-Short Act, division 5 of the *Welfare and Institutions Code*, division 5 enacted by Stats. 1967, Ch. 1667, amended by Stats. 1968, Ch. 1374.

Lebenbaum, M., Chiu, M., Vigod, S., & Kurdyak, P. (2018). Prevalence and predictors of involuntary psychiatric hospital admissions in Ontario, Canada: A population-based linked administrative database study. *British Journal of Psychiatry Open, 4*, 31–38. https://doi.org/10.1192/bjo.2017.4

Lee, G., & Cohen, D. (2021). Incidences of involuntary psychiatric detentions in 25 US states. *Psychiatric Services, 72*(1), 61–68. https://doi.org/10.1176/appi.ps.201900477

Leggio, M. (2012). A denial of being: Psychiatrization as epistemic violence. In B. A. LeFrançois, R. Menzies, & G. Reaume (Eds.), *Mad matters: A critical reader in Canadian mad studies* (pp. 122–129). Canadian Scholars.

Leifer, R. (1990). Introduction: The medical model as the ideology of the therapeutic state. *The Journal of Mind and Behavior, 11*(3), 247–258. https://www.jstor.org/stable/43854090

Light, E. (2019). Rates of use of community treatment orders in Australia. *International Journal of Law and Psychiatry, 64*, 83–87. https://doi.org/10.1016/j.ijlp.2019.02.006

Love, L. (2025, April 4). RFK Jr.'s 18th-century idea about mental health. *The Atlantic*. https://www.theatlantic.com/health/archive/2025/04/rfk-wellness-farms-mental-health/682293/. Accessed August 10, 2025.

Löve, L. E. (2023). Exclusion to inclusion: Lived experience of intellectual disabilities in national reporting on the CRPD. *Social Inclusion, 11*(2), 94–103. https://doi.org/10.17645/si.v11i2.6398

MacDonald, S. A., Fortin, V., & Houde, S. (2022). Therapeutic justice or epistemic injustice? In K. Fritsch, J. Monaghan, & E. van der Meulen (Eds.), *Disability injustice: Confronting criminalization in Canada* (pp. 164–186). University of British Columbia Press.

Macdonald, C., Weatherburn, D., Butler, T., Albalawi, O., Greenberg, D., & Farrell, M. (2023). Who gets diverted into treatment? A study of defendants with psychosis. *Psychiatry, Psychology and Law, 31*(1), 132–145. https://doi.org/10.1080/13218719.2023.2175070

Macdonald, C., Weatherburn, D., & Lappin, J. (2024). Diversion into mental health treatment: A survey of magistrates and treatment plans. *Psychiatry, Psychology and Law, 32*(3), 1–19. https://doi.org/10.1080/13218719.2024.2313985

Marr, C., Singh, S., Gaskin, C., Kasinathan, J., Lloyd, T., & Dean, K. (2024). Patterns of mental health service contacts for young people deemed eligible for court diversion. *International Journal of Forensic Mental Health, 23*(3), 204–216. https://doi.org/10.1080/14999013.2023.2276961

Martin, S. (2019). *Non responsabilité criminelle pour cause de troubles mentaux: Comparaison des pratiques de supervision des Commissions d'examen aux peines prononcées dans le système pénal* [Master dissertation, University of Montreal]. Papyrus. http://hdl.handle.net/1866/23719

Martin, W., & Gurbai, S. (2019). Surveying the Geneva impasse: Coercive care and human rights. *International Journal of Law and Psychiatry, 64*, 117–128. https://doi.org/10.1016/j.ijlp.2019.03.001

Mofette, D., & Bruckert, C. (2023). The violence of everyday police disrespect: Experiences of encounters with the police in Canada's Capital. *Deviant Behavior, 44*(10), 1443–1461. https://doi.org/10.1080/01639625.2023.2208254

Molyneaux, E., Turner, A., Candy, B., Landau, S., Johnson, S., & Lloyd-Evans, B. (2019). Crisis-planning interventions for people with psychotic illness or bipolar disorder: Systematic review and meta-analyses. *Bjpsych Open, 5*(4), Article e53. https://doi.org/10.1192/bjo.2019.28

Morehead, D. (2024). The horror of unjust psychiatric hospitalization. *Psychiatric times, 41*(12), 1.

Mowbray, C. T., Grazier, K. L., & Holter, M. (2002). Managed behavioral health care in the public sector: Will it become the third shame of the states? *Psychiatric Services, 53*(2), 157–170. https://doi.org/10.1176/appi.ps.53.2.157

National Council for Mental Wellbeing. (2025, February 26). *2022 Access to care survey results*. https://www.thenationalcouncil.org/resources/2022-access-to-care-survey-results/. Accessed August 10, 2025

New York State. (2025, May 9). *Governor Hochul Signs legislation to improve mental health care and strengthen treatment for serious mental illness as part of FY 2026 budget*. https://www.governor.ny.gov/news/governor-hochul-signs-legislation-improve-mental-health-care-and-strengthen-treatment-serious. Accessed August 10, 2025.

Nolan Jr, J. L. (1998). *The Therapeutic State*. New York University Press.

Nolan Jr, J. L. (2003). Redefining criminal courts: Problem-solving and the meaning of justice. *American Criminal Law Review, 40*(4), 1541–1566.

Nolan Jr, J. L. (2009). *Legal accents, legal borrowing: The international problem-solving court movement*. Princeton University Press.

Nolan Jr, J. L., (2020). The cultural constraints of legal transplantation a ten-year retrospective. *Cardozo Journal of Conflict Resolution, 21*, 641–662.

Nyvoll, P. (2025). Patient or prisoner? Perceptions of prison healthcare services in Norway and the conflict between care and control. *Incarceration, 6*. https://doi.org/10.1177/26326663241311554

Oaks, D. W. (2011). The moral imperative for dialogue with organizations of survivors of coerced psychiatric human rights violations. In T. W. Kallert, J. E. Mezzich & J. Monahan (Eds.), *Coercive treatment in psychiatry: Clinical, legal and ethical aspects* (pp. 185–211). https://doi.org/10.1002/9780470978573

Office of Mental Health of New York. (2022, February). *Memorandum: Interpretative guidance for the involuntary and custodial transportation of individuals for emergency assessments and for emergency and involuntary inpatient psychiatric admissions*. https://omh.ny.gov/omhweb/guidance/interpretative-guidance-involuntary-emergency-admissions.pdf. Accessed August 10, 2025.

Olmedo, M. D. L. A. R. (2023). Overprotected but unrepresented: An argument for mandatory appointment of counsel and against automatic general conservatorships in California. *Loyola of Los Angeles Law Review, 56*, 369–409.

Ouellet, G., Bernheim, E., & Morin, D. (2021). "VU" pour vulnérable : La police thérapeutique à l'assaut des problèmes sociaux. *Champ Pénal, 22*, 1–24. https://doi.org/10.4000/champpenal.12988

Pariseau-Legault, P., Pelosse, D., Bernheim, E., Goulet, M. H., Ouellet, G., Labrecque-Lebeau, L., & Holmes, D. (2025). When psychiatric services become a waiting room: Situational analysis of involuntary commitment and treatment as experienced by patients and nurses. *Clinical Nursing Research, 34*(3–4), 168–178. https://doi.org/10.1177/10547738251321067

Patel, V., et al. (2023). Transforming mental health systems globally: Principles and policy recommendations. *The Lancet, 402*(10402), 656–666. https://doi.org/10.1016/S0140-6736(23)00918-2

Perlin, M. L. (1992). On sanism. *SMULaw Review, 46*(2), 373–407.

Perlin, M. L. (1993). What is therapeutic jurisprudence? *New York Law School Journal of Human Rights, 10*, 623–636.

Perlin, M. L. (2013). Sanism and the law: virtual mentor. *American Medical Association Journal of Ethics, 15*(10), 878–885.

Perlin, M. L. (2017). The Insanity Defense : Nine Myths that will not go Away. In M. D. White (Ed.), *The insanity defense—Multidisciplinary views on it history, trends and controversy* (pp. 3–22). Bloomsbury Publishing. https://digitalcommons.nyls.edu/fac_articles_chapters/1128

Perlin, M. L. (2023). "In these times of compassion when conformity's in fashion:" How therapeutic jurisprudence can root out bias, limit polarization, and support vulnerable persons in the legal process. *Texas A&M Law Review, 10*, 219–267.

Pickett, M. (2023). Public defenders unwittingly face the homelessness crisis. *Criminal Justice, 38*(1), 44–46.

Polsky, A. J. (1991). *The rise of the therapeutic state*. Princetown University Press.

Principles for the protection of persons with mental illness and the improvement of mental health care, A/RES/46/119, 17 December 1991.

Rains, L. S., et al. (2019). Variations in patterns of involuntary hospitalisation and in legal frameworks: an international comparative study. *The Lancet, 6*(5), 403–417. https://doi.org/10.1016/S2215-0366(19)30090-2

Rasmussen, C., & Suslovic, B. (2025). Critiques of social work practice in carceral systems. In National Association of Social Workers (Ed.), *Encyclopedia of social work*. Oxford University Press. https://doi.org/10.1093/acrefore/9780199975839.013.1682

Rieff, P. (1966). *The triumph of the therapeutic: Uses of faith after Freud*. Harper & Row.

Robinson v. California, 370 U.S. 660 (1962)

Rossero, E. (2023). *Care in a Time of Crisis. An Ethnography of Coercive Practices in Italian Acute Mental Health Provision.* Palgrave Macmillan. https://doi.org/10.1007/978-3-031-34418-3

Rugkåsa, J. (2016). Effectiveness of community treatment orders: The international evidence. *The Canadian Journal of Psychiatry, 61*(1), 15–24. https://doi.org/10.1177/0706743715620415

Rusch, L., & Banner, F. (2024). Homeless group representation in Detroit's problem-solving court. *Law & Social Inquiry, 49*(1), 278–307. https://doi.org/10.1017/lsi.2022.68

Russo, J. (2023). Psychiatrization, assertions of epistemic justice, and the question of agency. *Frontiers in Sociology, 9*(8), 1092298. https://doi.org/10.3389/fsoc.2023.1092298

Sasso, L., Delogu, B., Carrozzino, R., Aleo, G., & Bagnasco, A. (2018). Ethical issues of prison nursing: A qualitative study in Northern Italy. *Nursing Ethics, 25*(3), 393–409. https://doi.org/10.1177/0969733016639760

Schneider, C. E. (2006). After autonomy. *Wake Forest Law Review, 41*, 411–443.

Schölin, L., Borschmann, R., & Chopra, A. (2024). Temporal patterns and individual characteristics of compulsory treatment orders for mental disorders in Scotland from 2007 to 2020. *Bjpsych Open, 10*(6), Article e204. https://doi.org/10.1192/bjo.2024.751

Schur, E. M. (1961). British Narcotics Policies British Narcotics Policies. *The Journal of Criminal Law, Criminology, and Police Science, 51*(6), 619–629.

Scrutton, A. P. (2017). Epistemic injustice and mental illness. In I. J. Kidd, J. Medina, & G. Pohlhaus (Eds.), *The Routledge handbook of epistemic injustice* (pp. 347–355). Routledge.

Scull, A. (1989). *Social order/mental disorder: Anglo-American psychiatry in historical perspective.* University of California Press.

Segal, S. P. (2013). Deinstitutionalization. In National Association of Social Workers (Eds.), *Encyclopedia of social work.* Oxford University Press. https://doi.org/10.1093/acrefore/9780199975839.013.101

Shdaimah, C. S., & McGarry, B. (2018). Social workers' use of moral entrepreneurship to enact professional ethics in the field: Case studies from the social justice profession. *British Journal of Social Work, 48*(1), 21 36. https://doi.org/10.1093/bjsw/bcx013

Simon, H. (1991–1992). Towns without pity: Constitutional and historical analysis of official efforts to drive homeless persons from American cities. *Tulane Law Review, 66*(4), 631–676.

Sisti, D. A., Segal, A. G., & Emanuel, E. J. (2015). Improving long-term psychiatric care: Bring back the asylum. *JAMA, 313*(3), 243–244. https://doi.org/10.1001/jama.2014.16088

Slate, R. N. (2003). From the jailhouse to Capitol Hill: Impacting mental health court legislation and defining what constitutes a mental health court. *Crime & Delinquency, 49*(1), 6–29. https://doi.org/10.1177/0011128702239233

Steele, L. (2020). *Disability, criminal justice and law : Reconsidering court diversion*. Routledge.

Sylvestre, M.-E., Blomley, N., & Bellot, C. (2020). *Red zones: Criminal law and the territorial governance of marginalized people*. Cambridge University Press. https://doi.org/10.1017/9781316875544

Sylvestre, M.-E., Damon, W., Blomley, N., & Bellot, C. (2015). Spatial tactics in criminal courts and the politics of legal technicalities. *Antipode, 47*(5), 1346–1366. https://doi.org/10.1111/anti.12161

Szasz, T. (1984). *The therapeutic state: Psychiatry in the mirror of current events*. Prometheus Book.

Szmukler, G. (2025). "Coercive" measures. In H. Helmchen, N. Sartorius, & J. Gather (Eds.), Ethics in psychiatry. *The international library of bioethics* (Vol. 110). Springer. https://doi.org/10.1007/978-94-024-2274-0_18

Thom, K., & Nakarada-Kordic, I. (2014). Mental health review tribunals in action: A systematic review of the empirical literature. *Psychiatry, Psychology & Law, 21*(1), 112–126. https://doi.org/10.1080/13218719.2013.790004

Torrents, E. G., & Björkdahl, A. (2024). Alternatives to coercion. In N. Hallett, R. Whittington, D. Richter, & E. Eneje (Eds.), *Coercion and violence in mental health settings: Causes, consequences, management* (pp. 373–403). Springer Nature.

Wexler, D. (1972). Therapeutic Justice. *Minnesota Law Review, 57*, 289–338.

Wexler, D. B. (1975). Reflections on the legal regulation of behavior modification in institutional settings. *Arizona Law Review, 17*(1), 132–143.

Wexler, D. (1981). *Mental Health Law: Major Issues*. Plenum Press.

Wexler, D. (1990). *Therapeutic jurisprudence: The law as a therapeutic agent*. Carolina Academic Press.

Wexler, D. B. (1988). Reforming the law in action through empirically grounded civil commitment guidelines. *Psychiatric Services, 39*(4), 402–405.

Wexler, D. B. (1992). Justice, mental health, and therapeutic jurisprudence. *Cleveland State Law Review, 40*(3), 517–526.

Wexler, D. B. (2008). Two decades of therapeutic jurisprudence. *Touro Law Review, 24*, 17–30.
Wexler, D. B. (2021). *Creating a therapeutic justice culture*. SAL Prac 20.
Wexler, D., & Winick, B. J. (1991). Therapeutic jurisprudence as a new approach to mental health law policy analysis and research. *University of Miami Law Review, 45*, 979–1004.
White House. (2025, July 24). *Ending crime and disorder on America's streets*. Executive Orders. https://www.whitehouse.gov/presidential-actions/2025/07/ending-crime-and-disorder-on-americas-streets/. Accessed August 9, 2025.
Whittington, R., Aluh, D. O., & Caldas-de-Almeida, J. M. (2023). Zero tolerance for coercion? Historical, cultural and organisational contexts for effective implementation of coercion-free mental health services around the world. *Healthcare, 11*(21), 2834. https://doi.org/10.3390/healthcare11212834
Wilson, A. (2023). *An alternative spotlight: Colonial legacies, therapeutic jurisprudence, and the enigma of healing*. In A. Aliverti, H. Carvalho, A. Chamberlen & M. Sozzo (Eds.), *Decolonizing the criminal question*. Oxford University Press. https://doi.org/10.1093/oso/9780192899002.003.0018
Wilson, J. Q., & Kelling, G. (1982, March). Broken windows—The police and neighborhood safety. *The Atlantic Online*. https://www.lakeclaire.org/docs/BrokenWindows-AtlantaicMonthly-March82.pdf. Accessed August 9, 2025.
Wilson, K. (2022). The CRPD and mental health law: The conflict about abolition, the practical dilemmas of implementation and the untapped potential. In *Disability law and human rights: Theory and policy* (pp. 171–197). Springer. https://doi.org/10.1007/978-3-030-86545-0_9
Winick, B. J. (1994). The right to refuse treatment: A therapeutic jurisprudence analysis. *International Journal of Law and Psychiatry, 17*(1), 99–117. https://doi.org/10.1016/0160-2527(94)90039-6
Winick, B. J. (1997). The jurisprudence of therapeutic jurisprudence. *Psychology, Public Policy and Law, 3*(1), 184–206. https://doi.org/10.1037/1076-8971.3.1.184
Winick, B. J. (1999). Therapeutic jurisprudence and the civil commitment hearing. *Journal of Contemporary Legal Issues, 10*, 37–60.
Winick, B. J. (2003). Problem solving courts: Therapeutic jurisprudence in practice. *Fordham Law Review, 30*(3), 1055–1103. https://ir.lawnet.fordham.edu/ulj/vol30/iss3/14

Winkler, P., Barrett, B., McCrone, P., Csémy, L., Janouskova, M., & Höschl, C. (2016). Deinstitutionalised patients, homelessness and imprisonment: Systematic review. *The British Journal of Psychiatry, 208*(5), 421–428. https://doi.org/10.1192/bjp.bp.114.161943

Wipond, R. (2023). *Your consent is not required: The rise in psychiatric detentions, forced treatment, and abusive guardianships*. BenBella.

Wu, C. (2023). Out of sight, out of mind: Removing unhoused people by proxy of mental illness. *University of Pennsylvania Journal of Law & Social Change, 26*(3), 333–368. https://doi.org/10.58112/JLASC.26-3.2

Zimonjic, P. (2025, April 23). *Poilievre promises to let police dismantle encampments, arrest occupants*. Canadian Broadcasting Corporation. https://www.cbc.ca/news/politics/poilievre-public-order-dismantle-encampments-1.7516297. Accessed August 10, 2025.

4

Investigating Mental Health Courtrooms

> Doing an ethnography is equal parts exhilarating, exhausting, and exasperating—Leslie Paik. (2021: 133)

The first time I walked into a mental health courtroom, I had no idea what I was going to experience there. In an earlier study, I interviewed judges about their relationship with psychiatric experts. They described involuntary commitment procedures as particularly complicated and emotionally draining: the evidence was incomplete, the hearings were short, and they could not take sufficient time to deliberate. As civil judges, accustomed to disputes over property and contracts, they were uncomfortable making decisions that infringed on freedom. They did not see why this task should fall to them and did not feel prepared or qualified. They recounted how distressed some of their colleagues were when faced with such decisions.

With this in mind, I entered the courtrooms for involuntary commitment hearings with the theoretical questions of a legal sociologist about

E. Bernheim, *Therapeutic (In)justice and the Shadow Carceral State*, The Politics of Mental Health and Illness, https://doi.org/10.1007/978-3-032-16186-4_4

the pluralism of norms (von Benda-Beckmann, 2002) and the effectivity of the law (Fryer et al., 2018). I wanted to see how the right to freedom of defendants would be balanced against their right to be protected, and how individual rights would be weighed against the rights of society. I wanted to listen to the legal arguments and pleadings of the petitioning hospitals and the defendants. And I wanted to document how judges came to their decisions: which arguments did they consider and why? What was their legal reasoning? How did they explain it to the defendants? I knew in advance that nearly 95% of hospital petitions for involuntary commitment were granted. I wanted to know why and how.

Unfortunately, what I observed in the courtrooms did not allow me to answer—at least not directly—my questions. The law is largely absent from mental health courtrooms. It is only implicitly present, but is not the subject of arguments, pleadings, or reasoning. Law is used as an accessory in mental health courtrooms; it mandates the hearing, but it does not determine its outcome. As a doctoral student who only knew the law in its written, theoretical form, what I saw in the courtrooms the first few times I attended seemed like an anomaly, very far from what I had been taught. Where was the "Law" with a capital L—noble, prestigious, powerful?

I quickly understood that the Law was hardly ever to be found in mental health courtrooms. The dozens of hours I spent there in the following years in various contexts of civil and administrative justice confirm this observation: the law is largely absent, sometimes instrumentalized, replaced by organizational constraints, sanist prejudices, and the logic of the market.

These realizations and experiences were deeply disturbing—both intellectually and on a human level. Not only is the legal debate absent from these courtrooms, but more importantly, the judicial process invalidates the defendants' knowledge, experiences, and preferences. Yet, defendants are the only ones in the courtroom with experiential knowledge of coercion and psychiatric treatments. While the conversation is about them, the defendants often cannot take part. They must "wait their turn" and witness the judicial conversation about them without being able to rectify erroneous facts or share their point of view. When they express their lack of understanding of the court procedure, they are most often ignored, even by their own lawyers. Judicial decisions are rarely explained to them. After their hearings, the defendants find themselves in the corridors of the courthouse, often alone, without fully understanding what has just transpired.

The courtroom experience was also emotionally disturbing, due to hearing about the precarious living conditions of the defendants, discussed throughout the hearings as evidence of their social dysfunction and mental health problems, and also due to the overwhelming distress for which no solution is provided. The defendants are often in situations of personal, material, and relational crisis. Some say they need help. In most of the time, judicial actors try to convince them that hospitalization or psychiatric treatment will provide relief and solve their problems, while the inequalities, poverty, and discrimination—including violation of rights—experienced by defendants are systematically ignored.

A Taboo Subject

Law and justice are individualistic in nature. This is nothing new, but is taken a step further by therapeutic jurisprudence, which promotes the individualization of legal processes to "support vulnerable persons" (Perlin, 2023). What is striking in mental health courtrooms, however, is the obvious disadvantage faced by the defendants. They are disadvantaged by their social class, gender, race or cultural difference, which has been documented many times in various judicial contexts (Berdejó, 2018; Kang et al., 2011; Leckey et al., 2022; Lens, 2019; Neitz, 2013; Sandefur, 2008; Thompson, 2018), while also being labeled as mentally ill. Due to the ongoing stigma surrounding mental illness, a psychiatric diagnosis typically affects credibility in the courtrooms (MacDonald et al., 2022; Smith, 2009), including for jurors (Levi & Golding, 2024).

Credibility is a fundamental element of the judicial process. The fact that defendants are not believed when they tell their stories undermines their ability to defend themselves, but it also determines an important part of the narrative around mental health, including the narrative promoted by research. For researchers, taking defendants' words and experience seriously calls into question their own credibility, as if their own credibility is tied with that of the defendants. In mental health research, political considerations generally take center stage. It is mandatory for researchers to "choose sides": the side of Mad people—associated with the Mad movement (Starkman, 2012), often labeled as "radical" or "antipsychiatry"—or the side of those who know how to help them (e.g., mental health professionals), generally associated with science and objectivity. These are two irreconcilable worldviews.

This circular and binary reasoning has been a constant in my research experience, where I was quickly labeled "pro-patient," or "antipsychiatry"—an experience that several researchers have undergone (Burston, 2018; Cohen, 2017; Szasz, 2008). These labels are used to discredit research results (Burston, 2018; Schramme, 2004; Szasz, 2008, 2010), as well as to cut short any conversation that does not support the urgency of the mental health crisis and the therapeutic role of the courts. The field of mental health is unique in this sense. I have conducted studies, including judicial ethnographies, on other social topics, and I have never experienced or witnessed similar obstruction. In addition to my research being denigrated for "believing mad people," I have been subjected to tactics aimed at silencing me. I received a formal notice from a mental health law firm after giving an interview to a journalist about my research, requesting a retraction. Hospital lawyers heckled a public presentation of research results that I gave, aggressively monopolizing the question period. Other hospital lawyers wrote a document disputing research result, which they distributed to participants in a training session I was providing. Judges have publicly stated that they did not believe my research results, claiming that I was lying, or that I was manipulating the results. Some of the judges I have spent hours with inside courtrooms and offices have refused to speak with me in over 15 years. And some courts today have closed their doors to research, prohibiting both courtroom observations when hearings are not public and judges' granting interviews.

These tactics of discrediting and silencing are not confined to the research community. Some legal professionals have confided in me that they are uncomfortable with the way things are done in mental health courtrooms. Judges and lawyers who try to bring the Law back into the courtroom are ostracized and subject to complaints. They are seen by their colleagues as wasting everyone's time and as preventing the system from working. They often end up conforming or changing their field of practice. The same applies to the media. In recent years, I, along with lawyers and community groups, have tried to draw the media's attention to the situation in mental health courtrooms. Some journalists were interested, and one has even initiated an investigation. But one by one, all media outlets retreated without explanation.

In recent years, scandals have multiplied, calling into question the practices of psychiatric and social institutions. These included abuses in the use of power and of coercive measures, botched investigations, fabrication of evidence, and perjury before the courts. Academic studies, as well as public institutions, community groups, and media investigations have brought to light practices that violate professional ethics, that are often discriminatory against marginalized groups, and result in rights violations (Appelbaum, 1992; Catallo, 2024; Levy, 2022; McIntosh, 2025; New Zealand Royal Commission of Inquiry, 2022; Panorama & Lee, 2022; Roxburgh & Sinclair, 2024; The Office of the Ombudsperson, 2019; Wipond, 2023). This can partly explain why many professionals working in these institutions are in defensive positions. The courts, however, have not been subjected to the same level of scrutiny.

But this is certainly not the only reason contributing to the reluctance to disclose courtroom practices. On several occasions during data collection, and in the context of training and research activities organized by the legal community, I have observed that legal practitioners expressed a lack of consideration, or even contempt, for defendants. Conversations about defendants and the judicial procedures concerning them, from which they are systematically absent, reflect ordinary sanism, tinged with common prejudices related to mental health. Because several legal professionals consider the judicial process to be unsuitable for individuals with mental health issues and because they do not recognize defendants as parties, they feel comfortable making "procedural accommodations," drawing parallels with children during divorce court proceedings. Denying the status of defendants does more than divert attention from the absence of the law during these hearings; it denies the defendants' judicial experience.

The disregarding of the value of the defendants' experiences goes far beyond the judicial process. In several contexts, lawyers and judges have told me, for example, that defendants could not participate in my research. On the one hand, it was claimed that the defendants were too unwell to give quality interviews, and that their input would be erratic, false, or incomprehensible. Yet the vast majority of these individuals are legally competent. On the other hand, it was claimed that the research might "destabilize" them. In this context, I was told that satisfaction forms filled out by court users are not made available to defendants subject to mental health procedures to avoid destabilization.

Attending hearings was a formative experience. Up until that point, I had conducted interviews with judges and psychiatrists, which helped answer my questions about the implementation of the law. The first hearing I attended was a shock; nothing in the interviews had prepared me for what I was about to witness and experience—the intricate and unspoken layering of social issues such as class, gender, and race relations, combined with the inherent violence of the judicial process. I expected to see justice; I experienced power relations and sanism. I therefore changed the focus of my observations to make the judicial narrative process that produces "mental health" and the "other" as the focus of my research. Since my earliest mental health courtroom experiences fifteen years ago and following Sarah Klosterkamp and Tasniem Anwar (2023: 50), my research seeks to "nam[e], analyz[e] and critiqu[e] power and domination relations and subsequently linked to a practice that considers power relations even within social fieldwork situations and academic knowledge production."

Form the onset, observing and experiencing court hearings has been central to my research standpoint (Haraway, 1988): interviews failed to capture the full complexity of the issues and interactions unfolding simultaneously during hearings, and court hearings provided me access to a social universe far removed from my own. My only personal experiences regarding mental health are those outlined in this book's introductory chapter. I have never been subjected to coercion in psychiatry or been personally involved in any legal disputes. Analyzing law and judicial or psychiatric decisions is relatively straightforward: it is about intellectualizing and rationalizing—while ignoring the people involved—which is what I have been trained to do. Experiencing law as it is lived and endured is another matter altogether.

Observing hearings has also been a way for me to break away from the dominant paradigm in mental health. Studies based on the views of legal, psychiatric, and social work professionals on mental health and coercion are numerous and dominate the literature on the subject. Being in a courtroom made me aware of the suppressed points of view, knowledge, and experiences. It also helped me understand the importance of judicial practices in the production of hegemonic discourse about mental health and defendants, which is poorly documented. As part of a tradition of critical ethnography (Thomas, 1993), my research explores this hegemonic narrative, while at the same time aiming to be useful for people involved in the mental health justice system for the purpose of emancipation (Bassett, 2020; Becker, 1967).

However, I am aware of my social status and my privileges and their effects in terms of power relationships, particularly their epistemological consequences in a research context, and in judicial ethnography in particular (Klosterkamp & Anwar, 2023). As a white person, descended from French settlers and living on the unceded indigenous territory of Tiohtià:ke, cisgender, heterosexual, member of a middle-class family, legal scholar, researcher, and academic, I am aware of the intellectual and personal limits in the work I do. I also understand that research can contribute to the positive or negative identification of social groups, either by promoting their visibility or by entrenching their non-existence.

Since my early days as a researcher, I have conducted research through collaboration or partnership with civil society groups, such as community organizations, advocacy groups, and legal clinics. These partnerships ensure the relevance and social usefulness of research, and the co-construction of projects incorporating the knowledge and concerns of the people judicialized in mental health. They are also tests of humility, when reality is often far removed from the pretensions of academic or legal circles.

This engaged and allied research posture does not mean that I do not recognize the highly challenging practice context faced by the various professionals involved in mental health—police officers, psychiatrists, emergency physicians, nurses, social workers, judges, and lawyers—particularly when it comes to coercive practices. Challenges that I learned about from hours of observation in courtrooms and interviews with these professionals, especially on psychiatric wards, include the inconsistency of the mandates they receive, their frustrations when services are non-existent or inadequate, the ethical dilemmas when the only services available are coercive, and the pain of seeing people they care about sink into extreme poverty, struggling, and sometimes die. Neoliberal policies target and directly affect the most marginalized people, and those who seek to care for, support, and help them. I am acutely aware of this reality.

Four Judicial Ethnographies

My research took place in Tiohtià:ke, in the judicial district of Montreal, Canada. Tiohtià:ke is an island and Canada's second-largest city by population. Located in the province of Quebec, it is North America's largest French-speaking city. Successive provincial reforms of health and social service systems implemented since the 1990s have resulted in diminished service accessibility, alongside a decline in available social housing. Approximately 29% of residents experience poverty, while homelessness rates have increased substantially since the early 2010s. Indigenous individuals comprise 13% of the homeless population, a proportion five times greater than their representation in the general population (Government of Quebec, 2023). To address the situation, municipal authorities have established court diversion program spanning mental health, homelessness, substance use disorders, and subsistence theft, alongside integrated police response units for mental health crises. However, community-based organizations addressing poverty and homelessness face significant challenges in meeting escalating service demands, and rates of involuntary commitment and treatment have increased significantly, with heightened application among severely impoverished and homeless populations (Action Autonomie, 2021).

I conducted four judicial ethnographies between 2009 and 2021. Being granted access to mental health courtrooms is no easy matter. In addition to the fact that hearings are often held behind closed doors, the presence of an observer is unusual and may be perceived by judicial actors as disruptive (Uhnoo et al., 2023). It was with the invaluable collaboration of the Chief Justices that I was able to conduct most of my research. Through them, I gained access to the courtrooms and had the opportunity to interview the judges. In most cases, I was only able to attend hearings and interview judges who had been hand-selected by the Chief Justices, which is a common situation in judicial ethnographies (Uhnoo et al., 2023).

My fieldworks focus on different judicial mechanisms in mental health, and they are closely interconnected in several ways mainly due to the fact that these are not criminal procedures but civil and administrative ones. Criminal justice is recognized as punitive and coercive and has been extensively researched in this regard for decades (Black, 1983; Sylvestre et al., 2020). It has been the subject of numerous judicial ethnographies and analyses from the perspective of therapeutic jurisprudence, particularly regarding mental health courts (Castellano, 2017; Cooper, 2018; MacDonald et al., 2022). Civil and administrative justice represents a blind spot in research on coercive and punitive judicial practices and therapeutic jurisprudence, yet it holds powers that are equivalent to that of criminal justice. It can restrict freedom and impose treatments and therapies, place of residency, home visits, changes in social relationships, diet, and personal budget management. However, defendants have far fewer rights and procedural guarantees in civil or administrative proceedings than in criminal proceedings. The judicial procedures I studied thus all constitute the "shadow carceral state" in that they can impose restrictions on rights akin to criminal sanctions (Beckett & Murakawa, 2012).

It was in the courtrooms, during my initial fieldwork experience, that my subsequent research fieldworks were constructed. It was there that I understood that defendants were involved in multiple judicial procedures, which remain under-documented (Paik, 2021). In this way, I identified early on in the fieldwork, the fieldworks I would later conduct, attempting to piece together a fragmented judicial narrative on mental health and on defendants in order to outline how judicialization leads to further judicialization. As the research progressed, it became clear that the results would be transversal. The substantial and procedural legal differences have marginal influence on the conduct of hearings, the subject of conversations, and the outcome of procedures, which is not particularly surprising given that the law is rarely discussed during hearings. The analysis I present here is the result of this transversal analysis.

The first two research fieldworks were carried out simultaneously as part of my doctorate research. They took place in the Civil Division of the Court of Quebec, the provincial court, in matters of involuntary commitment, and in the Superior Court of Quebec, the court of general jurisdiction, in matters of involuntary treatment. They built upon my master's research (Bernheim, 2008), where I analyzed case law and conducted interviews with judges regarding psychiatric expertise in different areas of judicial practice. The results of this initial research showed that expert testimony was perceived differently by judges in involuntary commitment cases compared to their colleagues practicing criminal or family law. One of the reasons cited by judges was that they did not have other evidence that would allow them to reconsider the weight of psychiatric expertise. Several judges reported feeling trapped due to gaps in these professional opinions, the absence of counter-expertise, and the fact that hospitals would sometimes withdraw their petition for involuntary commitment when they asked for additional evidence. Following this initial study, I undertook my doctoral research to analyze how psychiatrists and judges made their decisions regarding involuntary commitment and involuntary treatment.

In Quebec, involuntary commitment and involuntary treatment are subject to separate procedures[1]. Involuntary commitment refers to people who present a danger to themselves or to others due to their "mental state." It must be ordered by a judge of the provincial court, at the request of a hospital based on two psychiatric assessments. The *Civil Code of Quebec* stipulates that, regardless of the evidence submitted, the court itself must have "serious reason to believe" that the defendant is dangerous and that the involuntary commitment is "necessary" (Section 30). This unusual requirement demonstrates the exceptionality

[1] Legislation enacted in June 2026 and set to come into force in 2027 substantially amends this framework, most notably by vesting decisions concerning civil commitment and forced treatment in an administrative tribunal.

of this legal mechanism. Indeed, civil courts usually rule based on a preponderance of evidence, not based on the convictions of the judges, which is a less rigorous level of evidence. In practice, the concept of danger has never been defined by case law, which results in a variation in how the concept may be assessed and acted upon. The facts justifying a request from a hospital vary greatly, ranging from attempted suicide to altercations with neighbors, strange or disturbing behavior, unsanitary housing, or social isolation. Assessing psychiatrists are not present in court and the hospitals' evidence consists of two forms with checkboxes and a few lines of text. Hearings last an average of ten minutes, and involuntary commitment orders are for an average of 30 days but can also be issued for 60 or 90 days. In all cases, a reassessment of the danger must take place on day 21, and persons admitted involuntarily may obtain an administrative review at any time by an administrative tribunal. They must then demonstrate that their situation has changed, and that hospitalization is no longer necessary.

Involuntary commitment does not allow treatment to be imposed against defendants' will. With a few exceptions, treatment can only be imposed against a person's will in case they lack capacity for consent. In contrast to involuntary commitment, where mental state is a criterion, the situation of a person who lacks capacity for consent to treatment is governed by general legal provisions in Quebec that do not specifically focus on mental health. Lack of capacity for consent to treatment does not relieve physicians of the obligation to obtain free and informed consent before proceeding with treatment, and consent must be obtained from the person's legal representative, spouse, parent, adult child, or any person showing an interest in the person. However, those authorized to give consent on behalf of others must at least consider their wishes.

An involuntary treatment court order is required in three situations: (1) the legal representative is unavailable or unjustifiably refuses treatment; (2) an adult who lacks capacity for consent categorically refuses treatment; and (3) a minor aged 14[2] or older refuses treatment, unless there is an emergency, "in which case the consent of the person with parental authority or the guardian is sufficient" (*Civil code of Quebec*,

[2] Minors over the age of 14 consent to their own treatment in Quebec.

Section 16). The burden of proof rests with the hospital submitting the petition to the court, and the main evidence is the capacity assessment and the treatment plan provided by the attending physician of the defendant who testifies in person in court. The court can only order involuntary treatment if it is required by the defendant's state of health.

The capacity to consent is not defined in the Civil Code, and parliamentary debates show that it was not the legislators' intention to specifically target mental health through these provisions. However, an early involuntary treatment decision by the Quebec Court of Appeal set precedents by adopting the Canadian Psychiatric Association's capacity-to-consent test. The criteria applied by the Quebec Superior Court are as follows: "the person a) understands the condition for which the treatment is proposed; b) understands the nature and purpose of the treatment; c) understands the risks involved in undergoing the treatment; d) understands the risks involved in not undergoing the treatment; and e) whether their ability to consent is affected by their condition" (Institut Philippe Pinel de Montréal 1994). In practice, the court focuses on the first and last criteria, which results in most involuntary treatment orders involving psychiatric treatments or defendants with psychiatric diagnoses. On average, hearings last one hour to one hour and a half, and the authorizations are granted for an average of three years (Bernheim et al., 2016) with no legally required review process.

Involuntary commitment and involuntary treatment orders are the subject of conventional civil lawsuits, where the hospitals and doctors involved are the plaintiffs, and the targeted individuals are the defendants. Defendants have the right to be represented by lawyers and to present a defense to the court, including witnesses or counter experts. Lawyers' fees may be covered by legal aid if they meet eligibility criteria. There are two ways of obtaining free legal services. First, state-employed lawyers work in legal-aid offices; in the judicial district of Montreal, a legal-aid office is dedicated to mental health practice. These lawyers may represent defendants insofar as their eligibility for legal aid is established. They have fixed salaries that do not depend on the number of cases, although in recent years performance pressure has led them to take on an increasingly larger number of clients. Second, private lawyers can take on these cases and get paid by a public organization in charge of managing legal aid. Private lawyers are paid per case and therefore can have an incentive to take on more clients.

Involuntary commitment and involuntary treatment order petitions are subject to special procedural provisions: defendants must be notified in person 2 or 5 days before hearings; requests must be processed on the same day as they are submitted, as a matter of urgency; hearings take place behind closed doors, and the courts are obliged to hear the defendants (Code of Civil Procedure). These provisions are exceptional, as in civil matters there is no obligation to respond to a request, and the courts can make a decision against a defendant *in absentia*. In practice, defendants are absent in between one-third and one-half of cases most often without explanation. Judges sometimes ask hospital lawyers why they are absent, and the answer is usually that they do not contest. Studies have shown that legal practices vary widely from one hospital to another, and that the documents handed out to defendants by bailiffs are not consistently comprehensive in terms of how to obtain evidence and legal services (Bernheim et al., 2024).

The closed-doors rule, the redaction of decisions to protect defendants' identities, and the restrictions on access to court records are exceptional situations—given that open court is a constitutional rule in Canadian law and that exceptions are rare. This means that information about what happens in mental health courtrooms is difficult to obtain. To gain access to courtrooms, the closed-doors rule must be lifted, and in recent years, requests of this nature have been refused for journalists, and sometimes for community workers accompanying defendants.

Involuntary commitment and involuntary treatment order petitions are granted in around 95% of cases (Bernheim, 2015; Bernheim et al., 2016). Although defendants have the full right to appeal to the Quebec Court of Appeal, appeals, in practice, are rare. The high proportion of granted requests and the context in which hearings take place raise doubts about the integrity of the judicial process. Since the judicialization of civil procedures in mental health, similar observations have been made in several jurisdictions (Dix, 1967; Feldman, 1980; Oh et al., 2024; Winick, 2005). However, certain professionals and scholars argue that the high rate of granted petitions can be attributed to the advocacy efforts of hospital attorneys. In other words, the fact that more than

95% of requests are granted is explained by the fact that these requests are necessary, with hospital lawyers declining to present to the court petitions with no merit. This argument is dubious at best, insofar as ensuring there is merit to a case is the basic work of any lawyer in any matter, which does not prevent some parties from winning and others from losing. This brings us back to the binary conception of mental health, as if there existed only one truth: that of psychiatry, despite controversies associated with risk and capacity assessment scales, diagnostic tools and treatments, which I presented in the first chapter.

Over fifteen years, research conducted by community groups, public agencies, and academics has documented major and structural violations of rights in both hospital and judicial settings. These include time limits not met, illegal detentions, undisclosed information, consent to care not requested, and insufficient or incomplete evidence (Bernheim, 2015; Bernheim et al., 2016, 2024; Ombudsman, 2011; Quebec Ministry of Health and Social Services, 2011). A class-action lawsuit concluded in 2024 requires the Quebec government to compensate individuals who were unlawfully detained in hospitals under mental health law; their number is estimated at 50,000 people (Montreal City News, 2025). Research has also shown the overrepresentation of people living in precarious situations among those involuntarily admitted or involuntary treated (Action Autonomie, 2021; Bernheim, 2015, 2024), especially among people experiencing homelessness (Otero, 2016), which is consistent with international research findings (Haussleiter et al., 2022; Moloney et al., 2022). International studies also show the overrepresentation of racialized, Indigenous, or immigrant people subject to involuntary commitment or involuntary treatment (Barnett et al., 2019; Ogilvie & Kisely, 2022). Although data are scarce, the trends are the same in Canada (Lebenbaum et al., 2018; Salam et al., 2022), and in Montreal in particular (Knight et al., 2022; Tran et al., 2019).

During involuntary commitment and involuntary treatment hearings, I noticed that women regularly reported being involved in child-custody disputes, most often in matters of child welfare, and that men reported being subjected to criminal charges. This finding is consistent with the literature, as women are likely to be subjected to more interventions through social services and men through the criminal justice system (Datchis & Ancis, 2017; Payne, 1996). The relationship between mental health, child welfare services, and criminal justice is well known. According to studies, between 20 and 50% of children in contact with child welfare services have a mother who has had contact with mental health services (Hammond et al., 2017; O'Donnell et al., 2015; Palmer et al., 2024), while between 20 and 30% of people convicted by a criminal court have had such contacts (Michalski, 2017; Vogel et al., 2014). Studies most often focus on a causal link between mental health and parenting capacities or criminality, and very little on transinstitutionalization, or on the impact of social or mental health intervention, judicialization, and criminalization on the anxiety and emotional distress of the individuals. The dynamic relationship between involuntary commitment or involuntary treatment and interventions by social services or the criminal justice system is insufficiently documented. While the judicialization of marginalized social groups through civil or administrative justice has been increasingly studied, the trajectories within the justice system or between health services, social services, and the justice system have remained largely uninvestigated (Paik, 2021).

Following my fieldworks about involuntary commitment and involuntary treatment, I undertook fieldwork in child welfare at the Youth Division of the Court of Quebec. These hearings concern children whose security or development is "considered to be in danger" by child welfare services due to "abandonment, neglect, [serious risk of neglect], psychological ill-treatment, exposure to domestic violence or sexual or physical abuse, or if the child has serious behavioural disturbances" (Youth Protection Act, Section 38). To make its decision, the court considers evidence of danger to safety or development but must also assess the "best interests of the child" and the "parenting capacities." The observation of hearings reveals the significant overrepresentation of mothers, confirmed by a study of court files showing that mothers are present in 70% of hearings, while fathers are present in 53% of hearings (Coupienne, 2023). I also noticed during the hearings that the mental health of the mothers is often brought up in relation to parenting capacities, sometimes without any medical evidence.

Here as well, what constitutes danger is not clearly defined. Family situations targeted by judicial orders vary greatly, ranging from documented abuse to families not having the infrastructure considered essential to meet children's needs. Danger is inherently linked to the best interest of the child—a notion that is also insufficiently undefined and "morally" and culturally charged (Bala & Saunders, 2003; Littlechild & Housman, 2023). Apart from meeting basic needs, what constitutes the best interest of the child is indeed deeply rooted in what is regarded as a "good" family, with appropriate relationships, activities, and environment. Parenting abilities are also associated to what is considered a "good" family and a "good" mother (Fernance, 2024). Like risk and capacity-to-consent assessment scales, parenting capacity assessment scales structurally target marginalized people, including racialized individuals (Choate & Lindstrom, 2017; Roberts, 2022).

As in many countries, professionals working in the child welfare system base their interventions on attachment theory (Bowlby & World Health Organization, 1952), a theory that has been challenged for its lack of attention to cultural specificities in the development of mother-child relationships (Fernance, 2024; Keller, 2022). Adherence to this theory is not questioned, despite the overrepresentation of Indigenous children removed from their families by child welfare services across Canada (Sinclair, 2016). This observation is especially troubling given that Canada has committed to a path of reconciliation as a result of increasing awareness about abusive practices that took place in Indian Residential Schools until the early 1990s. In 2011, Indigenous children represented 7% of Canadian children, yet they represented 48% of children placed in foster care, with interprovincial variations between 0 and 100% (Turner, 2016). For many, child welfare service practices are a continuation of those of the Indian Residential Schools—colonial in nature (Robertson et al., 2022; Roxburgh & Sinclair, 2024).

In Quebec in particular, research shows that Black children are more than twice as likely as other children to be removed from their families, a proportion that rises to 6.6 for Indigenous children (Caldwell & Sinha, 2020; Lavergne & Dufour, 2020). Although they represent only 9% of the Quebec population, Black children are the target of 24% of child welfare services evaluation reports, the first step after a referral

(Boatswain-Kyte et al., 2020). Similarly, while 3.7% of non-Indigenous children were removed from their families in 2016, almost a quarter of Indigenous children (24.2%) were in foster care (Caldwell & Sinha, 2020). Black and Indigenous children are overrepresented in child welfare services at all stages of intervention, particularly before the Youth Division and in placement decisions. Compared to other children, Black and Indigenous children are more often placed in foster care, although foster care is known to have a negative impact on children's return to their families, as well as cutting them off from their cultural references, since they are most often placed with families who are not part of their communities (Boatswain-Kyte, 2018; Turner, 2016).

In matters of child welfare, the law explicitly states that judicialization is the last resort. Social workers must therefore favor the implementation of voluntary measures to which families agree. When no agreement is possible, it falls to the child welfare services to present a petition to the Youth Division. Several measures can be requested from the court, ranging from "ensuring that the child and their parents comply with the conditions imposed on them," to "removal of the child from their present environment," and "restricting contact between the child and their parents" (Youth Protection Act, Section 46). If the court accepts the child welfare services' request, the judge remains appointed to the case. It is therefore the same judge who will hear and decide during the successive stages of a case that consists of an initial request, often emergency-based, followed by hearings to examine the merits of the case, and hearings aimed at making and reviewing decisions. During this process, which can last several years, children and parents can petition the court at any time. However, I have not observed any hearings that took place at the request of children or parents.

In contrast to involuntary commitment and involuntary treatment, which are conventional civil adversary procedures, proceedings in the Youth Division are hybrid. Although the proceedings are adversarial, the Youth Division also has an investigative, inquisitorial role, which differs from that of the conventional arbitrator typically granted to the civil courts. This role is embodied in more flexible procedural rules, with parties not restricted by the facts alleged in the petition and therefore able, for instance, to invoke other factual elements during proceedings, present hearsay evidence in certain circumstances, or present oral arguments.

In practice, this reduction in procedural formalities works mainly to the child welfare services' advantage. Child welfare services are the most frequent plaintiff in the Youth Division and provide the main evidence to the court, consisting of the social assessment by the social worker of the services, often supplemented by psychological or psychiatric assessments or other evidence. The child's best interests and parental capacities are often evaluated by psychologists, but if one of the parents is under psychiatric care, a psychiatrist may provide their opinion. Alleging facts not previously disclosed in the claim can create a surprise effect that makes it difficult for defendants to prepare a defense. Similarly, the admission of hearsay allows the child welfare services to make their case based on statements reported by third parties and not on the observations of their own social workers, which is difficult for the defense to counter. The Supreme Court of Canada recognizes that child welfare intervention is a violation of parental rights but may be justifiable in the name of the best interests of the child, which are to be protected when their safety or development is in danger (Winnipeg Child and Family Services, 2000).

As with involuntary commitment and involuntary treatment, eligible defendants can benefit from legal-aid services. However, given that state-employed lawyers represent children in these proceedings, parents must find private attorneys willing to accept these mandates. Some lawyers have made child welfare their specialty, but many are reluctant to accept legal-aid mandates because they are not paid for case preparation, and the fees are negligible for both themselves and for any experts they might want to call upon. Unlike involuntary commitment or involuntary treatment cases, which generally consist of only one hearing, child welfare cases may last for years. Once lawyers have agreed to take these cases, they cannot withdraw easily if they end up not being paid or if they can no longer maintain contact with their clients without court approval. This situation results in many parents appearing at their hearings poorly prepared, or self-representing.

To protect the child's confidentiality, hearings are held behind closed doors, court decisions are redacted, and access to court records is restricted. As with involuntary commitment and involuntary treatment, these measures result in limited information about the process and content of judicial hearings being available to the public. In recent years, child welfare services have been the subject of multiple scandals, particularly in relation to the manipulation of evidence to facilitate the removal of children from families, as well as their adoption (Quebec Human Rights & Youth Rights Commission, 2025).

Due to its inquisitorial role, the Youth Division is not bound by the allegations and conclusions of the parties and has the power to investigate further to support its decision, either by seeking new evidence or by summoning witnesses. It has jurisdiction to rule on grounds of compromise and measures other than those requested by the parties and "may make any recommendation that it considers to be in the interest of the child" (Youth Protection Act, Section 91). However, it is up to the plaintiff to demonstrate, on a balance of probabilities, that there is a need to impose protective measures for the child due to danger to their safety or development. No proof of danger is required; proving that the child is "considered to be in danger" is sufficient.

The duration of hearings varies greatly, depending on the stage of the proceedings the case has reached. Cases regularly cannot be presented in their entirety before the end of a hearing, whether due to unforeseen circumstances, the fact that one of the lawyers is busy in another room, or a poor initial assessment of the time required. In this case, the child welfare services will sometimes have been able to present their evidence, while the parents will not have the opportunity to express themselves. Due to court overload and the need to find a time when the judge presiding over the case and all the lawyers (for the child welfare services, the child, and sometimes both parents) are available, the next hearing may be several months away. Because situations evolve quickly, all evidence usually needs to be presented again at the next hearing, and parents and their lawyers sometimes appear multiple times without being able to present all their evidence and arguments. These long delays have the effect of prolonging the measures put in place by the court and reducing the chances of parents regaining custody of their children.

Observations of the hearings, corroborated by a study of the court files (Coupienne, 2023), revealed that defendants presented little evidence and few grounds for contestation, and that the Youth Division generally accepts the evidence as presented by the child welfare services without requesting more. As for the grounds for compromise and the content of the orders, the Youth Division grants 93% of the petitions made by child welfare services, whether to get families to accept their services, to remove children temporarily or permanently, or to have them adopted (Coupienne, 2023). Defendants have the right to appeal to the Superior Court of Quebec on matters of fact and, with permission, to the Court of Appeal of Quebec on matters of law. Appeals are rare considering the high number of decisions made by the Youth Division.

Studies on child welfare services rarely focus on the role of the courts. Those that have done so have shown that courts are often reluctant to challenge the requests of child welfare services, and that the judicial process does not help to rebalance the power dynamics between child welfare services and families, especially mothers (Dumbrill, 2006; Masson, 2000; Roberts, 2022; Sinden, 1999). Judicial interventions generally align with social interventions, aiming to compensate for the perceived educational shortcomings of parents whose backgrounds are different from those of social workers and judges by promoting exemplary behavior. In this sense, the intervention by child welfare services reflects their historical mission of monitoring and controlling marginalized families and youth (Roberts, 2022; Robertson et al., 2022). Interventions targeting mothers—particularly poor and racialized mothers—are justified preventively by the perceived risks to children, especially boys, who might otherwise be left on their own with little or poor integration into school and social settings and may fall into delinquency (Ericsson, 2000; Van Krieken, 1986).

I conducted a fourth round of fieldwork at the Quebec Review Board, the administrative tribunal responsible for supervising and making decisions relating to people declared unfit to stand trial or not criminally responsible on account of mental disorder by a criminal court. According to the *Canadian Criminal Code*, unfitness to stand trial means being "unable on account of mental disorder to conduct a defense at any stage of the proceedings before a verdict is rendered or to instruct counsel to do so." To be fit to stand trial a person must: "(a) understand the nature or object of the proceedings, (b) understand the possible consequences of the proceedings, or (c) communicate with counsel" (Criminal Code, Section 2). Defendants unfit to stand trial do not receive verdicts but wait until they become fit before going to trial. Criminal charges remain pending against them. Non-criminal responsibility refers to having committed an act or omission while "suffering from a mental disorder" that rendered defendants "incapable of appreciating the nature and quality of the act or omission or of knowing that it was wrong" (Criminal Code, Sect. 16). The "right and wrong" test, used for over 150 years in certain common-law jurisdictions (Crotty, 1924; Platt & Diamond, 1966), has been criticized for the excessive burden of proof it places on the defendants, for the control left to psychiatrists in determining responsibility, giving rise to expert battles, as well as for the unjust convictions it produces (Denno, 2021; Law Reform Commission of Canada, 1976).

Observations at the hearings confirmed that men are significantly overrepresented before the Review Board; studies show that they make up 85% of defendants (Crocker et al., 2015). The offenses vary widely, from theft of sustenance to obstruction of police work to crimes against the person; violent crimes account for 6% of the not-criminally-responsible verdicts in Quebec. The observations also showed that involuntary commitment and involuntary treatment are regularly discussed during hearings. About a quarter of the defendants I observed before the Review Board had been, were, or were about to be subject to judicial orders for involuntary treatment.

In matters of mental disorders, because of the absence of a guilty verdict, the power Parliament holds over defendants is administrative rather than criminal. This power is based on the "threat to public safety" posed by non-criminally responsible defendants (Criminal Code, Section 672.54) on the one hand and on charges still pending against defendants unfit to stand trial on the other hand. Defendants found not criminally responsible on account of mental disorder who do not pose a "significant threat to the safety of the public," or whose threat can be controlled in society, must be discharged unconditionally (Winko, 1999). A "significant threat to the safety of the public" is defined in the Criminal Code (Section 672.5401) as "a risk of serious physical or psychological harm to members of the public—including any victim of or witness to the offence, or any person under the age of 18 years—resulting from conduct that is criminal in nature but not necessarily violent." However, defendants not criminally responsible on account of a mental disorder and who pose a significant threat to public safety and defendants unfit to stand trial may be released with conditions or kept in custody in a hospital. In addition to the safety of the public, "which is the paramount consideration" (Criminal Code, Section 672.54), the decision must consider the mental condition, the reintegration into society and the other needs of the defendants.

The decision to release, conditionally release, or detain may be made by the criminal court at the time of the verdict of not criminally responsible or of unfitness to stand trial. The court may also decide to refer the decision to the Review Board, the administrative tribunal specializing in mental disorders in criminal law. The Review Board consists of psychiatrists, lawyers, and professionals who "have training and experience in the field of mental health" (Criminal Code, Section 672.39). The Board sits in a panel of three: a lawyer who presides, a psychiatrist, and a psychologist or social worker. In practice, the criminal court generally imposes hospital detention on defendants pending a decision by the Review Board, which takes between 90 days and 3 months.

Unlike a criminal sentence or a civil order for involuntary commitment or involuntary treatment, the complete duration of the Review Board's supervision can never be known prior a complete release decision. The Board is required to hold hearings and renew its decisions concerning defendants every 12 months. The issue is that, here again, "significant threat" is not clearly defined in case law. The ambiguity of this notion is compounded by the fact that the French version of the Criminal Code speaks of "significant risk" instead of "significant threat," a distinction not addressed by the Supreme Court of Canada's bilingual decisions. The seriousness of the offense is not the issue here; rather, it is the significance of the threat at the time of the Review Board hearing. In addition to threat assessment, which has the flaws mentioned above, several factors may be considered: eating habits, including sugar, fat, and caffeine consumption; professional situation and activities; debts and financial situation; state of family and friendships; and drug and alcohol use. Lack of collaboration with the treating team, the challenge of psychiatric diagnoses and refusal of psychiatric medication are also routinely considered as threat factors, even in cases where the evidence presented at the hearing does not establish such associations. Studies show that the probability for non-criminally responsible defendants of being in custody for longer periods is three times greater than for defendants convicted for equivalent offenses, both in Quebec, in other Canadian provinces and in the United States (Martin et al., 2022; Perlin, 2017). The average duration of supervision by the Quebec Review Board is 7 years, with some defendants subject to it for over 40 years (Crocker et al., 2015).

With its inquisitorial mandate, the Review Board possesses the investigative powers provided by the *Inquiries Act*, including summoning witnesses, and having the authority to determine the procedural rules to be followed before it, with the Criminal Code providing that the procedure must be as informal as possible. The inquisitorial procedure means that the members of the Review Board oversee the investigation, and no burden of proof can be imposed on the defendants. It is therefore not an adversarial procedure, even if the defendants must be present, can be represented by a lawyer and can present evidence. The assessment of the "significant threat" is conducted and presented by the treating psychiatrists of the defendants, who act as witnesses summoned directly by the Review Board and not as plaintiffs as in cases of involuntary commitment or involuntary treatment. The hospitals caring for the defendants can be represented by lawyers; the Attorney General of the province may have the status of a party, and so does any person having a "substantial interest in protecting the interests" of the defendants (Criminal Code, Section 672.5). The people present at the hearings may therefore vary from case to case, but it is rare for defendants to present witnesses.

The inquisitorial mandate of the Review Board suggests that it should play an active role during the hearings. However, according to my observations, the procedure is applied differently depending on which lawyer is presiding over the bench of judges. In all cases, the hearing begins with the reading of the report of the treating psychiatrist, which is used as the primary evidence. Although judges lead the investigation, it is rare for them to begin by asking their questions first; instead, they generally let the lawyers ask their questions and intervene only after. The defendant is then questioned by their lawyer if they have one, and then by the judges.

Most often, hearings are conducted like a civil trial with judges referring to psychiatrists as "plaintiffs" and behaving as if they were judging a petition filed by a hospital. As in child welfare cases, the inquisitorial dimension of the procedure that should serve the "search for truth" is not implemented, as the Review Board is passive and is content with the evidence presented by the treating psychiatrist. Even though defendants have full right of appeal to the Quebec Court of Appeal, appeals are rare.

At the time of my fieldwork, hearings of the Quebec Review Board took place in hospitals[3] and lasted an average of one hour. Hearings were held in a wide variety of locations, from the conventional courtroom set up in the hospital, to a meeting room, and a storage area. In some cases, hearings took place with a setup similar to a courtroom, with the parties facing each other, while in other cases the defendants sat between their psychiatrist and their lawyer, close enough to the Review Board members that they could touch them.

Review Board hearings are open to the public, but information on schedule and locations is not readily available. During my fieldwork, I saw no one attending the hearings other than witnesses, psychiatrists', or lawyers' trainees. Review Board decisions are redacted to protect defendants' confidentiality.

Only one of the procedures studied allows for force treatment: the involuntary treatment order. In all other proceedings, defendants retain their right to consent to or refuse treatment, be it medication, consultation, therapy, or follow-up with any type of professional.[4] They also enjoy all the rights granted to users of the healthcare system, such as the right to confidentiality, to choose their healthcare professional and their healthcare establishment (defendants admitted involuntarily or under the control of the Review Board may apply to the court for a hospital transfer), to access their medical records and request rectification, and to be accompanied.

[3] Since the Covid-19 pandemic, the Quebec Review Board's hearings have been held online.
[4] They must, however, undergo psychiatric or social assessments.

In all the legal proceedings I have studied, judicial decisions are handed down on the bench at the end of the hearing. Although the Review Board suspends hearings for a few minutes to give its members time to deliberate, these decisions are made without the deliberation typical of court proceedings, which usually last several weeks and gives judges time to consult legal sources and reflect on decisions. This practice is warranted by the urgency inherent in the proceedings and the imperative for prompt decision-making. Furthermore, in contrast to standard judicial practices in civil and administrative law, these decisions are typically enforceable immediately, notwithstanding the initiation of an appeal process.

Table 4.1 presents the characteristics of the procedures studied.

In the case of hearings held in the courthouse and behind closed doors, the judges would lift the closed door at the start of the hearing and ask the parties if they consented to my presence. I usually sat in the section of the courtroom reserved for the public, so the parties could not directly see me unless they physically turned around. I could see the defendants from behind as they testified in the box. On occasion, some judges have asked me to sit next to the plaintiffs' lawyers. In these situations, I saw the people present much more closely, but the defendants sometimes mistook me for the plaintiff lawyers' trainee. When I sat in the part of the room reserved for the public, I took notes during the hearings, which I tried to make as exhaustive as possible, and when I sat with the parties, note-taking depended on the circumstances. In some situations, I was comfortable taking notes, but in other situations, I felt I was too visible and potentially disruptive to the defendants or the proceedings.

The judges who welcomed me into their courtrooms for observations were generous with their time. Several of them welcomed me into their offices and agreed to discuss the cases they had heard and decided on. They explained their decision processes, including their hesitations. Many told me that these exchanges were invaluable for them, as they found the work difficult but had no one to talk to about it.

For Review Board hearings, the process was completely different. Since the hearings are public, the Board members simply asked me to identify my name and role at the beginning of the hearings. Given that my research was being conducted in collaboration with a legal-aid office,

Table 4.1 Characteristics of the procedures studied

	1-Involuntary commitment	2-Involuntary treatment	3-Child welfare	4-Non-criminal responsibility & unfitness to stand trial
Tribunal	Civil	Civil	Civil	Administrative
Place	Courthouse	Courthouse	Courthouse	Hospital
Criteria	Danger to self or others	Incapacity to consent to treatment	Danger to children's safety or development	Threat to public safety
Procedure	Adversarial	Adversarial	Hybrid	Inquisitorial
Initiator of the procedure	Hospital	Hospital	Child welfare services	Result from a verdict of non-criminal resp. or unfit to stand trial
Parties	Hospital (plaintiff) versus defendant	Hospital (plaintiff) versus defendant	Child welfare services, children and defendant	No parties, the defendant must be present
Main evidence	Attending psychiatrists report	Attending psychiatrists report	CWS social worker report	Attending psychiatrists report
Regular witnesses	No witnesses	Attending psychiatrist summoned by the hospital	Social worker summoned by the child welfare services	Attending psychiatrist summoned by the tribunal
Bench	Judge sitting alone	Judge sitting alone	Judge sitting alone	Three-professionals bench
Closed doors	Yes	Yes	Yes	No
Can force treatment	No	Yes	No	No

the defendants were usually aware of my presence and had given their consent in advance. My place in the room depended on its layout. Sometimes I could sit in the back, and other times I found myself seated directly next to the defendants. Depending on the situation, I felt more or less comfortable taking notes during the hearings.

During the observation sessions, I took advantage of the opportunity to engage with as many people present as possible, whether they were defendants, lawyers, judges, families, psychiatrists, or social workers. Some of these exchanges were very brief and were included in my observation notes, while others took the form of informal interviews that were sometimes recorded. I also collected documents on site, such as documents found in courthouse or hospital lobbies, for example pamphlets providing information on procedures and rights. In some cases, I had access to documents contained in court files. I consider these data as part of the observational data.

At four research sites, I conducted ecological validations by presenting my preliminary analyses to individual participants, participant groups, or non-participating individuals with relevant experience, such as those who have been through the judicial system as defendants or who work with judicially involved persons. This important step in the research process helped ensure the relevance of the analytical orientations and the conceptual and theoretical choices.

My observational data are the primary data of my research and are at the heart of the analysis presented in this book. They were supplemented by a variety of complementary data such as individual or group interviews, court files, and judicial decisions.

Alongside the data collection process, I kept a research journal in which I noted my personal impressions. This journal allows me to reflect on my research practices and to maintain a healthy distance from the fieldworks, which was emotional, intense, and difficult. On several occasions, I was able to identify that my emotions or my sense of injustice were influencing my data collection, directing note-taking toward certain interactions and discourses. This led me to readjust while also supplementing my observational data with complementary data. For example, I found that hospital lawyers in involuntary commitment cases were aggressive with defendants, using strategies intended to destabilize and discredit them. Meeting some of them for interviews allowed me to document the context of their practice and to contextualize the observational data. In this way, I learned that they were under significant pressure to win their cases, and that those in private practice feared losing their livelihoods.

For each of these studies, I obtained ethics certificates from the universities I was affiliated with (University of Montreal, University of Quebec in Montreal, University of Ottawa). They were all funded by the Social Sciences and Humanities Research Council of Canada.[5] The four research fieldworks were conducted primarily in French; all translations are my own. Although I have formatted my notes to reproduce them for the purpose of describing my results, I have attempted to remain as faithful as possible to the original notes, particularly regarding the terms used during the hearings. When using observation notes, I generally chose not to assign pseudonyms to research participants but rather to refer to them by their role in judicial hearings—judge, lawyer, psychiatrist, social worker, defendant. This impersonal description seems to me to more accurately reflect the impersonal nature of judicial hearings. Regarding the gender of research participants, my notes reflect the gender attributed to each person during the hearings, and not the gender with which the individuals identify—which I do not know. Gender is central in exchanges during hearings, since defendants are often addressed by judicial actors as "Sir," "Madam," "Mr.," "Mrs.," "the mother," or "the father." I kept these words in the excerpt of my observation notes reproduced in the next two chapters.

The cross-sectional analysis of my data demonstrates that the four courtrooms investigated have primarily two functions: risk management and the framing of defendants and their behaviors through the psychiatric paradigm. It also reveals a justice system based on social class, gender, and race, in that the level of risk is strongly associated with the perception that mental health, social service, and legal professionals have of defendants. In my analysis, I refer to "class," "gender," and "race" as social constructs, with the attributes and performances commonly associated with them.

[5] 752–2009-1293; 430–2011-489; 201–2017-057; 435–2017-1150.

The Table 4.2 presents the details of the four judicial ethnographies I have conducted.

Table 4.2 Four judicial ethnographies

	1- Involuntary commit- ment	2- Invol- untary treat- ment	3- Child welfare	4-Non-criminal responsibility & unfitness to stand trial
Court	Court of Quebec (Civil Division)	Superior Court	Court of Quebec (Youth Division)	Review Board
Place	Montreal Courthouse		Montreal Youth Division	Montreal Hospitals
Year of collec- tion	2009		2012, 2019–2021	2017–2018
Number of hearings	187	14	70	51
Number of hours in hearing	56	18	50	57
Average duration of hearings	5 to 30 minutes	1 to 1.5 hours	5 minutes to 2 hours	1 to 1.5 hours
Defendants' gender profile	Men and women, split roughly evenly		Overrepresentation of women	Overrepresentation of men
Defendants' racial profile	Mostly white		Between one-quarter and one-third racialized	One-quarter racialized
Individual inter- views	Judges ($N = 15$), psychiatrists ($N = 7$)		Defense Lawyers ($N = 11$), mothers ($N = 10$)	Psychiatrists (N = 7), Defense Lawyers (N = 7)
Informal inter- views	Defendants ($N = 23$), Hospital Lawyers ($N = 6$)		Judges ($N = 12$)	Crown Lawyers (N = 3), Psychiatrists (N = 5), Hospital Lawyers (N = 4)

(continued)

Table 4.2 (continued)

	1- Involuntary commitment	2- Involuntary treatment	3- Child welfare	4-Non-criminal responsibility & unfitness to stand trial
Judicial decisions	100 randomly selected			
Other	Focus groups: defense Lawyers ($N = 7$) occasionally judicial records		Biographical interviews with mothers who were involuntarily admitted and had their children removed from their custody ($N = 3$)	Judicial records (N = 191)

The Context of Judicial Practice

The judicial context is similar in the four mental health courtrooms studied. For over a decade, the number of cases has risen sharply, while resources have not kept pace. Public institutions— including the courts, as well as hospitals and child welfare services—are subject to the efficiency and performance demands characteristic of New Public Management (Hood, 1991). The pressure and urgency are palpable.

The third Table 4.3 presents the increase in the number of judicial records in the four mental health courtrooms studied (Justice Quebec, 2018, 2021, 2022, 2023a, 2023b; Court of Quebec, 2010; Administrative Tribunal of Quebec, 2004, 2021).

The courts' schedules are extremely busy, and the time devoted to cases is generally set in advance, which means that judges have little room for maneuver if a case requires more time. Defendants may be meeting with their lawyers while judges are ready to hear cases. In such cases, it is sometimes requested that the meeting be cut short so as not to lose hearing time or cause the court to fall behind schedule. Lawyers generally accede

Table 4.3 Number of judicial records in the four mental health courtrooms studied

1-Involuntary commitment		2- Involuntary treatment		3- Child welfare		4-Non-criminal responsibility & unfitness to stand trial	
2012	5 720	2008	383	2001	4 916	2006	898
2015	5 958	2015	2 201	2015	7 420	2015	1 950
2021	8 821	2021	3 361	2021	10 687	2021	2 250

to these requests without arguing the rights of the defense. These pre-hearing meetings are often the first time defendants meet their lawyers and are thus the only opportunity to prepare for the hearing. Lawyers, however, are unrealistically expected to have the time to review the evidence with their clients, explain the procedure, advise them, receive their instructions, and prepare them to testify.

However, in many cases, the evidence is available only in the hours or minutes before the hearing. Not only are the defendants and their lawyers not always able to read the entire document before the hearing, but neither are the judges, who sometimes must react on the spot. If judges consider the evidence too weak or incomplete, they may request additional evidence, but they know that this request will have an impact on the number of cases presented in the coming days. In other words, they cannot afford to postpone too many hearings, since these cases will be added to the cases to be heard in the following days. For that reason, more often than not, judges accept the evidence as presented during the hearing.

Defendants usually have only their own testimony to present as evidence. Counter-expertise is presented in only about 3% of cases, due to practical reasons (the urgency makes it difficult to find experts) and financial constraints, and because it is challenging to find psychiatrists or other professionals willing to challenge a colleague (Bernheim et al., 2016, 2024). However, it appears that in cases where counter-expertise is presented, the defendants' chances of success increase dramatically.

Defendants are most often unprepared or poorly prepared to testify, even when they are represented by a lawyer. Their lack of preparation is often reflected in attitudes that show little respect for or knowledge of court decorum, for example, when some defendants might want to speak at any given moment, sometimes using inappropriately informal language. It is also a regular occurrence for defendants to make statements that can be harmful to their case, sometimes in response to questions from their own lawyers. These attitudes and remarks contrast sharply with those of the judicial actors—psychiatrists, social workers, lawyers, judges—who are judicial "repeat players" (Galanter, 1974). These professionals understand the operations of the court, can anticipate each stage of the process, and have no personal or emotional investment in the cases. They are therefore in control, due both to their professional training and their detachment, which greatly contrasts with that of defendants whose freedom, integrity, or family ties are at risk.

Additionally, the professionals who frequent mental health courtrooms are a small group. They all know each other and often have for a long time. They take advantage of idle moments or breaks to chat amiably, talk about their trips to Bermuda, the renovations to their homes or their new haircuts. For defendants, the complicity between their lawyer, hospital lawyers or social institutions' lawyers, and sometimes judges, leads to a loss of trust. They understand the familiarity created by these intense judicial practices but question their lawyers' ability to represent them effectively in this context. In the opinion of several defendants I have encountered in the courthouse corridors or in interviews, decisions are predetermined, and their lawyers have neither the will nor the capacity to defend them adequately. As a result, they approach the judicial process with few expectations and little hope.

References

Action Autonomie. (2021). *Trop souvent un abus, toujours un échec: portrait des recours aux autorisation de soins et d'hébergement en santé mentale par les établissements de santé montréalais* (Research Report). https://www.actionautonomie.qc.ca/portrait-de-situation-recherche/portrait-du-recours-a-lajsh-en-sante-mentale/. Accessed August 9, 2025.

Administrative Tribunal of Quebec. (2004). *Rapport annuel de gestion 2003–04.*

Administrative Tribunal of Quebec. (2021). *Rapport annuel de gestion 2020–21.* https://www.taq.gouv.qc.ca/fileadmin/user_upload/TAQ_Rapport_annuel_de_gestion_2020-2021-ecran.pdf. Accessed August 9, 2025.

Appelbaum, P. S. (1992). Forensic psychiatry: The need for self-regulation. *Journal of the American Academy of Psychiatry and the Law Online, 20*(2), 153–162.

Bala, N., & Saunders, A. (2003). Understanding the family context: Why the law of expert evidence is different in family law cases. *Canadian Family Law Quarterly, 20*(3), 277–338.

Barnett, P., Mackay, E., Matthews, H., Gate, R., Greenwood, H., Ariyo, K., Bhui, K., Halvorsrud, K., Pilling, S., & Smith, S. (2019). Ethnic variations in compulsory detention under the Mental Health Act: A systematic review and meta-analysis of international data. *The Lancet, 6*(4), 305–317. https://doi.org/10.1016/S2215-0366(19)30027-6

Bassett, M. T. (2020). Tired of science being ignored? Get political. *Nature, 586*(7829), 337–338. https://doi.org/10.1038/d41586-020-02854-9

Becker, H. S. (1967). Whose side are we on? *Social Problems, 14*(3), 239–248.

Beckett, K., & Murakawa, N. (2012). Mapping the shadow carceral state: Toward an institutionally capacious approach to punishment. *Theoretical Criminology, 16*(2), 221–244. https://doi.org/10.1177/1362480612442113

Berdejó, C. (2018). Criminalizing race: Racial disparities in plea-bargaining. *Boston College Law Review, 59*, 1187–1250.

Bernheim, E. (2008). Le psychiatre devant le juge: Entre pragmatisme et captivité, une communication aléatoire. *Canadian Journal of Law and Society, 23*(1–2), 37–61. https://doi.org/10.1017/S0829320100009571

Bernheim, E. (2015). Quinze ans de garde en établissement. De l'état des lieux à la remise en question. In *La protection des personnes vulnérables* (pp. 197–220). Quebec Bar Training Department Yvon Blais.

Bernheim, E. (2024). Extending the boundaries of the psychiatric hospital: The use and misuse of psychiatric coercion during the Covid-19 pandemic in Quebec and Ontario. In C. Flood, Y. Y. B. Chen, R. Deonandan, S. Halabi, & S. Thériault (Eds.), *Borders, boundaries and pandemics* (pp. 273–280). Routledge. https://doi.org/10.4324/9781003394006

Bernheim, E., Chalifour, G., & Laniel, R.-A. (2016). La santé mentale devant la cour: Invisibilité et déni de droits – Une étude statistique de la jurisprudence en autorisation de soins. *McGill Journal of Law and Health, 9*(2), 255–382.

Bernheim, E., Grisé, A.-D., & Perreault, E. (2024). Les pratiques des contentieux des Centres intégrés de santé et de services sociaux en matière d'autorisation de soins et les droits des parties défenderesses: une étude des dossiers judiciaires de Longueuil. In *La protection des personnes vulnérables* (pp. 90–116). Quebec Bar Training Department. Yvon Blais.

Black, D. (1983). Crime as social control. *American Sociological Review, 48*(1), 34–45. https://doi.org/10.2307/2095143

Boatswain-Kyte, A. (2018). *Overrepresentation and disparity of Black children reported under the child protection system: The need for effective cross-system collaborations* [Doctoral dissertation, University of Montreal]. Papyrus. http://hdl.handle.net/1866/21784

Boatswain-Kyte, A., Esposito, T., & Trocmé, N. (2020). A longitudinal jurisdictional study of Black children reported to child protection services in Quebec, Canada. *Children Youth Service, 116*, 105219. https://doi.org/10.1016/j.childyouth.2020.105219

Bowlby, J., & World Health Organization. (1952). *Maternal care and mental health: A report prepared on behalf of the World Health Organization as a contribution to the United Nations programme for the welfare of homeless children* (2nd ed.).World Health Organization. https://iris.who.int/handle/10665/40724. Accessed August 9, 2025.

Burston, D. (2018). Psychiatry, anti-psychiatry, and anti-anti-psychiatry: Rhetoric and reality. *Psychotherapy and Politics International, 16*(1), Article e1439. https://doi.org/10.1002/ppi.1439

Caldwell, J., & Sinha, V. (2020). (Re)conceptualizing neglect: Considering the overrepresentation of indigenous children in child welfare systems in Canada. *Child Indicators Research, 13*(2), 481–512. https://doi.org/10.1007/s12187-019-09676-w

Castellano, U. (2017). The politics of benchcraft: The role of judges in mental health courts. *Law & Social Inquiry, 42*(2), 398–422. https://doi.org/10.1111/lsi.12266

Catallo, H. (2024 February, 29). *Trapped in a psych ward: Michigan doc pre-signed blank forms that can rob you of your freedom*. American Broadcasting Company. https://www.wxyz.com/news/local-news/investigations/trapped-in-a-psych-ward-michigan-doc-pre-signed-blank-forms-that-can-rob-you-of-your-freedom. Accessed August 9, 2025.

Choate, P., & Lindstrom, G. (2017). Parenting capacity assessment as a colonial strategy. *Canadian Family Law Quarterly, 37*(1), 41–60.

Civil Code of Quebec, CQLR c CCQ-1991.

Code of Civil Procedure, CQLR c C-25.01.

Cohen, B. (2017). The importance of critical approaches to mental health and illness. In B. Cohen (Ed.), *Routledge international handbook of critical mental health* (pp. 1–12). Routledge.

Cooper, J. (2018). Unruly affects: Attempts at control and all that escapes from an American mental health court. *Cultural Anthropology, 33*(1), 85–108. https://doi.org/10.14506/ca33.1.04

Coupienne, M. (2023). Se défendre, se taire ou renoncer? Regards sur la participation des familles "négligentes" à la Chambre de la jeunesse. *Nouvelles Pratiques Sociales, 33*(2), 115–134. https://doi.org/10.7202/1107880ar

Court of Quebec. (2010). *Rapport public 2008–09*. https://courduquebec.ca/fileadmin/cour-du-quebec/centre-de-documentation/Publications/rapports-publics/RapPublic2009.pdf. Accessed August 9, 2025.

Criminal Code, RSC 1985, c C-46.

Crocker, A. G., Nicholls, T. L., Seto, M. C., Charette, Y., Côté, G., & Caulet, M. (2015). The national trajectory project of individuals found not criminally responsible on account of mental disorder in Canada. Part 2: The people behind the label. *The Canadian Journal of Psychiatry, 60*(3), 106–116. https://doi.org/10.1177/070674371506000305

Crotty, H. D. (1924). History of insanity as a defence to crime in English criminal law. *California Law Review, 12*(2), 105–122.

Datchis, C. C., & Ancis, J. R. (2017). *Gender, psychology, and justice: The mental health of women and girls in the legal system*. New York University Press.

Denno, D. W. (2021). How experts have dominated the neuroscience narrative in criminal cases for twelve decades: A warning for the future. *William & Mary Law Review, 63*, 1215–1288.

Dix, G. E. (1967). Hospitalization of the mentally Ill in Wisconsin: A need for a reexamination. *Marquette Law Review, 51*, 1–41.

Dumbrill, G. C. (2006). Parental experience of child protection intervention: A qualitative study. *Child Abuse & Neglect, 30*(1), 27–37. https://doi.org/10.1016/j.chiabu.2005.08.012

Ericsson, K. (2000). Social control and emancipation? Ambiguities in child welfare. *Journal of Scandinavian Studies in Criminology and Crime Prevention, 1*(1), 16–26. https://doi.org/10.1080/140438500501116237

Feldman, S. (1980). *The administration of mental health services.* Thomas Publisher.

Fernance, C. (2024). The discursive construction of 'good parenting 'in Australia's statutory child protection system: Impacts on First Nations families & ways to disrupt the discourse. *Social Work & Policy Studies: Social Justice, Practice and Theory, 7*(1), 1–21.

Fryer, B., Hunt, A., McBarnet, D., & Moorhouse, B. (Eds.). (2018). *Law, state and society*. Routledge. https://doi.org/10.4324/9781351053853

Galanter, M. (1974). Why the haves come out ahead: Speculations on the limits of legal change. *Law & Society Review, 9*, 95–160. https://doi.org/10.2307/3053023

Government of Québec. (2023). *Rapport de dénombrement 2022.* Data Report. https://publications.msss.gouv.qc.ca/msss/document-003630/. Accessed August 10, 2025.

Hammond, I., Eastman, A. L., Leventhal, J. M., & Putnam-Hornstein, E. (2017). Maternal mental health disorders and reports to child protective services: A birth cohort study. *International Journal of Environmental Research and Public Health, 14*(11), 1320. https://doi.org/10.3390/ijerph14111320

Haraway, D. (1988). Situated knowledges: The science question in feminism and the privilege of partial perspective. *Feminist Studies, 14*(3), 575–599. http://www.jstor.org/stable/3178066?origin=JSTOR-pdf

Haussleiter, I. S., Lehmann, I., Ueberberg, B., Heinz, J., Zielasek, J., Gouzoulis-Mayfrank, E., & Juckel, G. (2022). Homelessness among psychiatric inpatients in North Rhine-Westphalia: A retrospective routine data analysis. *BMC Psychiatry, 22*, 132. https://doi.org/10.1186/s12888-022-03786-6

Hood, C. (1991). A public management for all season? *Public Administration, 69*(1), 3–19. https://doi.org/10.1111/j.1467-9299.1991.tb00779.x

Institut Philippe Pinel de Montréal v. A.G., [1994] RJQ 2523 (C. A.).

Justice Quebec. (2018, May 16). *Demande d'accès aux documents – Décisions, Données sur les demandes d'autorisation judiciaire de soins*, Access to information report n° R-78666.

Justice Quebec (2021, March 12). *Demande d'accès aux documents – Décisions, Garde en établissement et autorisation de soins: statistiques*, Access to information report n° R-94748.
Justice Quebec. (2022, December 20). Demande d'accès aux documents—Nombre de demande d'évaluation psychiatrique, de garde en établissement et d'autorisation de soins. Access to information report n° BSM–2022–001682.
Justice Quebec. (2023a, October 19). *Demande d'accès aux documents – garde provisoire, ordonnance de soins et garde en établissement.* Access to information report n° BSM-2023–002984. https://cdn-contenu.quebec.ca/cdn-contenu/adm/min/justice/publications-adm/acces-information/decisions/2023/DAI_no_BSM-2023-002984.pdf. Accessed August 9, 2025.
Justice Quebec. (2023b, July 12). *Demande d'accès aux documents – Nombre de dossiers ouverts et al.* Access to information report n° BSM-2023–002689. https://cdn-contenu.quebec.ca/cdn-contenu/adm/min/justice/publications-adm/acces-information/decisions/2023/DAI_no_BSM-2023-002689.pdf. Accessed August 9, 2025.
Kang, J., et al. (2011). Implicit bias in the courtroom. *University of California Los Angeles Law Review, 59*(5), 1124–1186.
Knight, S., Jarvis, E., Ryder, A., Lashley, M., & Rousseau, C. (2022). Ethno-racial differences in coercive referral and intervention among patients with first- episode psychosis. *Psychiatric Services, 73*(1), 2–8. https://doi.org/10.1176/appi.ps.202000715
Keller, H. (2022). *The myth of attachment theory a critical understanding for multicultural societies*. Routledge. https://doi.org/10.4324/9781003167099
Klosterkamp, S., & Anwar, T. (2023). Positionality and research ethics. In L. Flower & S. Klosterkamp (Eds.), *Courtroom ethnography: Exploring contemporary approaches, fieldwork and challenges* (pp. 47–60). Springer. https://doi.org/10.1007/978-3-031-37985-7
Lavergne, C., & Dufour, S. (2020, January 20). *Les familles issues de la diversité culturelle et la protection de la jeunesse au Québec: constats et recommandations.* Quebec special Commission on Children's Rights and Youth Protection. https://www.csdepj.gouv.qc.ca/fileadmin/Fichiers_clients/Documents_deposes_a_la_Commission/P 068_Recommandations_Constats Familles_diversite_culturelle_PJ_Lavergne_Dufour.pdf. Accessed August 9, 2025.
Law Reform Commission of Canada. (1976). *Mental disorder in the criminal process.* Ottawa. https://publications.gc.ca/collections/collection_2022/jus/j32-1/J32-1-14-1975-eng.pdf. Accessed August 9, 2025.

Lebenbaum, M., Chiu, M., Vigod, S., & Kurdyak, P. (2018). Prevalence and predictors of involuntary psychiatric hospital admissions in Ontario, Canada: A population-based linked administrative database study. *Bjpsych Open, 4*(2), 31–38. https://doi.org/10.1192/bjo.2017.4

Leckey, R., Schmieder-Gropen, R., Nnebe, C., & Clouthier, M. (2022). Indigenous parents and child welfare: Mistrust, epistemic injustice, and training. *Social & Legal Studies, 31*(4), 559–579. https://doi.org/10.1177/09646639211041476

Lens, V. (2019). Judging the other: The intersection of race, gender, and class in family court. *Family Court Review, 57*(1), 72–87. https://doi.org/10.1111/fcre.12397

Levi, M. M., & Golding, J. M. (2024). Mental health in the courtroom: How victim mental health status impacts juror decision-making in a rape case. *Psychology, Crime & Law, 31*(7), 1–24. https://doi.org/10.1080/1068316X.2024.2316229

Levy, E. (2022). It's urgent! emergency decision-making, child welfare, and rethinking qualified immunity. *University of Illinois Law Review, 1*, 411–446.

Littlechild, B., & Housman, C. (2023). Applying universal principles of 'best interest': Practice challenges across transnational jurisdictions, cultural norms, and values. *Children, 10*(3), 537. https://doi.org/10.3390/children10030537

MacDonald, S. A., Fortin, V., & Houde, S. (2022). Therapeutic justice or epistemic injustice? In K. Fritsch, J. Monaghan, & E. van der Meulen (Eds.), *Disability injustice: Confronting criminalization in Canada* (pp. 164–186). University of British Columbia Press.

Martin, S., Charette, Y., Leclerc, C., Seto, M. C., Nicholls, T. L., & Crocker, A. G. (2022). *Not a "get out of jail free card": Comparing the legal supervision of persons found not criminally responsible on account of mental disorder and convicted offenders. Frontiers in Psychiatry, 12*, 775480. https://doi.org/10.3389/fpsyt.2021.775480

Masson, J. (2000). Thinking about contact: A social or a legal problem. *Children & Family Law Quartely, 12*(1), 15–30.

Michalski, J. H. (2017). Mental health issues and the Canadian criminal justice system. *Contemporary Justice Review, 20*(1), 2–25. https://doi.org/10.1080/10282580.2016.1226817

McIntosh, J. (2025, July 4). Forced hospitalization: Potential victims could receive compensation in Quebec. *Montreal City News*. https://montreal.citynews.ca/2025/07/04/forced-hospitalization-victims-quebec/. Accessed August 9, 2025.

Moloney, N., O'Donnell, P., Elzain, M., Bashir, A., Dunne, C. P., Kelly, B. D., & Gulati, G. (2022). Homelessness amongst psychiatric in-patients: A cross-sectional study in the mid-west of Ireland. *Irish Journal of Medical Science, 191*(1), 321–326. https://doi.org/10.1007/s11845-021-02546-x

Neitz, M. B. (2013). Socioeconomic bias in the judiciary. *Cleveland State Law Review, 61*, 137–165.

New Zealand Royal Commission of Inquiry. (2022). *Beautiful children: Inquiry into the Lake Alice Child and Adolescent Unit*. https://www.abuseincare.org.nz/reports/inquiry-into-the-lake-alice-child-and-adolescent-unit. Accessed August 9, 2025.

O'Donnell, M., Maclean, M. J., Sims, S., Morgan, V. A., Leonard, H., & Stanley, F. J. (2015). Maternal mental health and risk of child protection involvement: Mental health diagnoses associated with increased risk. *Journal of Epidemiology & Community Health, 69*(12), 1175–1183. https://doi.org/10.1136/jech-2014-205240

Ogilvie, J. M., & Kisely, S. (2022). Examining the health and criminal justice characteristics for young people on compulsory community treatment orders: An Australian birth cohort and data linkage study. *International Journal of Law and Psychiatry, 83*, Article 101813. https://doi.org/10.1016/j.ijlp.2022.101813

Oh, H., Cho, Y., Bae, J., Holley, L., Shafer, M., Kim, K., & Lee, Y. (2024). Impact of statutory revisions to family-petitioned civil commitment in South Korea. *International Journal of Law and Psychiatry, 94*, Article 101982. https://doi.org/10.1016/j.ijlp.2024.101982

Ombudsman. (2011, February). *Les difficultés d'application de la Loi sur la protection des personnes dont l'état mental représente un danger pour elles-mêmes ou pour autrui*. Special report. https://protecteurducitoyen.qc.ca/sites/default/files/pdf/rapports_speciaux/2011-02_P-38.pdf. Accessed August 9, 2025.

Otero, M. (2016). Traiter les intraitables : L'univers des autorisations judiciaires de soins à Montréal. *Nouvelles Pratiques Sociales, 28*(2), 203–226. https://doi.org/10.7202/1041188ar

Paik, L. (2021). *Trapped in a maze: How social control institutions drive family poverty and inequality*. University of California Press.

Palmer, L., Font, S., Eastman, A. L., Guo, L., & Putnam-Hornstein, E. (2024). What does child protective services investigate as neglect? A population-based study. *Child Maltreatment, 29*(1), 96–105. https://doi.org/10.1177/10775595221114144

Panorama & Lee, J. (2022, September 28). "Toxic culture" of abuse at mental health hospital revealed by BBC secret filming. *BBC News*. https://www.bbc.com/news/uk-63045298. Accessed August 9, 2025.

Payne, S. (1996). Masculinity and the redundant male: Explaining the increasing incarceration of young men. *Social & Legal Studies, 5*(2), 159–178. https://doi.org/10.1177/096466399600500202

Perlin, M. L. (2017). The insanity defense: Nine myths that will not go away. In M. D. White (Ed.), *The insanity defense—Multidisciplinary views on it history, trends and controversy* (pp. 3–22). Bloomsbury Publishing. https://digitalcommons.nyls.edu/fac_articles_chapters/1128

Perlin, M. L. (2023). "In these times of compassion when conformity's in fashion:" How therapeutic jurisprudence can root out bias, limit polarization, and support vulnerable persons in the legal process. *Texas a&m Law Review, 10*, 219–267.

Platt, A., & Diamond, B. L. (1966). The origins of the 'right and wrong' test of criminal responsibility and its subsequent development in the United States: An historical survey. *California Law Review, 54*, 1227–1261.

Quebec Human Rights and Youth Rights Commission. (2025, April 24). *Enquête systémique en protection des droits de la jeunesse – Mauricie-Centre-du-Québec*. Investigation report. https://cdpdj.qc.ca/fr/publications/enquete-dpj-mauricie-2025. Accessed August 9, 2025.

Quebec Ministry of Health and Social Services. (2011, January). *Rapport d'enquête sur les difficultés d'application de la Loi sur la protection des personnes dont l'état mental représente un danger pour elles-mêmes ou pour autrui*. https://publications.msss.gouv.qc.ca/msss/fichiers/2010/10-914-08.pdf. Accessed August 9, 2025.

Roberts, D. (2022). *Torn apart: How the child welfare system destroys black families–and how abolition can build a safer world*. Basic Books.

Robertson, S. C., Sinclair, C., & Hatala, A. R. (2022). Indigenous mothers' experiences of power and control in child welfare: Families being heard. *Journal of Social Work, 22*(2), 303–322. https://doi.org/10.1177/14680173211009187

Roxburgh, S., & Sinclair, M. (2024). Colonial constructions: Systemic racism in child welfare practice. *Journal of Social Work, 24*(1), 3–20. https://doi.org/10.1177/14680173231197988

Salam, Z., Odenigbo, O., Newbold, B., Wahoush, O., & Schwartz, L. (2022). Systemic and individual factors that shape mental health service usage among visible minority immigrants and refugees in Canada: A scoping review. *Administration and Policy in Mental Health and Mental Health*

Services Research, 49(4), 552–574. https://doi.org/10.1007/s10488-021-01183-x

Sandefur, R. (2008). Access to civil justice and race, class, and gender inequality. *Annual Review of Sociology, 34*, 339–358. https://doi.org/10.1146/annurev.soc.34.040507.134534

Schramme, T. (2004). The legacy of antipsychiatry. In T. Schramme & J. Thome (Eds.), *Philosophy and psychiatry* (pp. 94–119). Walter de Gruyter.

Sinclair, R. (2016). The indigenous child removal system in Canada: An examination of legal decision-making and racial bias. *First Peoples Child & Family Review, 11*(2), 8–18. https://doi.org/10.7202/1082333ar

Sinden, A. (1999). Why won't mom cooperate: A critique of informality in child welfare proceedings. *Yale Journal of Law & Feminism, 11*, 339–396.

Smith, D. M. (2009). The disordered and discredited plaintiff: Psychiatric evidence in civil litigation. *Cardozo Law Review, 31*, 749–822.

Starkman, M. (2012). The movement. In B. A. LeFrançois, R. Menzies, & G. Reaume (Eds.), *Mad matters: A critical reader in canadian mad studies* (pp. 27–370). Canadian Scholars.

Sylvestre, M.-E., Blomley, N., & Bellot, C. (2020). *Red zones: Criminal law and the territorial governance of marginalized people*. Cambridge University Press. https://doi.org/10.1017/9781316875544

Szasz, T. (2010). Psychiatry, anti-psychiatry, critical psychiatry: What do these terms mean? *Philosophy, Psychiatry, & Psychology, 17*(3), 229–232.

Szasz, T. (2008). Debunking antipsychiatry: Laing, law, and Largactil. *Current Psychology, 27*(2), 79–101. https://doi.org/10.1007/s12144-008-9024-z

The Office of the Ombudsperson. (2019, March). *Committed to change: Protecting the rights of involuntary patients under the mental health act*. Special Report N°42. https://bcombudsperson.ca/assets/media/OMB-Committed-to-Change-FINAL-web.pdf. Accessed August 9, 2025.

Thomas, J. (1993). *Doing critical ethnography*. Sage.

Thompson, M. K. (2018). Bias on trial: Toward an open discussion of racial stereotypes in the courtroom. *Michigan State Law Review, 5*, 1243–1307.

Tran, D. Q., Ryder, A. G., & Jarvis, G. E. (2019). Reported immigration and medical coercion among immigrants referred to a cultural consultation service. *Transcultural Psychiatry, 56*(5), 807–826. https://doi.org/10.1177/1363461519847811

Turner, A. (2016). *Living arrangements of Aboriginal children aged 14 and under*. Statistics Canada. https://www150.statcan.gc.ca/n1/en/pub/75-006-x/2016001/article/14547-eng.pdf?st=oJ-22ftL. Accessed August 9, 2025.

Uhnoo, S., Bladini, M., & Wettergren, Å. (2023). Negotiating access. In L. Flower & S. Klosterkamp (Eds.), *Courtroom ethnography: Exploring contemporary approaches, fieldwork and challenges* (pp. 33–46). Springer. https://doi.org/10.1007/978-3-031-37985-7_3

Van Krieken, R. (1986). Social theory and child welfare: Beyond social control. *Theory and Society, 15*(3), 401–429. https://www.jstor.org/stable/657324

Vogel, M., Stephens, K. D., & Siebels, D. (2014). Mental illness and the criminal justice system. *Sociology Compass, 8*(6), 627–638. https://doi.org/10.1111/soc4.12174

von Benda-Beckmann, F. (2002). Who's afraid of legal pluralism? *The Journal of Legal Pluralism and Unofficial Law, 34*(47), 37–82. https://doi.org/10.1080/07329113.2002.10756563

Winick, B. (2005). *Civil commitment: A therapeutic jurisprudence model*. Carolina Academic Press.

Winko v. British Columbia (Forensic Psychiatric Institute), [1999] 2 SCR 625

Winnipeg Child and Family Services v. K.L.W., 2000 SCC 48.

Wipond, R. (2023). *Your consent is not required: The rise in psychiatric detentions, forced treatment, and abusive guardianships*. BenBella.

Youth Protection Act, CQLR c P-34.1

5

Daily Life on Trial: When Poverty Is Evidence for Incapacity

> The defendant says that thirty days of hospitalization is too long because she has not paid her rent and is afraid that her home will be looted. She reports that homes are often looted when tenants are away in social housing buildings. She is worried about losing all her possessions and her home, and about becoming homeless again, as happened to her twenty years ago, when she was last involuntarily admitted. The hospital lawyer says to her, "The hospitalization you had twenty years ago that made you feel better for twenty years?" The lawyer questions the fact that she could lose her possessions or her home during her hospitalization. The defendant asks, "Have you ever lived in social housing?" The lawyer replies that she has not.—Excerpt of personal observation notes, Involuntary commitment hearing, Court of Quebec, Montreal courthouse.

My results are consistent with what is known about the socioeconomic profile of people subjected to involuntary commitment or treatment, child welfare services interventions or criminal proceedings (Clair, 2020; Eamon et al., 2004; Haussleiter, 2022; Moloney et al., 2022; Morris et al., 2018; Otero, 2016; Scott-Hayward & Fradella, 2019; Wacquant, 2009;). In all four legal contexts examined, the hearings are rich in

E. Bernheim, *Therapeutic (In)justice and the Shadow Carceral State*, The Politics of Mental Health and Illness, https://doi.org/10.1007/978-3-032-16186-4_5

information that demonstrates the poverty of defendants. Defendants are frequently characterized as transitioning between temporary shelters and relatives' residences, subsisting on social assistance, inhabiting substandard accommodations that may be plagued with mold or pest infestations, experiencing food insecurity, accumulating debt, facing eviction, or resorting to panhandling. This information is generally used as fact, and as evidence of social dysfunction resulting from mental health issues, especially when defendants have not applied for social assistance or sued their landlords for unhealthy living conditions. The ongoing housing and homelessness crisis, the inadequacy of social benefits and the minimum wage, the unavailability of services and the weakening of the social safety net are not mentioned during the hearings—let alone considered to explain the distressing situations in which the defendants find themselves. Poverty therefore constitutes an element of the definition and interpretation of the legal criteria of danger, "significant threat," and incapacity, rather than a contextual element (Roberts, 2002).

During hearings, the defendant's financial situation is not mentioned, and furthermore the judicial process tends to overlook social and economic realities. Although there is little discussion of the legal issues involved, particularly the rights at stake, judicial discourse deals with information only in technical terms. The facts are taken out of their social context; they are generally used as far as they constitute evidence against the defendants. However, even when rules of evidence and procedures are more flexible, they still have the effect of excluding the defendants' experiential knowledge. The conversation is framed using the evidence and arguments submitted by the hospital or child welfare services to which the defendants must respond—with the evidence and arguments interwoven with social elements and psychiatric and psychosocial interpretations. The defendants thus find themselves having to justify their homelessness, the insalubrity of their housing, their poor diet, the fact that they are being unemployed or family conflicts. In this respect, the hearings are a judgment on the defendants' living conditions, which are presented as a chosen lifestyle, being put on trial.

The political, economic, and social dimensions of mental health fall outside the legal framework of analysis and the role of the courts, due to the formalities of hearing procedures taking up all the space, and because they appear invisible to the judicial actors. Throughout the hearings, the judicial narrative on mental health constructs an "other" who is different, strange, and disturbing, effectively excluding the defendants' opinions and experience. However, the accumulation of mental health court orders produces tangible social and structural effects. Defendants are subject to multiple orders, which sometimes creates contradictory constraints on their daily lives, while impoverishing them. Moreover, the fact that courts almost systematically grant the petitions of hospitals and child welfare services contributes to the neoliberal discourse about the rise in the intensity and severity of the mental health crisis.

The Social Class Trial

During all the ethnographic fieldwork hearings I observed in the four courtrooms, only on a few occasions did situations or facts concerning a person's bodily integrity arise—whether of the defendants themselves or of third parties. Rather, court cases tend to be about erratic or disturbing behaviors leading to involuntary commitment or treatment, neglect or risk of neglect of children's basic needs in child welfare cases, and minor crimes such as thefts under $5,000 or obstruction of police work for defendants declared unfit to stand trial or not criminally responsible due to a mental disorder.

My observations highlighted two defendant profiles who are treated very differently by the courts: individuals who have no profession and presented a precarious socioeconomic profile, and professionals who fall under what could be described as the "middle class." The vast majority of defendants belong to the first profile. They have a low level of education, are unemployed, or work in what is often referred to in courts as "menial jobs." Several defendants demonstrate limited proficiency in French or English, utilize informal register in their speech, or appear before the court in attire deemed inappropriate for judicial proceedings, with some appearing in hospital garments. In several instances, the hearings are tied at least indirectly to their precarious circumstances, such as homelessness or social isolation, altercations on the street, in shelters, or in social housing, subsistence theft, behaviors deemed inadequate, erratic, or disturbing in public spaces, repeated moves or failing to meet their basic needs or those of their children. Defendants are often known to the police, who, in some cases, have been directly involved in the situation that brought them to court.

Various designations are used in the discourse of legal actors, which function to mask defendants' poverty. In the same way that coercion in mental health is erased through discourse using words relating to therapy (Rossero, 2023), poverty is concealed behind technical language. Judicial discourse euphemistically recast eviction as "housing instability" and small or unsanitary housing as "insufficient infrastructure," while avoiding any discussion of inadequate social benefits that perpetuate extreme poverty, simply noting that defendants were "unable to balance their budget."

Defendants are often asked to justify their living conditions, which were often treated as a deliberate lifestyle choice. Regarding housing, they have to explain their frequent moves and periods of homelessness without any consideration given to the exorbitant rental prices and well-documented eviction practices. Through their comments and questions, judges often show suspicion, seemingly convinced of the defendants' responsibility for their housing situation. For example, during a Review Board hearing, the lawyer presiding over the bench ask a defendant who had moved two times in four years because of evictions: "You move every two years, how do you explain that? Isn't it because you have problems with landlords or other tenants?".

Defendants have also to explain why they do not pursue legal action against their landlord for unsanitary conditions, why they do not receive the social benefits they are entitled to, or why they have not regularized their immigration status. They have to justify their living expenses, especially when they are in a homeless situation, have debts, or went bankrupt. In these cases, judicial actors share strong opinions about which expenses should be prioritized. For example, they consider it unnecessary and costly for a homeless person to have a dog, even though dogs offer protection, emotional benefits, and warmth, or believe that debts should be repaid before a cell phone is purchased.

Although the legal criteria are danger, incapacity, or threat, defendants are regularly confronted with statements about the abnormality of their situations and behaviors—statements that are also reflected in case law. What is normal or abnormal is never clearly defined, nor are the standards used to judge normality. Psychiatrists reported that defendants' functioning, perceptions or emotions are "not normal;" social workers assert that family relationships need to be "normalized;" lawyers plead "abnormal behavior" and lifestyle choices; judges ask defendants to assess the normality of their actions or thoughts, or even ask them: "Are you ready to live normally in society?" This is illustrated by the following excerpt from my observation notes during an involuntary commitment hearing, where the hospital's attorney asserted that the defendant lived "a life out of the norm:"

> Involuntary commitment is requested for 30 days following an altercation in a social housing apartment building, where the defendant threw a beer bottle onto his neighbor's balcony. Called to the scene, the police found the apartment to be unsanitary, with wet clothes everywhere and a great deal of dampness. The defendant, a man in his sixties with long white hair and wearing a fluorescent green bomber jacket, acknowledging that he had lost his temper, says that day noise is very high in social housing buildings, and that he could no longer tolerate hearing his neighbor screaming on his balcony. He also explains that he could not afford to go to a laundromat and must wash his clothes in his bathtub. He finally claims that because police officers once "flaged [him] as mental-health case," they routinely take him to the hospital. During her closing argument, the hospital's lawyer states, "we have here someone who doesn't seem to be mentally well" and asserts that "Mr. Bouchard could lose his apartment because of his attitude" and that he needs to "learn to respect the usual norms of behavior." The judge rejects the hospital's request, saying that just because "Mr. is special, unique, an artist and a philosopher" does not make him a danger.
>
> After the hearing, the judge tells me that "original" people are "regularly" subject to requests for involuntary commitment as a result of the confusion between disturbance and danger: "The defendant we just saw may be disturbing to some, precisely because he is original. He may pose a challenge to our philosophy of life, but how is he dangerous in the legal sense?" According to the judge, the "moral" or "human" dimensions of normality should not be confused with the legal requirements

for depriving someone of their freedom. He affirms that "the principle is freedom; deprivation of freedom is the exception."

Such an outcome is an exception. It was extremely rare for me to witness the rejection of arguments from a hospital or child welfare services during my fieldwork. I observe that questioning, or even rejecting, their arguments is done by only a small proportion of the judges. In most cases, judges opt for a therapeutic discourse, asserting that the court could act as a "framework" to normalize behaviors, relationships, situations, and even life itself.

The absence of clear criteria for normality essentially makes it into a moral category of analysis rooted in classism, with studies showing that legal, psychiatric and social work professionals base their interpretations on middle-class assumptions, practices, and lifestyles (Clair, 2020; Emmelman, 2003; López-Espino, 2024; Raz, 2013; Walkowitz, 1999). In many of the hearings I observed, the defendants' behaviors were examined and judged as more or less acceptable or normal, on a spectrum ranging from annoying to morally reprehensible. The defendants were just as likely to be reproached for using dating apps and playing video games as they were for being in debt, begging, or engaging in sex work. Any behavior, such as not locking doors, leaving for the weekend without telling friends and family, excessive intaking of coffee, soft drinks or junk food, overeating or driving in a bus lane, was likely to be reported and discussed. Among all the defendants' behaviors, the use of drugs and alcohol was systematically proscribed. Courts almost always require abstinence, even in the absence of evidence that drugs or alcohol were a problem in defendants' lives, which puts defendants living with addiction to substances in situations where they breached legal conditions simply by continuing to use substances.

The moral and classist aspect of the normality discussed in court is sometimes clearly assumed. A mother strip-dancing in bars was criticized as setting a bad example for her children; a young woman living in a squatter house was lectured about the illegality of this practice; a young man who did not work was labeled "idle." At an involuntary treatment hearing for a defendant who claimed to have contact with Jesus—which the defendant openly described as "not normal, it's abnormal, it's marginal, not everyone experiences that"—the question of behavioral conformity to social norms was openly discussed, as an excerpt from my observation notes shows:

> The psychiatrist asserts that, without psychiatric treatment, the defendant would certainly go on a pilgrimage "carrying his cross on his back." The judge says that the Compostela pilgrims "are not psychotic for all that," to which the psychiatrist replies, "But it's socially accepted in Compostela, not in Quebec. The definition of a delusion is that it doesn't meet social norms. It's my role as a psychiatrist to interpret behavior considering the social norm." The psychiatrist then states that, in accordance with "the principle of assigning the least severe and least compromising diagnosis," he is prepared to withdraw the diagnosis of psychosis in exchange for the defendant's cooperation. The defendant, a tall man in his fifties dressed entirely in leather, is unrepresented. He offers a well-articulated defense: several witnesses confirmed that he has an active, balanced life and that antipsychotics prevent him from working, after which he argued the case law. The judge nevertheless grants the petition, wishing him good luck. After the hearing, the judge confides in me that he does not understand how a woman engineer could be friend with the defendant and testify on his behalf: "How can this woman, who is an engineer, have so much consideration for this person? What is she defending? What is she looking for in this person? I would have understood better if she was someone uneducated, subject to influence and more naïve."

Like behavior, social relationships are also scrutinized against normality. The courts' conception of family relationships is highly conventional, in terms of parental roles, organization of daily life and type of interpersonal ties. Family relationships are viewed as essential and must be nurtured. When it comes to child welfare, the court views family relationships through the lens of a gendered and traditional conception of the roles of fathers and mothers, as well as routines that enable children to be cared for. Mothers are regarded as responsible for their children's basic needs, including the emotional dimension of family relationships, while the absence or non-involvement of fathers is simply noted. A routine that includes daycare attendance, playtime, family activities, shared meals, and supervised homework is considered essential to facilitate the child's "normal" development regardless of financial and time constraints. During hearings, arguments with family members, or a lack of family contact, were viewed with suspicion and require explanations from the defendants. The explanations provided, however, were often not believed, and situations were being regularly interpreted as evidence of paranoia or lack of insight on the part of the defendants, or as proof that they had exhausted their families who no longer want to see them. Although these interpretations were possible, they were rarely supported by formal evidence.

The courts are also interested in social relationships outside the family, especially when it comes to "bad company" and "bad influence." These relations are sometimes blamed for the defendants' use of drugs or alcohol, or for them not taking their medication, or being "idle."

In general, judicial actors—judges, but also lawyers, psychiatrists, and social workers—believe that defendants must work. Working is an essential part of the recovery approach and policies, but also a means of avoiding bad company and the use of drugs or alcohol, in addition to improving one's financial situation. Work is essential for a "normal life." In this respect, judges see court orders as a means of engaging defendants in the therapeutic process necessary to avoid homelessness or criminality. In a formal interview, a judge recounted the story of a defendant whose involuntary treatment order prevented them from being "arrested, caught in a conflict or having someone beat the crap out of them:"

> This guy could, at certain times in his life, if he took the right medication and had the right follow-up, almost manage a normal life, including working—obviously not a job that required high education, but working in restaurants, or doing things like that. Then, of course, you think: "If he has the support he needs and if he takes the medication and he can function and live a quasi-normal life, what else is there?"

The defendants' level of education or training is systematically questioned during hearings. Most of them have a high school education, whether completed or not, and have no specialized work training. Some have training in manual work in construction or factories. Many do not work or work only occasionally in restaurants or stores. Others are no longer able to work due to physical or mental health problems and live on social benefits. During hearings or in follow-up interviews, some defendants reported that psychiatric medication prevented them from working, as it exhausted them, interfered with their ability to concentrate, or made them sleepy. In fact, these debilitating adverse effects of medications are often the reason that defendants do not want to take them or want to reduce the dosage. These remarks are mostly ignored by the court, which reinforced that psychiatrists are in the best position to make decisions about the type of medication, its method of administration and its dosage. I will revisit this in Chapter 8.

Some defendants want to return to school. While such a goal should please the court, it is often met with skepticism. In many cases, it is suggested by judicial actors that school would be a "stressor" that could exacerbate mental health problems and risk factors. In other cases, the defendants' ability to complete their program is questioned, especially when they would have to work at the same time. In addition, judges sometimes question the defendants' program choices, for example by asking defendants to justify their choice to study plumbing or industrial design. When it comes to child welfare, judicial actors tend to believe that mothers will not be sufficiently available for their children if they go back to school.

In all the legal contexts studied, working and improving one's financial situation is considered necessary to meet judicial requirements. The poverty and destitution in which many defendants live are often seen as an indication of the extent of their social dysfunction and the abnormality of their behavior. The courts' ambivalence toward defendants pursuing education, while expecting that defendants will be able to improve their material conditions, demonstrates a disconnection from the realities of the job market for low-skilled workers, as well as the realities of the rental market.

This disconnection is evident throughout all the judicial processes inquired into and have concrete impacts on court orders. For example, psychiatrists sometimes claim to have recommended that defendants balance their diet by including more fresh vegetables, or join a gym, without considering the costs associated with such expenditures; similarly, child welfare services demand that every child should have their own room, an unattainable requirement for many defendants (and for many people in society in general). Judges generally endorse these requirements and relay them throughout the judicial process and orders. In many cases, the evidence show that the defendants' incomes do not allow for these expenses in light of rising living costs. The lack of judicial consideration for the general economic context and for the specific situation of the defendants means that the court's orders are based on unrealistic and unattainable considerations and requirements. This dynamic is illustrated by this excerpt from observation notes taken at the Youth Division of the Court of Quebec hearing in the matter of child welfare:

> The hearing concerns a young mother and her two-year-old daughter. The mother has come out of a domestic violence relationship that seems to have led to measures put in place by the child welfare services. The father is absent from his daughter's life, who is in the custody of her maternal grandmother. The mother has successfully participated in therapy to treat her emotional dependency. The hearing is about returning the child to her mother, although the social worker acting on behalf of child welfare services has expressed concern because the mother and grandmother plan to live in a three-room apartment and the mother is considering returning to school. The social worker's concerns are about sharing the apartment's only bedroom—when the grandmother, the mother and the little girl should have their own bedroom—as well as about the mother's absence due to her studies.
> The judge grants the return of the child to her mother, while stating in the same breath that the mother should find a larger apartment. The mother has no professional training and lives on welfare, but her plan to pursue studies to improve her financial situation constitutes, from the judge's perspective, a factor of instability for the child that will need to be monitored in the coming months.
> At the end of the hearing, I question the judge about the current context of housing scarcity and high costs. I ask if this is a factor that should be considered in this mother's situation. She replies that she has indeed vaguely heard about a housing crisis but does not know much about it.

This excerpt shows how court's housing requirements and reluctance to support training and education create an unsolvable situation. On the one hand, the mother must find a larger place to live, regardless of availability and cost; on the other hand, she cannot pursue professional training to give her the means to find a larger place to live. The court's desire to monitor the mother over the coming months suggests that more intervention could be possible, possibly to remove the child from her custody if she does not relocate to an apartment with a room for each person or if she is not sufficiently present. It should also be noted that the grandmother's availability seems to have made no difference to the social worker and judge, a phenomenon I have also observed in other contexts. The fact that defendants find ways to overcome their difficulties, particularly financial ones, such as using food banks or receiving financial or personal help from relatives, is generally ignored or used against them. While the presence of a family or other "social safety net" is generally recognized as positive, it is rarely considered a solution, and defendants are held individually responsible for making lifestyle changes and for self-empowering.

In most cases, judges believe that judicial decisions do not harm defendants but are instead helpful. Judges do not seem to know, understand, or consider the economic harm of judicial orders, or these harms do not appear to outweigh the expected benefit of therapy. In a formal interview, a judge discussing involuntary commitment declared that, "here, we don't deliver justice, we provide a service," explaining that they provide "room and board" to people experiencing homelessness or severe poverty. Another judge explained the benefit of involuntary treatment orders by stating that "decisions are made from the heart." During both hearings and interviews, defendants' rights were generally not a consideration in dismissing a petition.

However, during the hearings, defendants regularly explain the detrimental financial consequences of judicial orders. They report that hospital detention could lead to losing their housing if they are unable to pay their rent on time while being held in the hospital. This could also result in losing all their belongings. Some defendants claim to have been evicted during previous involuntary commitment and subsequently experienced homelessness. An involuntary commitment or detention order also frequently result in job loss and difficulty finding new employment, as explaining the situation to employers can be challenging. In child welfare cases, parents who lost custody of their children also lost their family allowances, which often made it impossible to pay for their housing or led to losing subsidized housing. Judges tend to systematically ignore defendants' statements as shown by this excerpt from the observation notes during an involuntary commitment hearing:

> The defendant is a 28-year-old man who is the subject of a 30-day-involuntary-commitment petition. He was arrested at his home by the police following a call from his parents, who were worried because he had not answered the phone for 2 days. Very calmly, the defendant explains that he is bipolar and has been taking his medication for years. He says, "I'm vulnerable and I know I'll fall back if I don't take my medication." He works in a factory and has been living in the same apartment for two years. He tells the court that he had gone to Quebec City for the weekend to meet up with a woman he met on a dating site, which explains why he did not answer the phone when his parents called. He described how the police brutally entered his home and confined him to the living room without an access to a telephone. They then took him to the hospital, where he says he was verbally aggressive because he knew "they were going to keep me." He says he refused the medication offered to him but changed his mind when he saw two nurses and two security guards arrive. The nurse reportedly said: "You had a choice, you didn't take it, it's too late." He was stripped naked by the security guards and restrained, and the medication was injected. The psychiatric assessment took place while he was under sedation.
>
> The defendant tells the judge that he had been involuntarily admitted a dozen times in his life, and that each time he lost his job. The defense counsel insisted on his "orderly life," the fact that he takes his medication; the hospital's lawyer, on the contrary, insisted on the fact that he refused to take medication upon his arrival at the hospital, which would demonstrate an "impaired judgment." Concerned about the refusal of medication on arrival at the hospital, and "taking into account the concerns of Dr. Moris, who is a psychiatrist, not a nobody," the judge grants the hospital's petition. After the hearing, she confides in me that if the defendant goes to appeal, she "would be overturned," as she "had no legal grounds."

The description of this hearing clearly shows how the defendants' rights and the consequences of judicial orders do not hold weight against the judges' conviction that therapy is good and necessary for people with mental health issues. In this case, the judge told me after the hearing that the fact that the psychiatrist could do a "review of the medication with Mr." seemed reassuring to her. She demonstrated no apparent concern for possible job termination, or rather, any such employment consequence appeared to be outweighed by the advantages of hospitalization. However, she legally had no power regarding treatment, and the refusal of treatment is not an indicator of danger according to case law. The fact that the judge stated they had no legal grounds to grant the request confirms that these practices take place with full knowledge.

Yet, judicial decisions have detrimental financial impacts on defendants, often further impoverishing them and leading to more legal proceedings. Failure to pay rent can lead to eviction, and the creation of a legal file which can then be accessed by potential future landlords. It is not uncommon for all belongings to be lost during an eviction, due to the lack of storage space. Losing one's job, and especially one's home, can lead to intervention by child welfare services, and living with rental instability compromises the possibility of retaining custody of children. In child welfare matters, while the size of the home is a factor considered by the court, court orders paradoxically have the effect of compromising parents' ability to keep a home large enough to accommodate their children, which can ultimately result in the permanent loss of custody. In a formal interview, a defense counsel offered an example of this situation:

> A father was granted custody of his five children at the last minute. He got a subsidized apartment. He wasn't perfect—he wasn't good at cleaning or helping with homework—but he made significant efforts. He was present for his children, and there was food on the table for every meal. He had five kids, all on his own. Then he lost custody of them. Without his children, he couldn't keep his subsidized apartment—he lost his family allowances and couldn't afford to rent such a large home anymore.
> It's a vicious cycle. After the removal of the children, the father had a major depression—he was out of contact with his kids for six months. For two years, he cared for his children seven days a week. For six months, he couldn't manage. He hit rock bottom and was completely shattered.

> When he returned after six months, the social worker told the court, "I am not going to check his new housing. What's the point? We're not there yet. The children are doing well in foster care."

For many defendants encountered in court, judicial processes occur back-to-back, creating an ever-deepening spiral of poverty: loss of housing, involuntary admissions, and interventions by child welfare services—all moments of disruption leading to increasingly compromised and precarious situations. However, in the eyes of the court, judicial intervention is seen as an opportunity, a chance to alter the course of one's life, a wake-up call to finally assume responsibility. This moral stance conflicts with decades of research on poverty, particularly concerning people experiencing homelessness, single mothers, and workers affected by the growing precariousness of the labor market (Broll & Huey, 2020; Cook, 2012; Feldman, 2019; Mayock et al., 2015; Piat et al., 2015).

In all the mental health courtrooms I investigated, I observed the presence of a small number of defendants with a very different profile: they hold a postsecondary education, are professionals working in a middle-class profession, or hold a position with important responsibilities. It is usually their first and only appearance at court. They are well dressed, articulate, and use refined language while addressing the judges with proper decorum. Their situation tend to be regarded as one-off or the result of a misstep. This was confirmed in a formal interview with a judge handling involuntary treatment decision who stated, "That's when you end up with a university professor, and then as a judge, you think to yourself: 'Come on, this doesn't make sense. You're a university professor, what's this? You're capable of holding a good job, it doesn't make sense.'" The communication in these cases go relatively smoothly, even in the absence of defense counsels, and defendants are considered credible and trustworthy, as if the danger, threat, or incapacity are inherently less severe. My formal interviews with psychiatrists, as well as studies (Lorant et al., 2007; Patel, 2020), confirm, however, that wealthier people are less often subject to coercive practices, not because they do not meet the criteria, but because alternatives are possible due to their financial and social resources. My observations show that when a professional defendant comes to court, the question of the impact of a court order on their income, as well as on their reputation, is a major concern. Judges are more inclined to not grant petitions, or to grant them only partially, to minimize their potential negative impacts, as shown by this excerpt from observation notes during an involuntary commitment hearing:

> The defendant is a 31-year-old engineer, father of two and owner of several apartments whose mother recently passed away and whose father is suffering from cancer. He describes being harassed at work and suffering from burnout. The hospital has requested 30 days of involuntary commitment, and his sister supports the request. Psychiatric reports state that the defendant is "bizarre, disorganized, has no food and is unclean;" that he "laughs alone, rubs a banana on a patient's stomach and goes down his knees at the nursing station." Psychiatrists conclude that he is "psychotic" and "delirious." The defendant reports having no support at work and problems with a tenant who did not pay their rent. He acknowledges that his situation is difficult, that he is exhausted, and said he wants help outside the hospital. The judge—asserting that "it's always difficult for a court to deprive someone of their liberty"—recounts "the escalation of events that led me to believe that you need help," and grants the motion, but reduces the duration to 14 days.
> After the hearing, the judge tells me that he had almost released the defendant but had changed his mind because of the sister's support for the hospital's petition. For the judge, it is necessary for the defendant to get help, and 14 days would have no impact on his work since he is currently on sick leave.

The Incapable Defendants

Communication between judges and defendants is often challenging, marked by frequent misunderstandings and mutual communication and comprehension difficulties that directly affected the hearings. These misunderstandings are often tied to vocabulary and social or cultural references, as illustrated by the reaction of a defendant during their involuntary treatment hearing, when the judge read the law to them: "I would need to have studied to understand what you're saying. I would need to go to school to be able to defend myself." Defendants regularly report feeling very stressed and anxious, not knowing how to behave or what to talk about.

Misunderstandings can also relate to the defendants' experiences, which are far removed from the judges' realities, as illustrated in this excerpt from observation notes during an involuntary commitment hearing at the Court of Quebec:

> The defendant, a 25-year-old man who spent his youth in child welfare services and is now experiencing homelessness, is the subject of an involuntary commitment request following an altercation at a shelter. During his testimony, he reports being harassed by the police while panhandling and having accumulated over $2,500 in fines. He states that upon his arrival at the hospital, he was restrained and forced to take medication he did not want. He has been in the hospital for six days, exceeding the legal time limits. He says, "I'm experiencing injustice," and that it makes him angry. He explains that he was forced to take Ritalin as a child while in youth centers [closed institutions where young offenders or youth under protection are confined]. He now says he wants to "try without medication." The judge states that the defendant has a behavioral disorder, is aggressive, and is psychotic, even though the evidence does not support this claim. She tells the defendant, "You have the right to refuse treatment until another judge decides otherwise." The defendant responds, "Can't you just let me live? I've been locked up for 10 years!" The judge replies in kind, "Maybe you're locked up in your own mind?"
>
> After the hearing, the judge confides in me that the fact that the defendant spoke of his placements in child welfare services showed that he was paranoid and aggressive. For her, the deprivation of liberty he had suffered for years was justified by what she had seen of him during the 20-minute hearing, ignoring the violation of his rights and the sense of injustice he had communicated. She exclaims, "I was afraid he was going to jump on my clerk!"

During hearings, defendants often talk about their experiences of detention, whether in psychiatric hospitals, prisons, or youth centers. Arrest, detention, involuntary commitment, restraint, and seclusion are common themes. Many bear witness to the ordinary violence of institutions, claiming that these experiences of violence are traumatic and aggravated their condition. Some state they would rather go to a shelter or prison than a psychiatric ward. At his involuntary treatment hearing, for example, a defendant told the judge:

> The hospital where I am confined is just tiles, white, metal. Your activity is when you eat, watch TV or read magazines. You don't hear the birds singing. You don't go outside. I'm in a prison, in fact. Even when I go outside, I'm in a prison. It's alienating. It should be illegal to build structures like this.

He finished by asking, "Maybe I've become psychotic since I've been here?" The judge replied, "That's good. Thank you, sir." The judge then suspended the hearing for fifteen minutes, and I found myself with the defendant in the corridor. He turned to me and said that he could see the judge was listening, but wondered if he really understood him, if he even knew what he was talking about.

In the discourse of several defendants, the violence experienced within institutions is relayed within the judicial institution, seen as a mere step on a continuum of coercion and not as a place of justice. Thus, many confided in me that hearings "serve no purpose" and that decisions "are made in advance." This was clearly expressed by a defendant found not criminally responsible at his Review Board hearing when he recounted feeling constrained by court hearings. He said that his story of coercion began twenty years ago, during his first experience in psychiatry, and that he was exhausted by the constant control exerted over him. The lawyer presiding over the judges' bench seemed offended; she told him, "But we're here for you sir."

Communication problems in the courtrooms are compounded by the fact that judges take for granted that the defendants' lawyers have done their job diligently, especially when it comes to providing information and preparing for hearings. Due to the nature of the procedures, which are often urgent, defendants often come to court poorly prepared and sometimes give testimonies that undermine their position without realizing it. Yet, a significant proportion of defendants are represented by a counsel. This lack of preparation can be partially explained by the urgency of proceedings, but it could also be intentional due to risks associated with mental illness, according to a defense lawyer interviewed:

> I know that in criminal cases or other matters, we prepare the client. We tell them: "Here's what you should or should not say." Not in mental health. And in our office, we never give the answer. We ask questions, they give us an answer, and they always ask me: "Is that okay?" If you think it's your right answer, if it's what you really think, then it's the right answer. I don't want to influence at all by saying: "You have to say you will take the medication." No. Never that. We are always very, very honest because we are dealing with mental health. Beyond the fundamental rights we must enforce, it is also a matter of public safety and a matter of care for themselves.

Most defendants formally interviewed or met in the courthouse corridors confirmed that they were not prepared by their lawyer, particularly regarding court procedures and the purpose of the proceedings. Only a few stated that they had been prepared to testify.

Some of the defense lawyers arrive at the courtroom with too little preparation for their client and with few arguments to present to the court. They are often passive during hearings, and one judge told me they had seen one of them fall asleep. They sometimes tell judges that they "like it when they ask [their clients] questions." Judges are well aware of the impact of defense lawyers on hearing. Some indicate in formal interviews that defense lawyers are there "for the fee," or that they "have rarely seen people well represented." A Court of Appeal judge explained:

> You see, the quality of our judgments depends on the quality of the pleadings we hear. That's very important. And often, the lawyers who work in this field may not be the big stars of the Bar. You don't know how much the quality of our judgements depends on the quality of their presentations. Because we don't have the time. And that's what the system is based on. The British system we have is based on that, on the quality of the barristers.

In an adversarial system, judges let lawyers argue their cases; they intervene very little. When the case is poorly prepared, this results in issues not being examined by the court, a situation I have observed on several occasions involving procedural irregularities. At times, time limits are not respected, the evidence is incomplete, or the defendants were illegally detained for several days or even weeks. But because the defense counsels do not raise this issue during the hearing, or because the defendants are absent and unrepresented at their hearing, these situations are generally not considered by the court. Repeatedly throughout the proceedings, judges assert that they had failed to observe these procedural irregularities and justified their oversight by citing the defense attorneys' failure to raise such issues. When defendants are absent and lacked legal representation, judges typically neglect to ensure adherence to proper procedure.

The work of defense lawyers also has an impact on defendants' credibility. Not only does being poorly prepared or unprepared, not understanding court proceedings, or communicating poorly make a bad impression on judges, but they tend to attribute these issues to defendants' mental health problems. However, in the justice system, credibility is the crux of the matter. There is only a small step between not being credible and not being believed, as demonstrated by this excerpt from my observation notes regarding an involuntary commitment hearing:

> The defendant is a 34-year-old man who has been under psychiatric care for fifteen years. He was first diagnosed with a psychotic disorder but is now being treated for bipolar disorder. He has been taking medication for several years. He works and writes poems but has not slept for five days. He was brought to the hospital by his mother-in-law after threatening their roommate with a kitchen knife and his sister with a plastic gun bought for his nephew. He says that psychiatric medication ruins his life by making him gain weight and preventing him from having erections and a sex life. He says, "for the first time in my life, things are going ok." He does not see why he should be hospitalized. The defense lawyer argues that "Mr. Jones acknowledges his illness and need for medication, which is good" and requests that the petition be dismissed. The judge addresses the defendant saying, "You will be disappointed with my decision. I have no grounds to reject the psychiatric reports. You have undermined your credibility by contradicting the psychiatrists' reports." The defendant asks

> the judge what "undermined credibility" means. After hearing the explanation, he asks if he could have witnesses; he is clearly angry, stating that he was told he could not have witnesses. The judge tells him "to check with his lawyer." The defendant and his lawyer leave the courtroom, and so do I.
> In the hallway, the lawyer asks the defendant who told him he could not have witnesses. The defendant responds that he was given this information by a nurse at the hospital. The lawyer states that "it wouldn't have made any difference anyway" and walk away. Later, the judge tells me he is "obligated to assume that the defense lawyer didn't think it was necessary to hear the witnesses that the defendant wanted to bring forward." He asserts that "if it were you or me, we would definitely come with witnesses," because "we are of sound mind." According to him, "these disturbed people might want to have their elementary school teacher testify that they were fine back then, which isn't relevant."

The defendants' word is often called into question, even when it came to facts and experiences that only they know in the courtroom. Hospitals and child welfare services regularly base their evidence on facts for which they have no witnesses: facts reported by neighbors, family members and police officers, and noted in medical records; facts described in police, school, or other reports, but not acted upon. These facts are regarded as established despite the absence of material or testimonial evidence, and any intervention on the part of the defendants to try to correct them tend to be considered proof of denial or lack of insight, and contribute to discrediting them.

The discrediting of the defendants' words contrasts with the high credibility accorded to psychiatrists, social workers and other experts from hospitals and child welfare services, including on matters which only the defendants know for sure. In interviews, lawyers described how difficult it is to advocate for their clients' perspective, stating, for example, that "clinical matters take up a lot of space," or that "judges don't care about the opinions of people on welfare." Defendants reported feeling ignored during their hearings, one mother recounting:

> The judge didn't believe my testimony because it wasn't credible, simply because I'm a parent, and he prefers to believe the child welfare specialists

rather than the parents. I immediately realized that no matter what I said, I had absolutely no credibility in front of the judge.

Thus, it is not uncommon for the court to ask professionals whether defendants use drugs or consume alcohol, attend their medical or therapeutic appointments, have taken steps to obtain social assistance, or even to confirm their addresses, while ignoring the defendants' own statements. Concerning the adverse effects of psychiatric treatments reported by defendants, the court systematically double-checks with psychiatrists whether the defendants' statements are true. Even though defendants are the only ones in the courtroom to have experienced psychiatric treatments and specifically experienced them on their own bodies, it is not uncommon for courts to conclude that they are exaggerating or simply to ignore them altogether. However, no medical evidence is generally submitted to the courts to demonstrate the effectiveness of the therapies psychiatrists or social workers want to impose on defendants, and in some cases, the quality of evidence is surprisingly low, to say the least. This is the case, for example, in child welfare matters when psychiatric diagnoses are alleged by social workers without medical evidence and based on their own observations, and the court generally do not require that evidence be properly presented. Although social workers are not legally qualified to make diagnoses, the fact that these diagnoses appear in their reports, and subsequently in judicial decisions, makes their statements a truth that becomes difficult to challenge and that comes to serve as a basis for interpreting the facts in the files and recommendations of psychiatric follow-ups or other interventions. Another striking example involves involuntary treatment, where only the psychiatrists' opinion is considered by the court in its decision, even in the most controversial cases, as shown in the following excerpt from my observation notes:

> The hospital's petition is to impose electroconvulsive therapy every two weeks for five years on the defendant, a man in his early twenties under public curatorship with diagnoses of intellectual disability, "medication-resistant disorganized schizophrenia," and hypermetabolism. He is handcuffed at the wrists and waist and shackled at the feet and is escorted by two security agents from the facility where he is detained. A special

constable has been called to the courtroom. However, the defendant walks dragging his feet and can barely hold his head up. Once seated, the two security agents stand behind him, wearing latex gloves, ready to intervene. The defendant is represented by a lawyer, and the public curator is also represented.

The public curator's lawyer wants to obtain a second opinion and requests a postponement; the hospital's lawyer states that an interim order is needed to allow treatment until the judgment on the merits of the case is rendered. The psychiatrist explains that electroconvulsive therapy is most often used for major depression and persistent psychosis, but that "for this patient, it's to reduce agitation." She explains that maintenance treatments aim for stability, but that acute treatments, administered three times per week up to twelve to eighteen treatments, can also be offered, and that if treatments are too spread out, acute treatments become necessary. The judge says, "That's a radical therapy," and the psychiatrist responds, "It's more effective than all known antidepressants." Faced with the judge's skepticism, the psychiatrist continues, "That's our collective unconscious speaking, your honor, because you've seen movies like "One Flew Over the Cuckoo's Nest," but electroconvulsive therapy has changed a lot." She says, "I agreed with a colleague that if I fall into depression, I want to have electroconvulsive therapy." The judge asks how the defendant feels after his treatments. The psychiatrist responds that he is disoriented for 24 hours, then "becomes more stable and smiles more." She says, "In acute treatment, the results add up; in maintenance treatment, the results are maintained, we reach a plateau." The judge turns to the defendant and asks, "Do you know why we're here?" The defendant, who struggles to lift his head, says something that remains incomprehensible; it seems his tongue is too thick. The judge says, "What? I don't understand you." The defendant, looking disappointed and discouraged, tries again to express himself without success. The judge, visibly uncomfortable, says "Given the circumstances, I don't wish to prolong the hearing" and adjourns *pro forma* to a later date.

After the hearing, the judge confides to me that he did not know how to respond "to a patient who cannot communicate." Although he is "reluctant about electroconvulsive therapy," the fact that "the patient cannot communicate convinces me greatly" of the need for treatment. He states, "I must defer to the expertise; I have no alternatives, I'm not being offered other treatments."

Psychiatrists, social workers, and experts who appear in court benefit from a credibility that is associated to their professional status and that is somewhat transferred to their opinions and statements. According to my observations, their assertions are rarely questioned, including when they are based on commonplaces—such as the claim that the reality depicted in "One Flew Over the Cuckoo's Nest" is outdated—when they are not supported by scientific data or when they are controversial—such as the claim that electroconvulsive therapy would be more effective than "all known antidepressants" (Read et al., 2023) for a defendant without a diagnosis of depression. This credibility is directly linked to judges' perceptions, backgrounds, and personal lives. In formal interviews, judges stated that psychiatrists are the best-positioned professionals to assess risk or incapacity, which is not confirmed by the literature and is contested by psychiatrists I interviewed who say that criminologists, psychologists, and nurses might be better positioned than they are to do so. Some judges referred to their "psychiatrist friend" to explain their general ideas on mental health and psychiatric treatment.

In addition to the credibility conferred by professional status, psychiatrists and social workers display an emotional detachment that the defendants do not have because their freedom, integrity and family ties are at stake in these hearings. It is common to see defendants in the courtroom express anger, sadness, distress, or anxiety: they intervene impulsively, interrupting others, speak loudly or rapidly, cry, and sometimes sob, shake, twist their hair or wring their hands. Through formal interviews or courtroom observations, defendants describe judicial hearings as a hardship that generates deep feelings of injustice and frequently triggers memories of other traumatic encounters with institutions such as police, schools, child welfare services, correctional facilities, or psychiatric services. "It brings stuff back up," a mother who had herself experienced foster care placement as a child told me. However, the slightest expression of anger or impatience, especially in men, is interpreted as aggressiveness, as a sign of an inability to control oneself. The expression of sadness or anxiety is interpreted as the manifestation of emotional distress or, more generally, as a state of depression. One of the major difficulties for defense counsels in the courtroom is related to managing their clients' emotions, especially in the context of child welfare, where they sometimes cannot express themselves for long hours. According to some lawyers, educating defendants about the importance of comportment to prevent possible situations in which the defendants “lose their cool” or “blow their top” is crucial. They reported trying to “prepare for the worst” with their clients to mitigate reactions of anger, frustration or despair before the court. While they described the lack of understanding from judicial actors regarding their clients’ emotions, they stated in the same breath that some intentionally “destabilize” them, even make them “explode”—something I have observed myself several times in all the courtrooms investigated. One lawyer practicing in child welfare matters explained in formal interview: “But when I know who we’re dealing with, I’ll prepare my clients: ‘Don’t be surprised, the judge is going to come at you hard.’”.

Several defendants I interviewed, or met during hearing observations, reported having been humiliated by the judicial process. No matter what they say, their poverty is treated as proof of a lack of willpower or of incapacity: having debts result from bad choices, or an incapacity to manage one’s budget; not working demonstrate a lack of empowerment or social dysfunction; the absence, abandonment, or failure to take steps to obtain social benefits (social assistance or family allowances) or low-income housing, to regularize immigration status, or to report unsanitary housing conditions to the authorities is a choice or proof of an incapacity to take charge of one’s life. How else can it be justified, in the eyes of legal practitioners, that available rights and remedies are not exercised? Yet the reasons for not taking or for abandoning the attempts to take the necessary steps to obtain benefits or status, or to exercise rights and remedies, are increasingly well documented (Herd et al., 2023; Tarshish & Holler, 2024). Studies show that some groups targeted by social programs benefit little or not at all from these programs due to difficulty accessing information, the complexity of administrative procedures, and the slowness of the processes. Passivity, incapacity, or lack of interest are therefore not the causes.

The mental health courtrooms I investigated are characterized by power relationships that exist prior to the legal process, resulting in an imbalance of power between the parties. Not only does the relationship between mental health or child welfare professionals and defendants constitute a relationship of authority, but coercion—formal or informal—may already have been used prior to court proceedings. Supported by several studies (Biland, 2023; Clair, 2020; Roberts, 2022; Ryo & Peacock, 2021), my observations have led me to conclude that the judicial process does not have the effect of rebalancing the imbalance of power—quite the contrary.

In addition to their private lives being displayed, discussed, and evaluated, the defendants experience the trial as a judgment of their personal worth. This is exemplified by Clara, a woman who has spent much time in mental health courtrooms and whom I met in a biographical interview. Clara was the mother of an 18-year-old daughter at the time of the interview and was herself placed in foster care by child welfare services at the age of four after being raped by her father. Also, she has been involuntarily committed several times. She lost custody of her daughter when she was two years old. She has long been a sex worker and was presently on welfare. Diagnosed with Borderline Personality Disorder and considered a polydrug addict by psychiatrists and social workers, Clara described herself as an "unworthy mother," an "asshole," a "nobody." She has been to court so many times that she could not recall the exact number. Clara had multiple hearings with as many psychiatrists, social workers, lawyers, and judges. She recounted meeting her lawyers at the last minute and being told to "keep quiet," with no information about her rights or the procedure. She explained that her diagnosis was used to interpret her entire life, especially her inability to assess her own needs and take care of her daughter. Speaking of court, she related her experience by saying, "everyone looks at you with disdain. 'What kind of goddamn horror is this.' That's what I feel. I don't feel listened to, I don't feel compassion, I don't feel sympathy." Her judicial experience was that of confirmation of her multiple incapacities, in every aspect of her life.

Many of the defendants I met in my research shared similar sentiments. The judicial process frequently appear opaque, complex, and incomprehensible to them. The failure of the judicial actors to explain it to them is interpreted as an assumption of their incapacity to understand it, as well as a lack of consideration. The court experience is commonly interpreted by defendants as a dismissal of their subjective realities, their opinions, and their preferences. For them, rather than constituting an experience of Justice—Clara, for example, said, "There is no justice on this *damn* Earth"—the judicial process formalize their incapacity, which further weakens them in the power dynamic with their psychiatrist or social worker.

Class Blindness

If defendants do not feel compassion through the judicial process, it may be because there is little or no compassion offered to them. Defendants are often ridiculed in court, even by their own lawyers, either for their lack of decorum, or for what they say. Knowing smiles, impatient sighs, eye-rolling: such manifestations of exasperation or mockery are numerous and relatively common. Defendants are often interrupted when they speak but are sharply called to order when they try to express themselves when it is not their turn. They are made to understand that they are wasting the court's time, that what they say is not relevant, important or credible. To illustrate these dynamics, here are two excerpts from my observation notes, first from a child welfare hearing, then from a Review Board hearing:

> The defendant, the mother of an 8-year-old boy, living with a disability and separated from the child's father, could not come to court and is participating in the hearing remotely via Teams. Her lawyer has to excuse themselves because they are representing another case, but states that "Mrs. is ready." The defendant is very emotional and has great difficulty following the proceedings from a distance. The child welfare services want to remove custody from the mother and give it to the father. The mother abruptly claims that the father is violent, and criminal charges against him are pending, a fact that will be ignored throughout the hearing. The lawyers for child welfare services, the child, and the father share several knowing glances and roll their eyes repeatedly. In the absence of her lawyer, the defendant must proceed with the cross-examination of her ex-spouse without counsel. The child welfare services lawyer constantly objects because her questions are leading. The defendant, who clearly

> does not understand what she is being accused of bursts into tears. She repeats while crying, "I'm sorry, Your Honor, I am scared to lose my child." The judge then states that she is suspending the hearing to allow her to compose herself. The defendant does not seem to have understood the reason for the interruption, and the child welfare services lawyer tells her, exasperated, that it is because of her incapacity to respect decorum, and then leaves the courtroom, ignoring the defendant's questions. The child's lawyer then approaches the screen and begins to speak, but the defendant, still sobbing, interrupts her. The lawyer then tells her that it is "normal" that no one wants to help her and also leaves the room. The special constable who was also present in the room for security reasons also turns her back on the defendant who sobs on the large screen, facing the empty courtroom.

> Regarding his failure to follow up with psychiatric care, the defendant, who is homeless and sleeps on park benches, explains that he had severe back pain, could not sleep or eat, and had respiratory problems. He reports having lost 100 pounds. He says, "I was scared. When you're suffocating, you're scared." Despite his repeated consultations at the emergency room, he had to wait 3 months to get X-rays and a diagnosis of lung infection. His lawyer looks him up and down with obvious skepticism. He turns to the hospital lawyer and rolls his eyes. The hospital lawyer grimaces in return, ignoring the documented obstacles faced by individuals with precarious socioeconomic status or mental health diagnosis in obtaining care (Knaak et al., 2017; Olah et al., 2013).

A large majority of the judges interviewed for my research stated that individuals involved in mental health courtrooms do not have a typical socioeconomic profile. Contradictorily, they stated that people from "wealthy neighborhoods" are among the defendants, which I have rarely seen. Defendants, meanwhile, are keenly aware of the classist dimension of their judicial experience. During the hearings, some stated, for instance: "I wouldn't be here if I had money" or "If I won the lottery, I wouldn't need medication." Following their hearing, one defendant explained to me that they were involuntarily committed because they lived in a squat and were thus "marginalized"; another, describing their intention to "fight until the end" against the involuntary treatment request, stated, "I don't have a bourgeois family and I have only a few friends. All I have is my integrity." During an interview, a mother-defendant asked me, "Which children do the *damn* child welfare services target? Do you think they go after children whose parents have PhDs and earn six figures?".

Research has shown that overlooking social class and its resulting stratification—which impedes critical analysis and reflexivity—promotes profiling and discrimination (Franklin, 2018). According to studies, people experiencing poverty are generally perceived as less intelligent, incompetent, lazy, untrustworthy, and lacking credibility (Durante et al., 2017; Lindqvist et al., 2017). In formal interviews, several judges stated that they were "afraid" or "uncomfortable" with mental disorders, or that the mental health defendants are "aggressive," "manipulative," or "liars." They reported that they did not believe what they were saying and "didn't want to play their game." Not only do judges consider defendants appearing in mental health courtrooms not credible and largely incapable of making decisions for themselves or their families, they also fail to recognize their position as defendants. In interviews, they systemically referred to defendants as "people living with mental illness," "poor patients," "poor little guy," "the weak in our society," "sick," "deranged people," and even "the bottom of the barrel," instead of "the defendant." Several judges have claimed to address defendants "with compassion" or "as if they were their children." This infantilizing and paternalistic approach have the effect of denying defendants their status as parties to a judicial proceeding about their own rights, reducing them to the status of the "other."

References

Biland, E. (2023). *Family law in action: Divorce and inequality in Quebec and France*. University of British Columbia Press.

Broll, R., & Huey, L. (2020). "Every time I try to get out, I get pushed back": The role of violent victimization in women's experience of multiple episodes of homelessness. *Journal of Interpersonal Violence, 35*(17–18), 3379–3404. https://doi.org/10.1177/0886260517708405

Clair, M. (2020). *Privilege and punishment: How race and class matter in criminal court*. De Gruyter Brill.

Cook, K. (2012). Neoliberalism, welfare policy and health: A qualitative meta-synthesis of single parents' experience of the transition from welfare to work. *Health, 16*(5), 507–530. https://doi.org/10.1177/1363459311434650

Durante, F., Bearns Tablante, C., & Fiske, S. T. (2017). Poor but warm, rich but cold (and competent): Social classes in the stereotype content model. *Journal of Social Issues, 73*, 138–157. https://doi.org/10.1111/josi.12208

Eamon, M. K., & Kopels, S. (2004). "For reasons of poverty:" Court challenges to child welfare practices and mandated programs. *Children and Youth Services Review, 26*(9), 821–836. https://doi.org/10.1016/j.childyouth.2004.02.023

Emmelman, D. S. (2003). The effect of social class on the adjudication of criminal cases: Class-linked behavior tendencies, common sense, and the interpretative procedures of court-appointed defense attorneys. In M. Pogrebin (Ed.), *Qualitative approaches to criminal justice: Perspectives from the field* (pp. 190–202). Sage.

Feldman, G. (2019). Neoliberalism and poverty: An unbreakable relationship. In B. Greve (Ed.), *Routledge international handbook of poverty* (pp. 340–350). Routledge.

Franklin, C. (2018). The New Class Blindness. *The Yale Law Journal, 128*(1), 2–98.

Galanter, M. (1974). Why the haves come out ahead: Speculations on the limits of legal change. *Law & Society Review, 9*, 95–160. https://doi.org/10.2307/3053023

Haussleiter, I. S. et al. (2022). Homelessness among psychiatric inpatients in North Rhine-Westphalia: A retrospective routine data analysis. *BMC Psychiatry, 22*, 132. https://doi.org/10.1186/s12888-022-03786-6

Herd, P., Hoynes, H., Michener, J., & Moynihan, D. (2023). Introduction: Administrative burden as a mechanism of inequality in policy implementation. *RSF: The Russell Sage Foundation Journal of the Social Sciences, 9*(4), 1–30. https://doi.org/10.7758/RSF.2023.9.4.01

Knaak, S., Mantler, E. D., & Szeto, A. (2017). Mental illness-related stigma in healthcare: Barriers to access and care and evidence-based solutions. *Healthcare Management Forum, 30*(2), 111–116. https://doi.org/10.1177/0840470416679413

Lens, V. (2019). Judging the other: The intersection of race, gender, and class in family court. *Family Court Review, 57*(1), 72–87. https://doi.org/10.1111/fcre.12397

Lindqvist, A., Björklund, F., & Bäckström, M. (2017). The perception of the poor: Capturing stereotype content with different measures. *Nordic Psychology, 69*(4), 231–247. https://doi.org/10.1080/19012276.2016.1270774

López-Espino, J. (2024). Giving and taking voice: Metapragmatic dismissals of parents in child welfare court cases. *Law & Social Inquiry, 49*(3), 1453–1478. https://doi.org/10.1017/lsi.2023.50

Lorant, V., Depuydt, C., Gillain, B., Guillet, A., & Dubois, V. (2007). Involuntary commitment in psychiatric care: What drives the decision? *Social Psychiatry and Psychiatric Epidemiology, 42*(5), 360–365. https://doi.org/10.1007/s00127-007-0175-2

Mayock, P., Sheridan, S., & Parker, S. (2015). "It's just like we're going around in circles and going back to the same thing…:" The dynamics of women's unresolved homelessness. *Housing Studies, 30*(6), 877–900. https://doi.org/10.1080/02673037.2014.991378

Moloney, N., O'Donnell, P., Elzain, M., Bashir, A., Dunne, C. P., Kelly, B. D., & Gulati, G. (2022). Homelessness amongst psychiatric In-patients: A cross-sectional study in the Mid-West of Ireland. *Irish Journal of Medical Science, 191*(1), 321–326. https://doi.org/10.1007/s11845-021-02546-x

Morris, K., Mason, W., Bywaters, P., Featherstone, B., Daniel, B., Brady, G., Bunting, L., Hooper, J., Mirza, N., Scourfield, J., & Webb, C. (2018). Social work, poverty, and child welfare interventions. *Child & Family Social Work, 23*(3), 364–372. https://doi.org/10.1111/cfs.12423

Olah, M. E., Gaisano, G., & Hwang, S. W. (2013). The effect of socioeconomic status on access to primary care: An audit study. *Canadian Medical Association Journal, 185*(6), E263–E269. https://doi.org/10.1503/cmaj.121383

Otero, M. (2016). Traiter les intraitables: L'univers des autorisations judiciaires de soins à Montréal. *Nouvelles Pratiques Sociales, 28*(2), 203–226. https://doi.org/10.7202/1041188ar

Piat, M., Polvere, L., Kirst, M., Voronka, J., Zabkiewicz, D., Plante, M. C., Isaak, C., Nolin, D., Nelson, G., & Goering, P. (2015). Pathways into homelessness: Understanding how both individual and structural factors contribute to and sustain homelessness in Canada. *Urban Studies, 52*(13), 2366–2382. https://doi.org/10.1177/0042098014548138

Patel, V. (2020). Income inequality and psychiatric admission in a rich country: Happiness does not guarantee mental health equity. *JAMA Psychiatry, 77*(3), 233–234. https://doi.org/10.1001/jamapsychiatry.2019.3638

Raz, M. (2013). *What's wrong with the poor?: Psychiatry, race, and the war on poverty*. University of North Carolina Press.

Read, J., Morrison, L., & Harrop, C. (2023). An independent audit of electro-convulsive therapy patient information leaflets in Northern Ireland. *Scotland and Wales. Psychology & Psychotherapy, 96*(4), 885–901. https://doi.org/10.1111/papt.12481

Roberts, D. (2022). *Torn apart: How the child welfare system destroys black families–and how abolition can build a safer world*. Basic Books.

Roberts, D. (2002). *Shattered bonds: The color of child welfare*. Basic Civitas Books.

Rossero, E. (2023) Care in a Time of Crisis. *An Ethnography of Coercive Practices in Italian Acute Mental Health Provision*. Palgrave Macmillan. https://doi.org/10.1007/978-3-031-34418-3

Ryo, E., & Peacock, I. (2021). Represented but unequal: The contingent effect of legal representation in removal proceedings. *Law & Society Review, 55*(4), 634–656. https://doi.org/10.1111/lasr.12574

Scott-Hayward, C. S., & Fradella, H. F. (2019). *Punishing poverty: How bail and pretrial detention fuel inequalities in the criminal justice system*. University of California Press.

Tarshish, N., & Holler, R. (2024). "You didn't ask, so you don't know": Information and administrative burden in social benefit claims. *Social Policy & Administration, 58*(5), 800–813. https://doi.org/10.1111/spol.12992

Wacquant, L. (2009). *Punishing the poor: The neoliberal government of social insecurity*. Duke University Press.

Walkowitz, D. J. (1999). *Working with class: Social workers and the politics of middle-class identity*. University of North Carolina Press.

6

Class, Gender, and Race: The Risk Triptych

The lawyers for child welfare services, the child, and the mother talk about a colleague's "large swimming pool" while the judge and court clerk review files. The atmosphere is light. The social worker and the parents for the next case enter the courtroom. The father has no lawyer and represents himself. The mother is holding a car seat with a 2-month-old baby sleeping in it. They recently separated. All judicial actors are white; the defendant parents are racialized. The hearing begins with the social worker's testimony. She reports a police intervention at the parents' home when they were living together. It seems the police took the father to the station, then released him with apologies. The facts of the case are unclear. The father testifies that he lost his job and emphasizes that he was released without charges. He says his family "has been suffering for months for no reason." The judge says, "We have to find out the truth about this situation," and orders a psychological evaluation of the parents, "which will provide a picture of the situation." After the hearing, the judge invokes the "cultural situation" to justify his decision. He claims the father is "too religious" and "feels he has the right of life or death over his wife" which presents a major risk for the child. None of this, however, was presented as evidence.—Excerpt from personal observation notes, Child welfare hearing, Youth Division, Court of Quebec.

E. Bernheim, *Therapeutic (In)justice and the Shadow Carceral State*, The Politics of Mental Health and Illness, https://doi.org/10.1007/978-3-032-16186-4_6

The court's treatment of poverty, discussed in Chapter 5, highlights how the ordinary prejudices associated with sanism reinforces power relationships. Through narratives about the defendants' precariousness, the reality of their incapacity takes shape over the course of the proceedings, which creates the impression that decisions need to be made for them instead of by them. For many judicial actors, the defendants' perceived incapacity legitimizes therapeutic justice interventions.

During interviews, most lawyers, psychiatrists, and judges maintained that their practice could preserve lives or help defendants rediscover purpose in their existence. Their narratives reveal two opposing perspectives: the principle of liberty versus the duty of protection. The former stance, representing a minority view grounded in strict legal interpretation, advocates for minimal and proportionate intervention solely to address clear and imminent risk. This approach prioritizes rights—particularly individual freedoms and informed consent to treatment—as the cornerstone of decision-making. The latter perspective, rooted in ethical considerations, presupposes that therapeutic interventions must serve the best interests of both individuals and society, embracing an expansive understanding of risk. Questions of rights become virtually irrelevant—except when framed as the defendants' entitlement to protection or to treatment. Within this framework, notions of best interests take precedence, with all interviewed professionals demonstrating confidence in their understanding of what serves defendants' optimal interests. These divergent viewpoints echo the consent debates in psychiatric care that emerged following transinstitutionalization, as discussed in Chapter 3. This reveals minimal advancement in resolving these fundamental tensions, particularly given that the paternalistic framework of best interest and right to treatment—acknowledged by its advocates since the 1960s as lacking substantial legal grounding (Birnbaum, 1960)—remains the dominant approach among most professionals, notably legal practitioners, in my research.

However, several inconsistencies are apparent in their discourse. Many lawyers, judges, and psychiatrists consider homelessness, precarity, or substance addiction to be the result of personal choices and that people in these situations must face the consequences of their choices—including judicial orders—to take their responsibility and get out of their situations. Simultaneously, they legitimize court orders by invoking the necessity of defendants' protection and arguing that court-imposed authority could motivate therapeutic participation that would assist them in surmounting their difficulties. From this perspective, the law can be both an obstacle and a lever for protecting and empowering defendants. Due to the rigidity of procedures and the right to consent to care, the law can be an obstacle in that it creates an antagonistic relationship with care professionals. At the same time, the symbolic and coercive force of law and the courts could facilitate individual responsibility-taking and engagement in therapies, which makes it a lever. Several research participants stated in formal interviews that the law must be interpreted and implemented in a manner that achieves the objectives of protecting and empowering defendants, including relaxing procedures and criteria, exceeding statutory deadlines, or using legal frameworks for purposes other than what is intended. This rationale is what led, for example, a judge to declare, "I don't get tangled up in procedural red tape: what matters to me is the individual, the fact that he has been illegally hospitalized for several days does not bother me." It is also what led a psychiatrist to affirm that "if we manage to work well with the system, [...we can] succeed in having a treatment plan where we have a bit more leverage over the patient."

In formal interviews, no psychiatrist or legal practitioner questioned the legal concepts of danger, significant threat, and incapacity, nor did they question the coercive practices, whether those of police, hospital, child welfare services, or courts. They also did not address the structural issues of coercion, even when they were asked direct questions about the topic.

Poverty as a Risk

Risk is ubiquitous yet implicit in discourse, both during hearings and interviews. It is invoked to justify the urgency and necessity of interventions, as well as violations of rights. Risk may constitute merely potential risk, with its severity unknown beforehand. Nevertheless, it lack clear definition regarding the specific behaviors or situations it encompasses. The risks invoked during hearings most frequently concern at least partly living conditions, conduct, or moral considerations rather than genuine threats to life or physical integrity.

The presence of risk creates a presumption of incapacity, and vice versa. On the one hand, putting oneself or others at risk demonstrates an incapacity to make good decisions that are in one's best interest. On the other hand, however, the incapacity to make decisions in one's best interest inherently generates a risk of not responding adequately to anticipated or unanticipated situations. One of the common findings within the mental health courtrooms I investigated is the indeterminacy of the criteria and notions on which judicial decisions are based. The legal criteria of "threat," "danger" or "incapacity," as well as "mental disorder," "mental state" or "best interest" are either not defined by law or case law, or their definition leaves room for interpretation. This indeterminacy explains the significant differences in the content of the evidence available to the court, and in the ways courts make decisions. In addition to the few cases of suicidal ideation, and physical assaults or threats, the behaviors or circumstances that courts examine and construct narratives around are varied, frequently bearing indirect connections to defendants' lifestyle or socioeconomic disadvantage. The risks encompassed scenarios such as accidentally igniting one's residence through careless smoking, maintaining poor nutritional habits, excessive consumption of sugary beverages, irresponsible financial management, or excessive gaming, as well as the prospect of a homeless defendant succumbing to exposure during winter months, the likelihood of exploitation due to defendant vulnerability, the possibility of assault resulting from defendant's confrontational or disruptive conduct, or the potential instability a child might face from their family's constant relocations.

It is rare for defendants to be associated with a single risk through judicial process; on the contrary, defendants are subject to a cluster of risks. Their living conditions entail preexisting risks, as well as generating new ones: homelessness in itself constitute a risk to life and health, especially in winter when defendants can develop frostbite, fall ill, or die without shelter. Being unhoused also generate potential risks such as being mugged, using drugs, not eating enough or not keeping up with therapy. Living in an unsanitary apartment can put the defendants and their children at risk of developing illnesses, which can then compromise their ability to work, to study, and to recover. Being socially isolated and not having a familial safety net to help take care of oneself or one's children put defendants at risk of burnout or depression, while creating a risk due to the absence of third parties to monitor and raise the alarm if necessary. Not working or studying increased defendants' risk of bad influences and drug or alcohol use, which, in addition to compromising recovery, increased the risk of psychosis or violence. While certain risks seem plausible, others remain purely hypothetical, such as inferring that a defendant who smokes might accidentally start a fire in residence or that a defendant contemplating relocation could experience a psychotic episode. Given that the underlying factors of these risks are frequently tied, wholly or partially, to living circumstances that defendants cannot easily modify—particularly in the immediate term—they are left with limited or no viable arguments to advance in their defense.

The accumulation of observational findings and judicial precedents demonstrates that mental health courts are progressively employed as mechanisms for addressing poverty and its perceived risks—whether immediate or anticipated, real or hypothetical. In the absence of adequate social services and infrastructure, courts deal daily with social misery. Impoverished and isolated elderly people who have fallen in their apartment are involuntarily housed in nursing homes to prevent new falls that could cause fractures; children are taken from their refugee parents who have not yet found housing; people experiencing homelessness are subjected to involuntary amputations, as a result of their legs freezing while sleeping outside in winter—after resisting amputation due to fear of being disabled while homeless. These extreme situations have multiplied before the courts since the early 2010s, coinciding with the worsening housing crisis and the increasing number of people living in precarious housing or experiencing homelessness. Largely unknown by the public, these situations are treated and adjudicated by the courts like any other situation. It is uncommon for judicial actors to question the use of judicialization in such situations, despite the limitations of court orders in producing structural and long term effects.

The nature and intensity of risk varies greatly depending on the defendants' socioeconomic profiles. I discussed in the preceding chapter how the judicial treatment of defendants is rooted in classism and sanism, particularly through the systemic indifference to the social conditions in which defendants lived and through the tendency to discredit their lived experience and opinions. My findings indicate that this treatment also depends on the perceived gender, race, and ethnicity of defendants, particularly regarding the evaluation of the risk that they or their situation may present.

Consistent with wide-ranging research, my analysis reveals that mental health courtrooms privilege violence-based risk narratives when assessing men—particularly young men of color (Ogilvie & Kisely, 2022; Barnett et al., 2019; Wong et al., 2019)—with their presumed dangerousness justifying protective interventions against them. In contrast, women are viewed through the lens of fragility (Burstow, 2015; Chunn & Menzies, 1998), where their perceived susceptibility necessitates safeguarding them, or shielding their children from them—especially male children, who might be drawn into criminal behavior or delinquency if exposed to maternal "deviance" (Ericsson, 2000; Van Krieken, 1986). Multiple studies have shown that perceived race is a risk factor that materializes differently for men and women in the judicial process (Williams et al., 2024; Roberts, 2022; Lens, 2019; Brown & Sorensen, 2013). Through their hearings and decisions, courts operationalize distinctions of gender and race at the intersection of class relations and sanism, thereby constructing the foundational narrative about "mental health" and the "other."

Violent Men, Fragile Women

The differentiated narrative of judicial actors toward the alleged risk posed by defendants according to gender manifests on two levels: the nature of the risk, and the judicial control measures put in place to monitor it. Thus, the association of men with risk of violence, and of women with risk to themselves or their children, is present in the four mental health courtrooms studied. However, the differentiated control measures are most evident in matters of defendants unfit to stand trial or not criminally responsible—where men are overrepresented—and in matters of child welfare—where women are overrepresented.

For all defendants, regardless of the specific situations in which they find themselves, there is an implicit presumption of risk, which stems from the fact that psychiatrists or social workers, and sometimes other experts, testify to this effect. For judges, the fact that the main witnesses are not judicial experts[1] but attending psychiatrists or social workers assigned to the defendants' situation creates a sense of trust: they are convinced that as professionals, they seek "the best interest" of their patients or that of the children. Judicial experts, on the contrary, are perceived as being "hand-selected" by the parties and as deriving financial advantage from the judicial process. In formal interview, judges therefore claimed to "constantly defer to the great concern of professionals for their patients." The credibility accorded to psychiatric and social work testimony appeared to increase when judges perceived these professionals as demonstrating "dedication" and care toward the defendants. The merits of the cases seemed very often to rely more on the dedication of the psychiatrists and social workers and on the superiority of their knowledge than on the evidence submitted to the court.

As mentioned earlier, only in exceptional cases I saw defendants who had committed acts of violence during my fieldwork, including in the Review Board. Threats or verbal altercations were much more common. These altercations regularly occurred in contexts related to the precarious situations of defendants. For example, one homeless defendant threatened to kill a bank clerk because his account had been closed, while another verbally assaulted his roommate with whom he lived in a studio apartment because of the loud music they imposed on him every evening that prevented him from sleeping. Many of these events took place in public spaces, shelters, rooming houses, or social housing apartment

[1] In an adversarial judicial system, experts are hired by the parties to produce reports, which they may or may not present as evidence. The experts have no connection, therapeutic or otherwise, with the defendants. Their expertise consists in answering one or more specific questions designed to enlighten the courts on a particular aspect of litigation (e.g. assessing criminal responsibility, fitness to stand trial or the risk posed by a defendant). In this context, they may have access to medical and legal records, in addition to interviewing defendants.

buildings. Incidents of serious violence, or those directed at strangers, family members, or acquaintances, were infrequent; among all the hearings I observed, I encountered only one defendant who had committed homicide, and another who had committed kidnapping.

The starting point of many of the judicial proceedings I attended is often police involvement. When these situations involve women, psychiatrists, social workers, or defense attorneys often emphasize that they are verbally aggressive, that they "speak loudly" or are "disrespectful," but not violent. The aggressiveness is attributed to the fact that the female defendants are "not doing well," "feel bad," or were "depressed." However, when these situations involve men, which is much more frequent, the discussion focus on the impulsivity and the unpredictability of their behaviors and the potential for violence. Even if no act of violence is committed, violence is explicitly considered as a possibility. In these situations, judges often ask treating psychiatrists for a "prognosis" on the expected evolution of the defendants' aggressiveness.

A multitude of facts, or even anecdotes, seem to create presumptions of risk of violence. These include facts reported by third parties absent from the hearing, such as disturbing, strange or unexpected behaviors; the indictment, incarceration, or hospitalization of defendants; documents emanating from authorities such as the police, schools, tribunals, or government agencies; drug or alcohol consumption, even without evidence of a relationship between consumption and violence; lack of "collaboration" with psychiatrists and social workers; and the refusal to take medication, or the suspicion that the defendants could stop taking their medication.

The attitude and appearance of men-defendants during the hearing is a key element in evaluating their aggressiveness. Actions such as interrupting, speaking loudly, or swearing, for example, are interpreted as indicative of challenges in self-control and thus risk of losing self-control. Clothing, tattoos, jewelry, and hair style may also contribute to projecting an unsettling image. During hearings, judges provide advice and recommendations regarding the attitude, language, and appearance of defendants. They encourage defendants to express themselves politely and calmly, in formal language, and only when invited to do so. Expressions of anger or frustration are strictly prohibited. For example, judges may explain to defendants that a spiked bracelet is frightening, or that graphic t-shirts of metal music bands can be interpreted as aggressive. Similarly, as discussed in the preceding chapter, when the defendants speak about their rights, even in the context where rights have been violated in the hospital setting or in the judicial procedure, it is considered as indicative of a demanding character, and a form of aggressiveness. In general, challenging authority is regarded by the court as evidence of aggressiveness and risk of violence. This authority is most often afforded to police officers, psychiatrists, social workers, and judges. I will deal with the challenge to authority in the next chapter.

Several defendants have had altercations with police officers, including verbal altercations, refusal to identify, and resistance to an intervention or a police arrest. Some defendants, especially those living on the streets, in rooming houses or in social housing, have regular contact with the police. At the Review Board, several defendants are there after being accused of obstructing police work and then being found unfit to stand trial or not criminally responsible on account of mental disorder. In most cases, the obstruction consisted of refusing to identify themselves or of having "disturbed" the police work, both of which do not involve any violence. The Review Board's supervision can then last for years, with no relation to the seriousness of the acts committed, as in this example from my observation notes:

> The hearing begins with the psychiatrist presenting his report. Five years ago, the defendant called 911 saying someone had been stabbed. That was not the case, but he wanted to lodge a complaint against his mother, who is also his landlord and had taken advantage of his involuntary commitment to have his apartment emptied. He has been under the control of the Review Board since then, on conditional release. He has been admitted to a psychiatric ward eleven times in the last twelve years. He lives on welfare. The psychiatrist report states, "If he doesn't use drugs and takes his medication, no problem; if he does use drugs, he risks becoming aggressive and not paying his rent." The defendant occasionally uses drugs, especially under the influence of "bad company." However, no incidents have occurred in the last five years.

> The psychiatrist-judge asks the defendant, "It isn't easy for you, is it?" The defendant replies, "I know, I got myself into trouble." He is on the verge of tears. The judge asks, "Do you have a mental illness?" The defendant says, "Yes, I'm depressed but not mean;" he explains he never meant to hurt anyone; he is wondering if it might be his size or strength that make him appear scary. The judge asks, "Is it a good idea to call 911 for no good reason?" The defendant responds no, but it has been a month since the police did anything in response to the fact that his mother stole all his belongings. He mentions he lives in an apartment belonging to his mother and has numerous physical health problems that prevent him from working. He also reports that his mother says he is "useless," a "good-for-nothing." The psychiatrist-judge cuts him off, "How are things going with your treatment team?" The defendant replies, "Fine, they're very nice," then recounts lying about his drug use. He says, "I know you want what's best for me, but I'm afraid of you." He is about to cry again.

Hearings concerning female defendants have several points in common with those concerning male defendants, including the nature of the facts or anecdotes reported, sometimes by absent third parties; contacts with other judicial authorities and previous hospitalizations; the entering into evidence of documents from different institutions, including the police, daycare centers, and schools, especially in child welfare matters; the alleged consumption of drugs or alcohol, whether or not it is related to the facts presented to the court; collaboration with the treatment team or the social team of child welfare services, and medication intake. However, the narrative developed by judicial actors concerning women is often one of help and protection, rather than of surveillance or control, as it is for men. The risk posed by women's behavior encompasses unstable or depressive moods, or conduct that could make defendants targets of violence. Judicial actors insist on the need for women to obtain support and to be protected, emphasizing their vulnerability, which medication can mitigate. Women are thus often presented as immature and unaware of the consequences of their actions and decisions, as shown in the following excerpt from my observation notes during an involuntary commitment hearing:

> The defendant is a 22-years-old woman. She faces a thirty-day involuntary commitment application stemming from conflicts with her parents and her unannounced trip to Toronto. The hospital's lawyer has announced that a petition for involuntary treatment will be filed with the Superior Court the following week. The defendant says she was beaten by her parents, lives in a shelter and has no suicidal thoughts. She was diagnosed with schizophrenia and offered medication but states that since no one explained the diagnosis and treatment to her, she refused treatment. The judge asks her, "Do you understand that you're still a young person, that you're vulnerable; do you understand the importance of telling a loved one that you're leaving town?"
>
> After the hearing, the judge contends he sees the defendant as "much more of a child" than a 22-year-old. For him, it is "very dangerous" for a young woman to be alone in a city like Toronto, something that a "person with good judgment who is not mentally ill would understand."

The contrast with the preceding case is particularly noteworthy. Whereas the male defendant exhibited considerable emotional distress throughout the proceedings—nearly breaking down on multiple occasions while describing what he perceived as traumatic experiences involving his mother—the female defendant presented herself as neither vulnerable nor requiring assistance. However, judicial responses inverted these presentations: the emotionally distressed male defendant's vulnerability was overlooked in favor of focusing on his occasional substance use, while the apparently self-sufficient female defendant was characterized as requiring child-like protection.

Female fragility assumes multiple dimensions. As illustrated in the preceding case, it may concern victimization risk, especially from males, particularly when defendants' appearance and behavior are characterized as provocative or sexualized. Fragility may also derive from depressive episodes, emotional instability, or hopelessness that could drive defendants toward self-harm, imprudent decision-making, or neglect of personal or parental responsibilities. Vulnerability may additionally relate to social disconnection, especially for aging women, encompassing risks of accidents, injuries, or unmet care needs due to absent support networks.

The narrative about women's fragility and need of protection tends to be somewhat modified when children are involved. In this case, the fragility of women is a threat to third parties, namely their children. Pregnant women, for example, are subject to requests for involuntary commitment due to behaviors deemed risky for the unborn child, such as drug use. During hearings, when women defendants expressed distress related to their pregnancy, they are generally ignored by the judicial actors. It is then agreed that the involuntary commitment will continue until delivery, and that child welfare services will take charge of the child after their birth. Child welfare hearings best exemplify gendered judicial narratives, centered around traditional parental roles. Mothers are responsible for education, health, schooling, nutrition, and affection. Thus, difficulties at school, unbalanced meals, and untidy housework are systematically blamed on them, even when the father is present. Among the criticisms often leveled at mothers is their lack of "availability" or "dedication" to their children, with judges telling mothers that they must have "the same level of commitment to their child as they have to their work." Fathers, on the other hand, are allowed to decide what role they wish to play and how. A large proportion of fathers are absent from their children's lives. For those who are present, the degree of involvement varies greatly but is not scrutinized or even comment on by the judicial actors. When parents are separated, judges sometimes stress the need for fathers (but not for single mothers) to receive help with the children from women, be it grandmothers, aunts, or spouses. As a result, mothers are systematically blamed for what goes wrong, including their spouse's violence, while fathers are regularly praised for accomplishing everyday tasks, as illustrated by the following extract from my observation notes during a child welfare hearing:

> The defendant parents are separated but appear together in court. They are a couple in their twenties. The child, a four-year-old boy who lives with his mother, is absent. The father, a person from Latin America who has difficulty expressing himself in French, is unemployed, and the mother, a French-speaking Quebecois, works as a nude dancer in bars. The social worker from child welfare services explains that before the separation, the father was physically violent toward the mother and that

> she had recommended anger-management workshops for him and code-pendency management workshops for her. The father has taken no steps to participate in these workshops, while the mother has attended a few sessions, but not enough in the eyes of the social worker. She says she fears that if the mother starts dating men again, she will once again "expose her son to violence." She also notes that the father, who sees his son under his sister's supervision for a few hours every other weekend, prepared him a Kraft-Dinner the last time. She says, "it's important to compliment him here, in front of everyone." The judge adds, cheerfully, "Bravo, sir!"
>
> During the entire hearing, the focus is on the mother, her unstable mental health and her occasional cannabis use. The social worker explains how the mother tolerating being physically abused by the father demonstrates her emotional dependence on him, as well as her lack of consideration for her child's development in her decision to stay with a violent partner. She is extremely concerned. She proposes psychiatric monitoring of the mother and a psychological evaluation of the child regarding attachment, in addition to the obligation for the mother to disclose any future romantic relationships and undergo random drug testing, as well as random home visits from child welfare social workers. She states that if the mother does not comply with these measures, the child could be removed from her care. The judge, who says she is equally concerned, grants all the requests of the child welfare services.
>
> After the hearing, the judge explains that the history of violence of the father towards the mother does not make him a bad father. For her, the concern in this case is the mother's incapacity to prioritize her child, which represents the main risk for the future.

Child welfare hearings are often filled with gendered stories of domestic and family violence. Most of the time, these facts are ignored by judicial actors, even when criminal charges have been brought against fathers. Child welfare services often insist that children who do not want to see their violent fathers be forced to do so, often questioning whether the mothers are manipulating the children or engaging in parental alienation, even when the children are teenagers and testify at the hearing themselves. Furthermore, mothers' shortcomings in raising their children are often seen as evidence that they are not as fully devoted to their children as they should be, or as indicative of mental health issues, including personality disorders. Little evidence is typically presented to support these diagnoses.

More generally, women who do not fit the model of the traditional, present, and loving mother are considered deviant and problematic in child welfare hearings. Many of the women defendants are single mothers living in extreme poverty or working long hours, some use drugs or alcohol, and others have romantic or sexual relationships with men who are not their partners or the fathers of their children. These situations are considered as evidence of instability or lack of insight and it may happen that the "very open sexuality" or "strong libido" of defendants are discussed during hearings. The mothers who are members of the LGBTQIA2+ community also appear to be outside the norms promoted by child welfare services and the courts. This was the case for Agnès, a transgender woman in a relationship with a woman and whom I interviewed after she lost custody of her two children. She was born intersex, and recounts that when she was operated on "at two months old, [her] doctors flipped a coin to decide whether [she] was a boy or a girl." She explains,

> I was forced to be a boy for years. At forty-five, I said, "Okay, enough." When my children started school, I wanted them to make two Mother's Day cards, but the school refused. Then, for Father's Day, the school made them make cards that said: "Happy Father's Day, Dad." They forced the children to call me "Dad." The children never called me that. It was always "Mom" or "Agnès." The children were not even aware of my gender change; it was the school that made them aware of the situation. To them, they had two moms, and that was completely normal. It was the school that traumatized them with this. I even met with the administration to tell them, "Stop making Father's Day cards," and they told me that we had to tell the truth to the children. They reported me to child welfare services, who wrote in the report that I had changed sex. "Changed" is a big word. The situation is much more complex than that. Then they said the children had been traumatized by the situation.

The differentiated judicial narrative between men and women, between risk of violence and need for protection, produces differences in the way control is exercised on defendants. The Review Board, where men are overrepresented, exercises control more similar to criminal law, focused on social life and public space, by imposing conditions that restrict contact with certain people or access to certain public places. In child welfare matters, where women are not only overrepresented but more targeted by judicial orders even when fathers are present, the control focuses on the domestic sphere and personal relationships. Youth Division orders are intrusive and impose a level of daily surveillance, whether through participation in workshops, therapies, and follow-ups, the imposition of surprise visits, or the demand for disclosure of personal life details such as romantic relationships.

My research also uncovered how the risk of violence from men is treated differently depending on whether it affects the public, as in involuntary commitment or the Review Board hearings, or whether it targets women, particularly spouses, as in the case of the Youth Division. In matters of involuntary commitment or before the Review Board, the potential risk of violence, which is in most cases not directed toward a known person and is often poorly supported by evidence or facts, is considered by the courts as justifying the exercise of control and surveillance. In contrast, in child welfare matters, the documented violence of fathers toward mothers is attributed to mothers who must take measures to protect their children and heal their emotional dependence. For the court, the fact that a mother is, or even has been, in a violent relationship demonstrates her incapacity to prioritize the best interests of her children, thus compromising her parental capacities and eventually the possibility for her to maintain ties with them (Lapierre & Cadrin, 2022). While the potential violence of men justifies their involuntary commitment or their remaining under the control of the Review Board, the proven violence of fathers is not considered to be an indicator of their parental incompetence and does not prevent them from seeing their children, or even in some cases from being entrusted with their care by the court.

The "Race Factor"

As well as the social condition and gender of the defendants, race and ethnicity also come into play during the hearings and reinforce the dynamics I described above, especially for men. Thus, men of color are treated as more threatening and presenting a higher risk of violence than white men. In line with what has been documented in other studies, racialized women, on the other hand, appear to deviate from gender stereotypes associated with fragility (Fernance, 2024; Roberts, 2022; Hannah-Moffat, 2007). The narrative surrounding them leans rather toward a risk similar to that of men, rooted in violence, or in negligence and abandonment of responsibility. The perceived risk they represent to their children is situated in the educational sphere and in the teaching of inadequate values, and not in exposure to their own vulnerability.

In addition to race, certain ethnic and religious beliefs are associated with an increased risk, particularly the practice of Voodoo or Islam. In matters of child welfare, values different from those associated with the "good family," from the perspective of judicial actors, highlight the moral dimension of risk discussed in Chapter 5. While judicial actors have a gendered conception of parenting, they are also suspicious of families they perceive as too traditional or too religious. The court may consider devoutly religious family dynamics, especially with stay-at-home mothers practicing homeschooling, as presenting a danger to children's development, due to lack of peer contact, under stimulation or overly patriarchal values.

As with social conditions and gender, race and ethnic differences are rarely discussed in the courtroom and even less often named as such. Rather, it is through the facts mentioned by psychiatrists and social workers, or through comments made during hearings, that the intersectional links between mental health, risk, poverty, gender, ethnicity, and race are woven. However, I once witnessed a situation where the risk presented by the defendant due to their skin tone was explicitly named. These remarks were not made during a hearing but referred directly to the exchanges that took place during a Review Board hearing concerning a tall, racialized man in his forties wearing his hair in locs, and who had been unhoused for several years.

> The defendant had been diagnosed with schizophrenia, pathological gambling, and substance abuse. He has been under Review Board supervision for eight years, is on conditional release but is currently hospitalized. Within the span of eight years, he was incarcerated about ten times, most often for breach of conditions of release. The treating psychiatrist would like him to be placed in detention to treat his gambling problem, which the defendant refuses to collaborate with. The Review Board does not have the power to order treatments.
>
> At the beginning of the hearing, the judges state that the defendant aggressively begs in the streets: they draw this information from police records, but no charges have been filed. The defendant recounts being harassed by shopkeepers and police officers when he begs, directly referring to racial profiling. The lawyers, the psychiatrist, and the judges look at each other, smiling knowingly; it seems they have never heard of the numerous reports on the profiling practices of the Montreal Police Service (Rutland, 2020). The judges maintain that police reports constitute evidence of the defendant's aggressiveness and the risk he poses. They not only dismissed his words on profiling but also insinuated that they show paranoia, thus diminishing his credibility. The defendant raises his voice, "I'm tired of being controlled by the system. Yes, we must respect the law, but I also have rights." The psychiatrist-judge responds with a surprised look that he "seems frustrated" and asks him to remain calm. She tells him with a smile, "We are here for you."
>
> While the Review Board deliberates, all those present in the room must go into the hallway. Upon leaving the room, the defense attorney tells the defendant in front of everyone, referring to the exchange about police reports: "You must stop with this profiling story. You are tall; you are Black; you're scary." The discomfort was palpable for the 10 minutes that the deliberation lasted.
>
> Back in the courtroom, the judges announce that they will follow the psychiatrist's recommendation and place the defendant in detention in hospital without outing privileges for one year, "Good luck, sir!"

Although such remarks are exceptional, they reflect unspoken dynamics that I have observed repeatedly. During hearings, the appearance of male defendants constitute an important element of risk assessment, where skin tone, tattoos, piercings, height, clothing choices, and hair style added up to create a threatening image in the eyes of the judges—in the case of the defendant I just mentioned, the judges advised them to cut their hair. In addition, courts generally do not consider defendants' allegations of discrimination, racism, or profiling to be credible, in the same way that they do not consider their statements regarding rights violations. On the contrary, these elements appear to the court as evidence of aggressiveness or lack of insight. These observations are particularly evident concerning police services. When defendants report being harassed, profiled, or even assaulted by police officers, their statements are not only disbelieved but are considered as evidence of defiance toward authority. Courts thus consistently tend to believe that police interventions are justified and conduct according to best practices, despite literature, public reports, and press articles that have been documenting for years that people experiencing homelessness and racialized people are subject to police profiling and violence (Rutland, 2020; Laurencin & Walker, 2020; Hayle et al., 2016).

Cultural or religious beliefs and practices are also factored in alongside defendants' race, and in some cases are viewed by the court as carrying particular risks. It is especially the case for Muslim men, with courts seeming to associate Islam with different types of risk. In matters of child welfare, Muslim fathers seem to be considered by the court as potentially strict in their educational methods, or as exercising psychological violence on their children, especially girls, through increased surveillance and control. In the other mental health courtrooms that I observed, the practice of Islam in itself seem to raise fears of violence and to be perceived as a potential risk to relatives or more broadly, even in the absence of past or contemporary facts to support this idea. The mere mention of the practice of Islam or mosque attendance during the hearings raise immediate questions and concerns, as illustrated by this excerpt from my observation notes during a Review Board hearing concerning a defendant originally from Senegal who arrived in Canada six years earlier:

> The hearing begins with the reading of the psychiatrist's report. The defendant, a racialized man in his mid-thirties, is a statistician and is married to a woman who "supports him" and who "will be there when he gets discharged." He made threats to a 911 agent and a police officer four years ago and was found not criminally responsible on account of mental

> disorder. At the time of the hearing, he has been voluntarily hospitalized for five months as a result of depression "due to financial stress," but returns home every weekend. For the attending psychiatrist, the defendant needs to find work "to feel useful." She states that he could be released under conditions, including specifically not consuming drugs or alcohol. She explains that even though he has never consumed them, the restriction is "just in case."
> It is now the defendant's turn to be questioned. He appears very polite and deferential to the judges. He says, "I don't want to be considered dangerous to society because I am not." He asserts that he is taking his medications and is following all his psychiatrist's recommendations and explains that it was "financial hardship" that caused his depression. Through the account of his daily life, he mentions attending a mosque. The social-work judge immediately intervenes by asking if he does not consume alcohol due to "conviction or religion." The defendant responds that he has "never had any interest in it." The judges are clearly relieved.

Hearings concerning racialized women showed similar trends. Perceived race and culture can lead the court to quickly reach conclusions about the presence of risk, with the claims of discrimination and racism evoked by the defendants ignored, thus diminishing their credibility in the eyes of the court. However, unlike what I have observed with white women defendants, who are in the majority at court, racialized women are much less often seen as fragile and in need of protection. While women's aggressiveness is generally attributed to the fact that they are depressed or that they "fe[lt] bad" as I explained above, this is not necessarily the case for racialized women for whom aggressiveness can instead be considered a risk of violence. Although the number of racialized women I encountered in my research fields is relatively small, this trend concerns all the mental health courtrooms investigated. For example, the educational methods of Haitian women are often scrutinized for signs of violence during child welfare hearings; in a hearing for involuntary treatments, the fact that a Haitian woman practiced Voodoo was sufficient to establish that she could become delusional, and possibly become aggressive, even violent, or set fire to her apartment due to the candle she lit. In both cases, the courts quite readily accepted the reasons and arguments presented by social workers and psychiatrists, although the evidence did not establish a risk of violence. Similarly to the case involving the male defendant wearing his hair in locs, or the one who frequented the mosque, racial or ethnic dimensions seem to play a leading role in the courts' assessment of risk in these cases.

In child welfare matters, interventions with racialized mothers are generally focused on educational approaches, often because those used by the mothers are often different from those promoted by child welfare services and judicial actors. In addition to particular attention given to religious beliefs and potential psychological or physical violence, the involvement of extended family members or siblings with children was often approached with suspicion by judicial actors. That grandparents, or uncles and aunts, contribute significantly to the education of children, or that siblings participated in the care of younger children, is considered inadequate from the Western-centric perspective of attachment theory principles, as demonstrating a lack of dedication from mothers, or as an indicator of potential danger to children's development. Judicial actors often consider these situations as demonstrating the parental incapacity of mothers, or even as demonstrating mental health problems. Ironically, child welfare services themselves sometimes use extended family when they place children outside their family, and they encourage extended family women to support single fathers in some cases.

In addition to the educational dimension, it seems that racialized mothers are often held responsible, or at least seen as having some involvement, in the delinquency of their sons. Thus, the fact that a teenage boy faced criminal charges, or even a conviction, seem to raise suspicions that mothers are not strict enough, might be trying to protect them, or hiding information from child welfare services and the court. The intervention of child welfare services then aim to protect other children not only from contact with criminalized peers, but also with the mother who would not be able to protect their sons from their bad influence, or who would herself present a risk.

In hearings, racialized women reported being subjected to coercive measures or to surveillance in hospitals or by child welfare services more often than white women, which research consistently shows (Baughman et al., 2021; Harp & Bunting, 2020). These practices are generally not discussed during hearings, and judicial decisions tend either to reinforce coercive measures via court orders or to implicitly allow their continuation.

Besides being risk factors, perceived race and culture can lead to inappropriate comments and attitude, such as a judge asking a defendant "what he is waiting for to return to his country," another insisting on knowing the citizenship status of a defendant's relatives, or yet another referring to the "culturally problematic practices" of the defendant. The following excerpt from my observation notes during a Review Board hearing exemplifies such a situation:

> The hearing begins with an intervention from the psychiatrist who explains that the defendant is Cambodian and that "in his culture, mental health is a taboo." He mentions that they have a "good therapeutic alliance," but that the diagnosis of schizophrenia is very difficult for the defendant to accept. He also says that "for cultural reasons" he has not talked about it with his family back in Cambodia or with his friends. He is before the Review Board for having thrown a piece of furniture out of his apartment window and injuring a passerby. The psychiatrist recommends unconditional release, insisting that the defendant does not pose a significant threat to public safety.
>
> During his testimony, the defendant says that he works in a factory and wishes to go to Cambodia to get married, to which the psychiatrist-judge responds quickly, "Why? Are the women here not beautiful enough for you?" He then bursts out laughing at his own joke. The defendant remains silent, staring into space. The psychologist-judge intervenes to say that "going abroad to get married" is not a constructive personal project given the situation. The lawyer presiding over the bench asks the defendant if he has told his colleagues about his schizophrenia diagnosis. The defendant responds no, embarrassed. The psychiatrist intervenes to remind the judges that for cultural reasons, the defendant is not comfortable talking about his diagnosis. However, the lawyer-judge insists. He says, "If you talk about it with your colleagues, they can warn you about the symptoms' onset next time." The defendant clearly does not know what to answer. The judges insist, however, stating that "a safety net is essential to avoid new problems."

At this hearing, not only did the judges indulge in offensive remarks, but they also disregarded the cultural background and characteristics of the defendant that would have been beneficial to consider, which is a common situation. There were instances where psychiatrists or social workers tried to put a situation in its cultural context to provide the courts with relevant elements to consider in their decisions. For example, as in the excerpt above, they may explain that mental health is highly stigmatized in the defendants' community, which constituted an obstacle when it comes to securing the cooperation of relatives. However, the courts generally consider the cooperation of relatives to be a means of mitigating risks, and the nuances of the defendants' situation are generally not deemed relevant in the eyes of the court, or at least not sufficiently relevant enough to be considered. Thus, the court generally treat this information as contextual but do not seek to ensure that the judicial process is adequate as well as culturally sensitive and safe.

Defendants with limited proficiency in French or English face compounded difficulties. The involvement of interpreters disrupt courtroom exchanges, potentially compromising testimonial coherence and necessitating extensive time for clarification. Defendants who forgo interpreter services—typically believing that their language skills are adequate for proceedings in French or English—yet struggle with the language, often deliver labored testimony wherein their inability to convey intended meanings becomes apparent. Such circumstances disadvantaged defendants, who cannot adequately comprehend procedural exchanges or effectively communicate with the judges. Language barriers are occasionally cited in court as impediments to therapeutic intervention, in situations in which psychiatric and social work professionals could not engage in direct communication with defendants. In child welfare proceedings, home visits reportedly failed to document improvements in parental capacity when mothers interacted with children in languages unfamiliar to supervising social workers. Courts typically construe these factors as barriers to therapeutic efficacy yet fail to recommend that psychiatric or child welfare services engage linguistically or culturally competent professionals.

Defendants' cultural safety is typically not one of the issues considered in mental health courtrooms, which is easily demonstrated by the situations involving Indigenous defendants. I attended a hearing regarding an involuntary commitment petition for a 68-year-old Indigenous woman who fled from a hospital in Winnipeg, Manitoba, and at the time of the hearing was unhoused in Montreal. According to the psychiatric reports to which I had access before the hearing, she was taken by police to the hospital emergency room because she was wandering the streets and refused to provide identification to police officers. The reports emphasized that she was distrustful and "paranoid against the psychiatrist from Winnipeg," that she ran away from police, and that she was bipolar and "jumped from one subject to another" without logic. The two psychiatric reports, which said she should not testify because she was "too disorganized," did not mention that she was a member of the Ojibway First Nation, which I understood only at the beginning of the hearing.

> The defendant has no lawyer to represent her and speaks in limited English. The hearing nevertheless proceeds primarily in French, even though she does not speak the language. As she has no lawyer, the judge prompts the hospital's lawyer to ask questions. The defendant recounts having been placed in restraints upon her arrival at the hospital and being released only several hours later when staff understood she was not violent. She does not want to take medication because of the adverse effects.
>
> Typically, when defendants are unrepresented, judges are more proactive and ask questions themselves, something I have seen this judge do on a few previous occasions previously. But the judge remains silent during this hearing, which ends after five minutes. The hospital's lawyer simply says that the defendant is "disorganized" and that nobody knows where she would go if she left the hospital. The judge grants the petition without giving any explanation to the defendant.

While the psychiatric reports stated that the defendant was dangerous to others, and that she was placed in restraints upon her arrival at the hospital, the facts that explain her presence at the hospital were rather her distrust of police and psychiatrists. This distrust was not mentioned during the hearing, nor has it been placed in its colonial context by the psychiatrists in their reports or by the judicial actors despite the direct participation of public institutions—police, justice, child welfare services, health—in colonial practices and the resulting intergenerational trauma for Indigenous people (Matheson et al., 2022; Sinclair, 2016; Bombay et al., 2009). The court simply ignored the fact that the defendant was a member of an Indigenous Nation, which was also the case for other hearings involving Indigenous defendants that I observed, including before the Review Board. Although the Supreme Court of Canada decreed in 1999 (*R. v. Gladue*) that criminal courts bear responsibility for considering systemic and historical factors relevant to Indigenous defendants during sentencing to mitigate their disproportionate presence in correctional systems, logical consistency would suggest that equivalent considerations should inform every court when adjudicating matters that compromise Indigenous peoples' rights, beginning with liberty (Laskin, 2021; Martin, 2020). However, this Supreme Court ruling has failed to achieve its intended outcome of lowering Indigenous incarceration rates. Conversely, these figures continue to escalate (Statistics Canada, 2023; McGuire & Murdoch, 2022), with Indigenous overrepresentation in Canadian correctional institutions increasing by 14% between 2019 and 2021 (Statistics Canada, 2023). Assigning courts the duty to account for historical and structural discriminatory factors fails to acknowledge that legal systems, rights frameworks, and judicial institutions constitute integral components of oppressive structures (Oudshoorn, 2024)—a reality that mental health courtroom observations demonstrate remains unrecognized. Judicial color-blindness, like class-blindness, fosters conditions that are conducive to systemic discrimination and enables the manifestation of classist, sexist, racist, and sanist practices.

Lacking systemic critique, judicial proceedings function within an integrated apparatus of police, social service, and psychiatric interventions that systematically target marginalized communities, while judicial actors remain oblivious to this pattern. Moreover, judicial narratives surrounding mental health mirror the political and media narratives examined in Chapter 2: centering on risk constructions rooted in elite definitions of acceptable behavior and normality, while claiming objectivity. Therefore, what distinguishes defendants encountered during my research is neither the acuity of their psychiatric conditions nor their alleged conduct. It is their repeated institutional contacts—particularly with law enforcement—which explain their courtroom presence. Rather than illuminating genuine mental health related risks, mental health court operations expose how routine socioeconomic, gender, and racial marginalization becomes organized and amplified through public institutional interventions across the care continuum.

References

Barnett, P., et al. (2019). Ethnic variations in compulsory detention under the mental health act: A systematic review and meta-analysis of international data. *The Lancet, 6*(4), 305–317. https://doi.org/10.1016/S2215-0366(19)30027-6

Baughman, C., Coles, T., Feinberg, J., & Newton, H. (2021). The surveillance tentacles of the child welfare system. *Columbia journal of Race and Law, 11*(3), 501–532. https://doi.org/10.7916/e0de-de42

Bombay, A., Matheson, K., & Anisman, H. (2009). Intergenerational trauma: Convergence of multiple processes among first nations peoples in Canada. *International Journal of Indigenous Health, 5*(3), 6–47.

Brown, J. M., & Sorensen, J. R. (2013). Race, ethnicity, gender, and waiver to adult court. *Journal of Ethnicity In Criminal Justice, 11*(3), 181–195. https://doi.org/10.1080/15377938.2012.756846

Burstow, B. (2015). *Psychiatry and the Business of Madness: An Ethical and Epistemological Accounting*. Palgrave Macmillan.

Chunn, D. E., & Menzies, R. (1998). Out of mind, out of law: The regulation of criminally insane women inside British Columbia's public mental hospitals, 1888-1973. *Canadian Journal Women and the Law, 10*(2), 241–279.

Ericsson, K. (2000). Social control and emancipation? Ambiguities in child welfare. *Journal of Scandinavian Studies in Criminology and Crime Prevention, 1*(1), 16–26. https://doi.org/10.1080/14043850050116237

Fernance, C. (2024). The discursive construction of "good parenting" in Australia's statutory child protection system: Impacts on first nations families & ways to disrupt the discourse. *Social Work & Policy Studies: Social Justice, Practice and Theory, 7*(1).

Hannah-Moffat, K. (2007). Gendering dynamic risk: Assessing and managing the maternal identities of women prisoners. In Hannah-Moffat, K. & O'Malley, P. (Eds.), Gendered risks (pp. 237–256). Routledge-Cavendish. https://doi.org/10.4324/9780203940556.

Harp, K. L., & Bunting, A. M. (2020). The racialized nature of child welfare policies and the social control of black bodies. *Social Politics: International Studies in Gender, State & Society, 27*(2), 258–281. https://doi.org/10.1093/sp/jxz039

Hayle, S., Wortley, S., & Tanner, J. (2016). Race, street life, and policing: Implications for racial profiling. *Canadian Journal of Criminology and Criminal Justice, 58*(3), 322–353. https://doi.org/10.3138/cjccj.2014.E32

Laskin, R. (2021). Expanding the reach of Gladue: Exploring the use of Gladue reports in child protection. *Appeal: Review of Current Law & Law Reform, 26*, 25–50.

Laurencin, C. T., & Walker, J. M. (2020). Racial profiling is a public health and health disparities issue. *Journal of Racial and Ethnic Health Disparities, 7*(3), 393–397. https://doi.org/10.1007/s40615-020-00738-2

Martin, A. F. (2020). Creative and responsive advocacy for reconciliation: The application of Gladue principles in administrative law. *McGill Law Journal, 66*(2), 337–376. https://doi.org/10.7202/1084134ar

Matheson, K., Seymour, A., Landry, J., Ventura, K., Arsenault, E., & Anisman, H. (2022). Canada's colonial genocide of indigenous peoples: A review of the psychosocial and neurobiological processes linking trauma and intergenerational outcomes. *International Journal of Environmental Research and Public Health, 19*(11), 6455. https://doi.org/10.3390/ijerph19116455

McGuire, M. M., & Murdoch, D. J. (2022). (in)-justice: An exploration of the dehumanization, victimization, criminalization, and over-incarceration of indigenous women in Canada. *Punishment & Society, 24*(4), 529–550. https://doi.org/10.1177/14624745211001685

Ogilvie, J. M., & Kisely, S. (2022). Examining the health and criminal justice characteristics for young people on compulsory community treatment orders: An Australian birth cohort and data linkage study. *International Journal of Law and Psychiatry, 83*, 101813. https://doi.org/10.1016/j.ijlp.2022.101813

Oudshoorn, J. (2024). Theorizing a way out of reformist reforms: Gladue reports and penal abolition. *Punishment & Society, 26*(2), 243–260. https://doi.org/10.1177/14624745231208177

R. v. Gladue, [1999] 1 S.C.R. 688.

Roberts, D. 2022. *Torn apart: How the child welfare system destroys black families–and how abolition can build a safer world.* Basic Books.
Rutland, T. (2020). Profiling the future: The long struggle against police racial profiling in Montreal. *American Review of Canadian Studies, 50*(3), 270–292. https://doi.org/10.1080/02722011.2020.1831139
Sinclair, R. (2016). The indigenous child removal system in Canada: An examination of legal decision-making and racial bias. *First Peoples Child & Family Review, 11*(2), 8–18. https://doi.org/10.7202/1082333ar
Statistics Canada. (2023, July 12). *Over-representation of Indigenous persons in adult provincial custody, 2019/2020 and 2020/2021.*. https://www150.statcan.gc.ca/n1/en/pub/85-002-x/2023001/article/00004-eng.pdf?st=F3B63sXN (accessed August 9, 2025).
Van Krieken, R. (1986). Social theory and child welfare: Beyond social control. *Theory and Society*, 401–429. https://www.jstor.org/stable/657324
Williams, M. T., Faber, S., Zare, M., Barker, T., & Abdulrehman, R. Y. (2024). Intersectional racial and gender bias in family court. *Discover Psychology, 4*(1), 178. https://doi.org/10.1007/s44202-024-00282-8
Wong, A. H., Taylor, R. A., Ray, J. M., & Bernstein, S. L. (2019). Physical restraint use in adult patients presenting to a general emergency department. *Annals of Emergency Medicine, 73*(2), 183–192. https://doi.org/10.1016/j.annemergmed.2018.06.020

7

The Magic Pill

> The lawyer representing the Crown [the prosecution office] pulls out of her briefcase all the files concerning the defendant. It is quite an impressive stack. She flips through pages, searching for specific information. She asks the defendant what the medication does for him. He replies that it helps him sleep. She asks, "That's all?" She follows up with a series of questions, and eventually asks if the medication is only for sleeping. That is not what the defendant said, but he finds himself a bit stuck. He says, "That's not what I meant, but that I'm unable to clearly express my thoughts, I am not a psychiatrist. But when I sleep next to someone I love, I do not need medication." The lawyer replies that she does not want to know what the medication does on a chemical level, but rather what it changes for him. The defendant says he feels better with the medication without elaborating further. The lawyer gives the judges a knowing look.—Excerpt of personal observation notes, Review Board hearing, Department of Psychiatry, General Hospital.

In recent years, Quebec and Canadian mental health courtrooms have been repeatedly put on the spot by the media and politicians in connection with dramatic events involving people with prior court involvement.

E. Bernheim, *Therapeutic (In)justice and the Shadow Carceral State*, The Politics of Mental Health and Illness, https://doi.org/10.1007/978-3-032-16186-4_7

Legislative reforms inspired by therapeutic jurisprudence, aimed at facilitating the sharing of personal information between police, health, social, and legal professionals on the continuum of care, as well as at tightening control and surveillance, have been put in place or have been under discussion in several provinces. Recent provincial and federal election campaigns have made promises to increase the use of forced treatment, conflating homelessness, mental health, and addiction (Bernheim, 2024a), which has been similarly observed in the United States (White House, 2025).

Risk occupies the central position in these discussions, and its depiction is deeply troubling. Risk is described in a manner that is magnified, intensified beyond previous levels, and encompassing more severe and frightening psychiatric conditions. Within this social climate, public anxiety escalates, with citizens reluctant to walk in the streets or utilize public transportation. Legislation is simultaneously characterized as overly restrictive, permitting involuntary commitment and treatment only under extraordinary circumstances, while community-based monitoring and control mechanisms are deemed inadequately robust and dependable. Judicial decision-making capacity faces scrutiny, and courts are characterized as permissive or incompetent, inclined to release dangerous individuals with mental disorders into the streets too readily. When questioned regarding proposed legislative changes, political leaders typically cannot affirm that the incidents prompting reform demands were preventable.

Scientific controversies about risk assessment are generally absent from the public conversation. On the contrary, it is often suggested that risk assessment is simple, almost a formality, and that police officers will soon have to use risk assessment tools during their daily interventions. Nevertheless, beyond the reliability concerns and biases inherent in the previously examined risk assessment instruments, ethnographic observations reveal that mental health courtrooms' risk determinations frequently derive from singular incidents, hypothetical future scenarios, or circumstances directly attributable to defendants' impoverished living situations. The connection between risk assessment and socioeconomic conditions became particularly evident during the COVID-19 pandemic, when involuntary commitments and treatments were implemented because defendants' housing circumstances precluded adherence to public-health protocols (Bernheim, 2024b).

In formal interviews, several psychiatrists expressed discomfort with the judicial institution's requests for risk assessments, a sentiment also documented in a few studies (Wangmo et al., 2021; Lesse, 1982). For them, these binary risk/no risk evaluations do not correspond closely enough to any clinical reality. They ignore the complexity of mental health issues and of the psychiatric practice, which is characterized by the absence of reliable examinations to establish pathology, and which places a disproportionate responsibility on their shoulders—a burden that is discussed in research demonstrating the limited reliability of psychiatric risk assessments (Reyes, 2017; Swanson et al., 2015; Fazel et al., 2012). One psychiatrist I interviewed explained:

> Psychiatry, now, is experienced as a kind of radiography of the patient's soul, and if the patient has been seen by a psychiatrist, the entire system, both families and the psychiatric system and the legal system, assumes it's absolutely certain that this guy won't commit suicide, that one won't do such and such, this one will do that, etc. And the psychiatrist bears the burden of this enormous responsibility, that is, in 35 minutes, to predict what will happen in people's lives.

The discomfort of psychiatrists is compounded by that of judges, who claim they do not have the knowledge to judge risk. In formal interviews, several judges deplored the absence of defense evidence and having to rely on evidence presented by hospitals and child welfare services. In addition to this context, the judicial practice is affected by reforms inspired by the approach of new public management (Hood, 1991)—they must demonstrate accountability grounded in efficiency and efficacy, which means judges have neither the time nor the resources to formulate legally supported decisions. In interviews, some reported not having the option to adjourn cases to obtain additional evidence due to pressure to "close cases." Many denounce the fact that the significant increase in the number of cases in recent years has not been matched with new judicial resources and question the quality of work accomplished in such a context. Some judges said they question whether their decisions truly help defendants, in a context where public services are overwhelmed. One judge, for example, said they were not familiar with the conditions of psychiatric hospitalization, wondering if people were simply "parked on stretchers" without psychological support or activities.

Ethnographic observations revealed a significant gap between what was said in interviews and actual practices during the hearing. In interviews, many legal and health professional participants were critical of the processes in mental health courtrooms and asserted that the defendants' rights were central to their practices. During hearings, however, I observed that their reservations and criticisms generally were not expressed. On the contrary, my fieldwork demonstrates fluidity and continuity between the claims of psychiatric and child welfare services institutions, the conduct of hearings, and judicial decisions.

The Courts' Adherence to the Psychiatric Paradigm

Procedural rules create conditions where hospital and child welfare service claims constitute the primary substance of courtroom debate, effectively silencing defendants' attempts to raise other matters. The procedural architecture of legal debate, in conjunction with evidentiary frameworks that privilege certain subjects and evidence while marginalizing others, produces the dominant judicial narrative on mental health. As I explained above, a significant portion of hearing time is devoted to evidence presented by psychiatrists, social workers, and possibly other experts. This primary evidence, introduce at the outset, form the cornerstone of the case, and defendants find themselves in situations where they must respond to allegations. They are caught in a logic of trial, even when the process is not adversarial.

However, evidence frequently remain fragmentary or relies exclusively on opinions that lack scientific foundation, which explain why psychiatric diagnostic, practice, and treatment controversies often fail to reach judicial consideration. The content of evidence varies greatly depending on the psychiatrists and social workers who employ different assessment methods and different methods of documenting their cases. Assessments of danger, threat, and incapacity therefore vary in content and in form but are received in the same manner by courts—that is, without questioning methods and foundations. While judges expressed concern about inadequate or incomplete evidence during formal interviews, ethnographic observations demonstrate that judges comment on evidentiary quality only infrequently and engage in only minimal questioning of psychiatrists and social workers regarding specific reports or testimony details. Judicial requests for supplementary evidence occur exceptionally rarely. Defense counsels replicate this pattern, infrequently challenging evidentiary adequacy despite encountering incomplete, dated, or legally non-compliant evidence.

The issue of evidence highlights a fundamental characteristic of mental health courtrooms and therapeutic jurisprudence more generally. First, these judicial processes rest on a therapeutic objective based on the premises of recovery theory or attachment theory, which I detailed in Chapter 4, without questioning their foundations. Second, the criteria of danger, threat, and incapacity are at the heart of judicial decisions despite their absence of legal foundation. Third, these criteria lack substantive clarity and escape legal professionals who must rely on psychiatrists and social workers for assessment. One might think this is not specific to mental health courtrooms; courts hear cases of all kinds in which the legal practitioners involved are not subject-matter experts, and several observers argue that courts defer their adjudicative power to expert witnesses (Canale, 2021; Sutherland, 2005; Skurka & Renzella, 1998; Stefan, 1992). In mental health courtrooms, however, the asymmetrical power dynamics between hospitals and child welfare services, which furnish the predominant evidence, and defendants, who generally possess only their own testimony, are exacerbated by psychiatric and social work professionals' characterizations of defendants as demonstrating "poor judgment" and "lack of insight," which erodes their testimonial credibility. Mental health courtrooms operate on psychiatric categorizations that construct defendants as unpredictable and threatening, incapable of making sound decisions for themselves, and in need of psychiatric treatment—creating an institutional bias that privileges the allegations made by hospitals and child welfare services. Thus, although psychiatrists and social workers provide opinions supported by minimal evidence on scientifically controversial subjects such as danger, threat, or incapacity, and despite their known affiliation with more or less security-oriented and interventionist schools of thought—explaining why psychiatrists, for instance, testify exclusively for either prosecution or defense in criminal matters, a reality with which legal practitioners are well acquainted—their opinions are almost invariably considered more credible than those of defendants, who base their testimony on lived experience. This pronounced tendency persists even when defendants are the sole possessors of knowledge regarding issues such as the adverse effects of psychiatric medication or of the electroconvulsive therapy. It should be noted that judges lack the capacity to assess the reliability and rigor of evaluations submitted to them, having no scientific training (Haack, 2004; Skurka & Renzella, 1998). Modifications to expert evidence admission rules in certain jurisdictions have not resolved this problem (Bernstein, 2007; Kovera et al., 2002; Gatowski et al., 2001).

Across all courtrooms examined, legislation mandates the requirement of professional opinions while simultaneously empowering judges to render decisions that contradict such professional assessments, particularly in matters concerning individual rights, with statutory interpretation favoring rights protection. Formal interviews clearly establish that in the eyes of judges, professional opinions constitute the valid evidence, and that it can only exceptionally be set aside in favor of lived experience. However, it is during hearings that the arbitration between professional opinions and lived experience takes shape. Defendants thus very often reported painful hospitalization experiences or debilitating adverse effects of medications. Many offered reasoned justifications for declining psychiatric consultations, psychiatric hospitalization, or psychiatric interventions, including pharmacological treatments or electroconvulsive therapy. They recount the trauma of seclusion rooms and straps used to restrain them; the weight gain, insomnia, and brain fog related to medication; the fact that psychiatric hospitalization and treatments did not help them feel better—experiences that resonate with scientific literature. These statements are often ignored or sometimes questioned or minimized. It is suggested, for example, that seclusion rooms are not used for no reason, implying that defendants would have deserved it;

that weight gain is a frivolous and superficial concern; or that no solution other than psychiatric treatments would be more appropriate. The fact that a psychiatrist or social worker asserted that the defendants' statements are false is generally sufficient for judges to agree with them.

Defendants' experience and knowledge are therefore not only ignored throughout the judicial process but are contested, denied, and devalued. It is often the case that defendants' words are used against them to show their "poor judgment" or "lack of insight." As if what they experience and understand from their psychiatric experience is wrong or false; this is indeed what some judges confided to me in interviews. For them, it is unlikely to hear that defendants could have been traumatized by coercive practices in psychiatry; they were convinced that there was an explanation, that they did not have the whole story, or were manipulated. Yet an increasingly significant part of the mental health literature makes room for lived experience, recognizing its importance and scope (Beresford & Russo, 2021; Faulkner, 2017). Apart from including experiential perspectives in legal and policy creation, some authors deem it essential for producing robust and meaningful mental health insights, in conjunction with professional knowledge (Russo, 2023; Veldmeijer et al., 2023; Sunkel & Sartor, 2022; Porter, 2013).

The tendency to devalue defendants' statements is not limited to their experiences with psychiatry or child welfare services. For instance, psychiatrists and social workers routinely describe situations, including incidents or defendants' lifestyle, which alone cannot justify their positions, yet help paint a problematic picture of the defendants. These assertions are rarely supported by evidence, as they are often reported by third parties—police officers, family members or others—who are absent. When defendants disputed these facts, or offered a different explanation or interpretation, they often face the same reaction by the court, which consider it to be either denial, lack of insight, or lies and manipulation. Judges rarely recognize that situations may be understood or experimented in multiple ways, or that coherent explanations could be offered. They rather approach psychiatrists' and social workers' words as confirmed truth rather than professional opinions, including concerning circumstances they have not personally observed.

As I have already briefly discussed in the two preceding chapters, defendants generally face a devaluing response from the court when they talk about the infringement of their rights and their experiences of discrimination. The courts readily embrace psychiatric interpretations of paranoia, lack of insight or manipulation when defendants describe for instance, being physically restrained after questioning their involuntary commitment, distrusting their social worker due to statements or behaviors suggesting classist, racist, sexist, or sanist prejudice, or when they articulate beliefs and preferences rooted in traditions or beliefs that diverge from the cultural norms of judicial actors. In some cases, these psychiatric explanations are not offered by social workers or psychiatrists, but are suggested by lawyers or judges, demonstrating the judicial actors' adherence to the psychiatric paradigm. In interviews, defense lawyers claimed to have developed "the necessary knowledge to understand and explain medical reports," and "to form their own idea of their clients' mental condition." In the exchanges I had with some of them during the hearing observations, they sometimes described their clients' behavior as "poor judgment," "paranoid," "delusional," or "lacking insight." The observations and interviews with judges demonstrate their weaker mental health knowledge base and understanding. However, they generally portray themselves as bearing ultimate authority and decisive power that must operate to strengthen the work and credibility of psychiatrists and social workers.

During hearings, judges verbally condemn what they saw as defiance of the authorities—be they psychiatric, police, child welfare, or judicial—and seek to reinforce the power of these authorities as much through their words as through their decisions. Multiple circumstances, including the mere exercise of fundamental rights, may be interpreted by courts as challenges to authority, including defendants articulating their positions or narrating their experiences during hearings—which represents, essentially, the standard procedure of legal proceedings intended to adjudicate between divergent claims. Situations may include contesting a diagnosis, refusing treatment, or attempting to negotiate medication dosage; failing to comply with instructions from police officers, immigration agents, or security guards; resisting police arrest or hospital restraint; or not complying with a court order. The explanations provided by defendants, even those based on the specific circumstances, generally do not constitute valid arguments from the courts' perspective. Judges rarely hesitate to rebuke defendants by insisting on the importance of complying on principle, and are sometimes particularly harsh in their attitude and decisions. A 23-year-old defendant with Tourette's syndrome whose predominant symptom consisted of screaming at two-to-three-second intervals, significantly impeding their ability to provide court testimony and who stopped their medication to take cannabis because, in their words, it "works better than medication and gives me some respite from my very invasive symptoms" was told by the judge that "the medication works very well" and that an involuntary commitment "will allow you to become aware of it;" a defendant who repeatedly asserted their "right to refuse medications" was told by a judge, "yes, until another judge decides otherwise;" a judge said about a defendant who refused to take their hands out of their pockets at a police officer's request that they "require behavioral containment" and orders detention for a year; a judge stated that a 15-year-old's non-attendance at school in violation of a court order constituted grounds for removal from the family "as a matter of principle," regardless of the family's ongoing efforts to find appropriate schooling that would meet their child's needs. The judge then explained to me that challenging the court's authority was unacceptable and indicated a need to "learn a lesson."

Not only do courts condemn what they see as open defiance of any authority, but they expect that defendants "fully cooperate" with psychiatrists, social workers, and professionals in general. The level of cooperation is therefore subjected to careful scrutiny, and defendants are often criticized for "mixed," "fluctuating," or "inconsistent" cooperation. Here too, the defendants' previous experiences, preferences, or opinions are given little consideration or are ignored. Rather, it is on the basis of the objectives set by the professionals themselves that the quality of cooperation is evaluated, and judges regularly ask psychiatrists or social workers whether the cooperation is "good" or "satisfactory." Not adhering to or questioning the psychiatric diagnosis and the treatment plan, the opinions expressed by social workers, or the recommendations of health or social services; seeking a second clinical opinion; refusing to engage in therapy; or "negotiating" medication dosage are regarded as lack of cooperation. To assess the level of cooperation, for example, judges ask direct questions to psychiatrists such as whether defendants "willingly take their medication, or if they bargain" and if they "reliably keep their appointments." But cooperation is also assessed beyond concrete behaviors, relying on professional impressions that defendants lack "true engagement" due to maintaining "their own vision of things" and therefore tend to "omit details" about their personal lives. Cooperation is deemed "excellent" or "exemplary" when defendants "conceal nothing" and proactively contact hospital or child welfare services "whenever any changes occur in their circumstances."

The narrative about mental health and defendants that unfolds in the courtroom revolves mainly around insight and cooperation, including full disclosure of one's personal life. Similar to what several other studies have highlighted (Beaupert & Brosnan, 2021; Brosnan & Flynn, 2017; Case, 2016), my observations show that psychiatrists, social workers, and experts not only appeal to patients' lack of insight to explain non-cooperation but also, using circular reasoning, talk about non-cooperation as evidence of lack of insight. Lack of insight is a central element of the evidence, even though it is not part of the legal criteria, as it is associated with a certain incapacity to understand and make sound decisions, and thus with unpredictability and, consequently, risk. The pattern whereby psychiatrists and social workers initially establish, through their testimony, the lack of cooperation, and consequently the lack of insight, after which defendants' statements are construed as evidence of the lack of insight, is commonly observed. That pattern undermined defendants' credibility and capacity for defense, while also strengthening the power dynamics that preceded the hearings and will persist subsequently. These findings are in line with those made by Merrick D. Pilling and colleagues in their study of 120 medical records:

> Psychiatrists use insight as a discursive means to delegitimize patient perspectives that diverge from the medical model of mental illness, particularly those that are more likely to be held by marginalized people, such as cultural or spiritual beliefs about sources of distress, and trauma narratives. Patients who expressed the logics and lived realities of white, middle

class, male heteronormativity were often accorded more respect and were more likely to be perceived as insightful. (Pilling et al., 2018: 192)

Therefore, courtroom observation demonstrates, as Eleonora Rossero (2023) observed in a psychiatric hospital ethnography, that coercion becomes masked, through discursive processes around "therapeuticization," "relationalization," and "proceduralization," as pathological symptoms such as denial, disorganization, paranoia, or lack of insight. Refusing treatment or intervention—though a right—is framed as lack of cooperation, thus shifting the discourse into the relational register. The use of coercion then appear as a consequence of the defendants' refusal to seriously engage in therapeutic relationships, and legal proceedings function to authenticate its legitimacy and security. The imperative for therapy is assumed, arising both from lack of insight and from non-cooperation.

Due to their therapeutic dimension, these legal proceedings have been profoundly changing the meaning and role of legal actors and courts. Both formal interviews and court observations highlighted how lawyers and judges have transgressed the roles they traditionally play to take on the role of intermediary between defendants and psychiatrists or social workers, advocating for recovery or attachment theories. For many, their role is to give space to defendants so that they "feel like they've been listened to," while fostering the therapeutic relationship with psychiatrists or social workers and encouraging cooperation. Lawyers and judges thus often seek to convince defendants of the need for hospitalization, detention, care, or social intervention, giving them advice of a personal nature often well outside the scope of legal proceedings. They sometimes directly ask defendants what they could do to get them to consent. Consistent with the opinions of psychiatrists and social workers, lawyers and judges insist on four elements: (1) the need to comply with the therapeutic recommendations, (2) the need to cooperate completely and therefore to refrain from expressing disagreement or different personal opinions, (3) to abstain from drugs and alcohol, and 4) to find a job and lead an active life. According to legal practitioners, these elements are as much a guarantee of good mental health as they are of mitigating risks.

In interviews, several judges strongly expressed their belief in the positive and transformative potential of the judicial process and court orders to enhance defendants' mental health, while managing their risk. They argued that the authority of the court could persuade reluctant defendants to accept measures they would otherwise refuse. This perspective is illustrated by a judge discussing involuntary commitments:

> That's why, for me, it's important to gain the person [defendant]'s consent. I don't always succeed, but I often do. Often. Because of the court's authority, the whole decorum, the fact that I am a judge. In society, judges are somewhat perceived as the fathers and mothers of society, right? We are kind of like the parents of society. So, there is that authority that plays a role.

In interviews, many judges spoke of the therapeutic significance of their work, of the fact that they believed the court process can have beneficial effects on defendants' therapeutic relationships with their psychiatrist or social worker, not the least because the court plays, as one judge asserted, "the role of the villain." While judges decide on and order the use of coercion and psychiatrists and social workers formally only carry out court orders, many judges imagined that their decisions help persuade the defendants that their psychiatrist or social worker is not responsible for the coercion, thus preserving the therapeutic relationship. Legal proceedings thus become a "lever" for care and social intervention teams who use the court to relieve themselves of formal accountability for the decision to employ coercion. However, this legalistic approach is at odds with the experience of several defendants and psychiatrists. Observations and interviews show that defendants do not cope well with what psychiatrists and social workers say about them during hearings. Pre-hearing preparation differ substantially based on the involved psychiatrists and social workers, as some dedicate time to explaining their professional opinion and report to defendants, whereas others offer no such briefing. Some defendants are therefore taken by surprise during hearings, especially as their lawyers do not always have the time to go over the details of the evidence with them. Many regard the fact that their psychiatrists and social workers share certain information as betrayal, as they revealed things that the defendants confided in them believing that their confidentiality would be respected, or that they were there to help them. Several psychiatrists confirmed that after court hearings, the bond of trust is broken and needs to be rebuilt.

Judges generally do not regard defendants as legitimate parties within mental health courtrooms. Beyond the labels they apply to describe them—"patients," "sick individuals," "persons with mental illness"—this stance manifest most clearly through actions and verbal communication during hearings. Under the guise of the informality required to "individualize the judicial process," judges may be both familiar and authoritarian toward the defendants. They lecture them, show empathy or, on the contrary, are cold and brittle, depending on their own assessment of the defendants' needs. In other words, the fact that judges do not see defendants as parties helped them to step out of their traditional role as adjudicators and offer their opinions on the right way to live, on mental health, and on treatments. In formal interviews, several of them justified this departure from their traditional role in the name of defendants' "right to treatment." Without acknowledging that this constitutes no legally sanctioned right, the right-to-treatment rhetoric—with medication at its core—permeates the entirety of judicial proceedings to advance defendants' best interests as defined by the judges themselves.

The Poor, the Risk, and the Pill

Of the four mental health courtrooms investigated, only the one where civil proceedings for involuntary treatment take place is where treatment can legally be imposed on defendants. Yet treatment, and more specifically medication, is the most recurrent topic in every courtroom I have been in, and the course of discussions regularly suggest that treatment has been ordered by the court. It is implicit in the narrative develop during court hearings that psychiatric drugs are a means of containing risks, whatever they may be, or improving parental capacities or capacity to consent to treatment. Medication is regarded as a kind of guarantee against problematic behavior, whether violent acts or inappropriate lifestyles. It controls mood swings and anger, prevents aggressiveness and soothes distress, and is therefore regarded as prerequisite for a return to a "normal" or acceptable life. Treatment compliance is thus view by psychiatrists, social workers, and judicial actors as the key to improved cooperation, understanding of the importance of abstaining from drugs and alcohol, and engagement in active life. It is therefore the most important requirement placed upon defendants.

In numerous instances, the central concern driving the proceedings is not the specific therapeutic approach (which medications are to be prescribed) but rather securing defendants' acceptance not merely that they must undergo treatment, but that they must do so indefinitely. The court's first concern is therefore to determine whether the defendants are genuinely complying with the treatments. Simply following medication regimens do not necessarily represent real therapeutic adherence, and the court examines whether defendants are willingly participating in treatment or acquiescing only due to judicial coercion—including where the court has no formal power to order involuntary treatment. Wanting to negotiate the dosage of a medication, or expressing a preference for one medication over another, are indications of potentially poor compliance in the eyes of the court. Sometimes, the clues to a defendant's true willingness to undergo treatment are more subtle, based on the impressions of psychiatrists, social workers, lawyers, or family members. When psychiatrists are present in the courtroom—for involuntary treatment and before the Review Board—they describe how their treatment-related conversations with defendants play out. They report the defendants' comments on adverse effects, their attempts to negotiate, and of course their refusal to take medications. When psychiatrists are not present, other witnesses give their opinion on the matter. In child welfare cases, the court often have no direct evidence. Social workers could invoke in their report and testimony psychiatric diagnoses without evidence of a physician's diagnosis—in Quebec, social workers are not authorized to make diagnoses. When these diagnoses are mentioned, the conversation turn to the need for the defendant to consult a psychiatrist and take medication to protect their children. These diagnoses and the need for psychiatric treatment are then reflected in court decisions, and even if they do not contain formal orders for psychiatric consultation, follow-up, or treatment, they formalize the psychiatric dimension of the case. This practice has implications for subsequent involvement with child welfare services, which will require psychiatric monitoring and treatment, but it can also affect defendants' interactions with other social institutions or judicial processes, as the diagnoses are taken for granted. Defense lawyers criticize this practice, as it requires them to challenge the diagnoses provided in social workers' reports. Such challenges are not necessarily covered by legal aid, which can explain their rarity. In involuntary commitment hearings, hospital attorneys could present arguments drawing from medical documentation that have not been formally entered as evidence or relying on discussions with nursing staff. In both child welfare cases and involuntary commitments, the court often lack direct evidence and readily defer to the statements of social workers and lawyers without any verification.

Defense lawyers frequently intervene on the issue of treatment compliance. They report having spoken with their clients and, for example, state that they are now willing to take medication or that they understand the importance of doing so. Court observations show that they regularly discuss treatment with their clients—even when it is not the focus of the legal proceedings, and even when the evidence presented by the hospital or child welfare services do not center on that issue. In formal interviews, defense lawyers acknowledge the judicial emphasis on medication compliance and report preparing their clients to respond to this expectation. During hearing, they try to use their clients' commitment to treatment compliance as evidence of good faith and cooperation, as well as a bargaining tool—for instance, to reduce the number of days of involuntary commitment, to obtain conditional release, or to allow more frequent contact between defendants and their children. Although this type of strategy is routine in criminal cases for plea and sentence bargaining, it is particularly striking within civil or administrative judicial contexts, where punishment is not the objective. This reveals that, in mental health courtrooms, defendants are treated as if they are at fault and must therefore prove their commitment to change. Observations and interviews with the judges confirm that some of them consider that the defendants' presence in court is due to their "bad actions," or "bad decisions," and that it is up to the court—using its authority—to make them accept, or not to challenge, their responsibility to change. They also view medication as a kind of insurance policy against these behaviors and decisions. Interviews with defense lawyers point in the same direction, showing that most of them believe treatment is often necessary for their clients and regard their role as helping to convince them to comply. In their view, encouraging clients to maintain medication compliance will reduce their trajectory toward repeat court involvement. They do not necessarily see their role as voicing their clients' wishes in court, especially when those wishes are seen as "unreasonable" or "unrealistic," but rather as protecting their clients' best interests and those of society. This means fully cooperating with psychiatrists and social workers and accepting the therapeutic measures they recommend—starting with medication—without challenging them.

Family members of defendants occasionally attend proceedings, typically to provide testimony favoring the hospital or child welfare services, or at minimum to adopt a cooperative stance with these institutions. They commonly speak about medication, voicing endorsement and illustrating—through specific instances—how medication aids defendants or provides their family with peace of mind. They also convey their observations concerning treatment compliance, including whether they consider it sincere. Like psychiatrists and social workers, they base these impressions on behavior or statements made by defendants, but also on their intimate knowledge of them. Family members often present themselves as "experts" on the defendants' illness and treatment, stating, for instance, that even when they do not know whether the defendants are taking their medication, they can tell just by observing their behavior. They often agree to monitor the defendants by being present when they take their medication and by reporting to the psychiatrists if they do not. The family's involvement in monitoring defendants can sometimes be decisive—for example, judges may deny requests for involuntary commitment based on relatives' engagement to supervise medication intake. The surveillance carry out by families around medication can also extend to everyday life, including monitoring diet, leisure activities, and alcohol or drug use. Although only rarely, some families reported controlling the defendants' movements or having installed surveillance cameras throughout the house, stating, for example, that "in our home, it's worse than in prison."

Several reasons explain defendants' resistance to medication, ranging from a refusal to recognize the psychiatric diagnosis—and therefore the need for medication—to debilitating adverse effects. Despite the notable difference between these two types of arguments, courts most often reach similar conclusions about the defendant's lack of insight and about the risks associated with it. In the case of reluctance to acknowledge the psychiatric diagnosis, defendants generally offer explanations that differ from the psychiatric interpretations given to their personal situation, or recent events. Their statements often contradict those provided by third parties such as neighbors, police officers, or relatives, who are absent during the hearing but whose accounts are included in the reports and testimonies of psychiatrists and social workers. This is particularly true in cases involving complex or tense family relationships. Defendants often find themselves trying to explain family disputes or distant, sometimes dramatic, past events. These statements, even when realistic, are usually unsupported by evidence and are thus most often interpreted as evidence of paranoia. Defendants sometimes report having seen the psychiatrist for only about fifteen minutes, claim that another psychiatrist gave them a different diagnosis, or challenge the facts used by psychiatrists to make their diagnosis. Here again, the defendants' claims confirm in the eyes of the court the defendants' lack of insight and are most often doomed to fail. Nonetheless, there are instances where defendants succeed in demonstrating the accuracy of their assertions. One example involved a defendant for whom an involuntary commitment was being sought based on "grandiose delusions" and "loss of contact with reality" partly because of their claim that they had a degree from Harvard University—only for the claim to be confirmed by the defendant's sister during the hearing. These situations, however, are not typical, as most defendants have neither witnesses nor tangible evidence to support their assertions. They nonetheless show that third parties are typically deemed more trustworthy than defendants concerning their own experiences and personal lives.

However, it is rare for defendants to completely deny having personal or psychological difficulties. During hearings, some report traumatic events or describe the hardships of their daily lives. Others say they need help but explain that what psychiatry offers them do not suit them or is not what they are looking for. Several defendants indicate that they have attempted to obtain psychiatric services voluntarily but have failed; some of them were, at the time of the hearings, on waiting lists for services they wish to obtain. Numerous defendants explicitly express their desire to access particular types of services—predominantly psychotherapy. In interview, judges reported experiencing powerlessness when encountering such help-seeking requests. They are bound to rule on petitions with minimal flexibility to suggest alternative solutions, and moreover, psychotherapy access remains severely restricted in Canada's public healthcare system, requiring private insurance plans. Unlike the mental health professionals, social workers, legal counsel, and judicial officers functioning in mental health courtrooms, most defendants lack private healthcare access. They face not only the restricted availability of psychotherapy but also exclusion from the growing range of medical treatments now deliver through the alternative private healthcare sector. Hence, in many circumstances, medication emerge as the predominant—if not sole— therapeutic option available within mental health courtrooms.

Refusal of medication based on adverse effects is much more common than refusal of diagnosis. Most often, defendants have already taken psychiatric medication and sometimes have tried several. In some cases, they agree to take medication but refuse the one prescribed by their psychiatrist or the method of administration, such as long-acting injections. Defendants report documented adverse effects such as loss of energy and fatigue, weight gain that is disabling and harmful to their health, as well as disturbances in sleep, concentration, appetite, and libido. These adverse effects have real impacts on their daily lives and on their ability to carry out activities, including the ability to work, study, care for children, and, in some cases, live independently. These arguments are most often minimized or treated as a lesser evil, even as exaggeration. Sometimes psychiatrists claim that the adverse effects reported by defendants are not real or are insignificant. In cases involving electroconvulsive therapy (ECT), where defendants' situations are presented as severe and likely to deteriorate, defendants report adverse effects such as memory loss, which are in some cases denied by psychiatrists and by the court (Bernheim, Ferron-Parayre & Gauthier-Boiteau, 2025). The side effects described by defendants regarding medication and electroconvulsive therapy are comprehensively documented in scientific studies that are never presented to the court. Much like the harm associated with court orders—which is considered minor for defendants who are not employed or are not professionals as discussed in Chapter 5—the harm caused by adverse effects is downplayed throughout the judicial process. It is rare for the court to seriously attempt to understand the consequences of these adverse effects or to consider alternatives to a specific psychiatric medication or to psychiatric medication in general (Boyle, Walsh & Nelson, 2021).

The evidence supporting the appropriateness of medication relies entirely on the opinion and experience of psychiatrists. The court do not require medical evidence, nor do defense lawyers typically raise it as an argument—even when the list of prescribed medications resembled a "cocktail." Yet, as explained in Chapter 2, there are numerous scientific controversies regarding the effectiveness of psychiatric medications, and their adverse effects are well documented and have been the subject of successful class-action lawsuits brought by patient advocacy groups. The practice of the judiciary of relying on the reports of psychiatrists and social workers, observed by other researchers in different jurisdictions (Boyle, Walsh & Nelson, 2021; Jobling, 2019; Henwood, 2008; Hiday, 1981), raises concerns about the fairness of judicial procedures targeting marginalized social groups within a context of psychiatric coercion. Not only are the hearings short and expedited, with evidence often made available only at the last minute and defense lawyers working under difficult conditions, but judicial decisions are also made without considering fundamental scientific data.

Moreover, I have observed that courts regularly go beyond their jurisdiction, especially when it comes to medication—which is documented in other studies (Jobling, 2019; Thom & Nakarada-Kordic, 2014). As previously mentioned, in the investigated mental health courtrooms, only involuntary treatment hearings can legally result in an order to take medication against a person's will. Nevertheless, I have observed—and case law confirms—that other mental health courtrooms routinely include medication in their rulings, either explicitly or implicitly. In involuntary commitment cases, judges sometimes wrote in their decisions that the purpose of the commitment is to begin or continue treatment. In child welfare cases, the court could recommend—or even order—parents to see a psychiatrist and take psychiatric medication. The Review Board regularly order defendants to "comply with treatment teams' recommendations."

An analysis of my observation fieldnotes from the four mental health courtrooms investigated, supplemented by interviews with judges and lawyers, reveals that the central objective of these legal proceedings is to secure defendants' compliance with psychiatric medication—in certain cases, by maintaining ongoing judicial oversight. From the perspective of judicial actors, medication is positioned as an instrument for regulating defendants' conduct and judgment, purportedly to address diverse risks. Medication therefore functions, in effect, to expand judicial authority and surveillance over defendants beyond hospital boundaries into their everyday existence. It is further portrayed as a vehicle for encouraging individual responsibility and motivating defendants to accept their need for transformation. A refusal to take medication—though constituting a valid assertion of rights—is interpreted not only as evidence of mental disorder, but also as moral deficiency, suggesting defendants are avoiding accountability for their personal health and for public safety.

The narrative that emerges from mental health courtrooms is considerably reductive, if not fundamentally simplistic—connecting mental health, risk, and medication in an unchallenged causal sequence. This narrative ignores scientific debates and controversies, defendants' lived experiences and viewpoints and their legal rights, as well as the structural issues that run through these legal processes. In this setting, medication assumes "magical" properties—serving as both a risk-management tool and accountability mechanism, while justifying varied judicial strategies designed to compromise defendants' self-governance and autonomy.

Judicial Strategies for Thwarting Treatment Refusal

Observation of court proceedings revealed that courts employ strategies to lead defendants to relinquish their right to consent to treatment—and, by extension, their right to refuse treatment. As in psychiatric settings, where formal and informal coercion coexist (Rossero, 2023; Oaks, 2011; Szmukler & Appelbaum, 2008), judicial practices operate along a spectrum that ranges from explicit forms of coercion to more implicit mechanisms.

Defendants' consent is rarely addressed directly during hearings—instead, it is framed in terms of cooperation. Information regarding defendants' willingness to cooperate is assessed through the testimony of psychiatrists, social workers, and occasionally lawyers—without first establishing whether the standards for free and informed consent have been met. Courts do not verify whether complete information about the mental health condition and proposed treatment—including its benefits, risks, the risk of not being treated, and available alternatives—has been conveyed in accessible language, nor do they ensure that defendants are not subject to undue pressure. Similarly, during hearings, no clear information on treatment is offered to defendants, even when it is one of the main topics of conversation.

Paradoxically, it is not uncommon for judges to ask defendants directly what could be done to persuade them to consent to treatment, or to state that they would endorse a therapeutic plan if the defendant are to give their consent. As such, negotiations could take place during hearings to convince defendants to accept measures that they initially refuse, such as medication, ECT, psychiatric supervision and, in child protection matters, parenting competency workshops, social worker household visits, and monitored parent-child contact. Judges could seek to identify the specific points of resistance expressed by defendants and encouraged hospitals or child welfare services to offer alternative proposals, or to withdraw certain therapeutic demands in exchange for agreement on others. Judges also sometimes suggest that the hearing be suspended to allow time for the parties to reach a settlement. These practices could occur even when the court formally recognizes the defendant's incapacity to consent to treatment or, in child protection matters, their parental incapacity. Through this process, legal proceedings recognize the consent of someone adjudicated as incapable—even when the agreement pertains exactly to the matter on which incapacity was adjudicated. Certain judges describe this practice as a therapeutic technique, aimed at safeguarding or reestablishing trust between defendants and their psychiatrist or social workers.

Sometimes, defendants' consent, whether expressed in the courtroom or beforehand, is considered to be "strategic consent," and therefore a "false" consent. A few court hearings took place after the defendants had accepted the proposed therapeutic measures. In other cases, consent was expressed during the hearings, usually following testimony from psychiatrists or social workers. Consent was considered strategic when it followed hesitation, or when defendants had in the past consented to care but had not "kept their word"—even though legally, consent to treatment is non-binding and may be revoked at any moment. According to social workers, psychiatrists, defense lawyers and judges, the purpose of strategic consent would be to avoid court orders. Here too, the court rely on the interpretation of psychiatrists and social workers, and the mere allegation of strategic consent makes the courts wary of the defendants' word.

Generally, courts employ four strategies to lead defendants to relinquish their own will—and, by extension, their right to consent to care: threat, undue pressure, paternalism, and confusion. Threats are expressed openly by both lawyers and judges. For example, in private meetings before hearings, defense lawyers may tell their clients that if they do not cooperate with their psychiatrist or social worker, their hospitalization or the placement of their children will be prolonged. Hospital lawyers may announce during hearings that a petition for involuntary treatment will be filed with the court if the defendant continues to refuse treatment. Judges may make dramatic declarations, such as warning defendants that if they do not cooperate, they will go "from hospital to prison," but that if they do cooperate, they will "live a normal life." Defense attorneys, whether in interviews or during hearing observations, generally fail to advocate for their clients' right to consent to or refuse treatment when faced with arguments from hospital lawyer, child welfare services, or judges. Rather, they voice the perspective that the faster defendants conform, the more they will avoid the wider effects of legal involvement and psychiatric coercion.

Undue pressure is exerted by judges, who assert that judicial measures cannot be lifted until defendants comply with treatment in contexts where the court lacks jurisdiction over treatment decisions, be it in involuntary commitment, child welfare, and Review Board cases. This practice is widespread in Review Board and child welfare proceedings, where judges incorporate treatment-related factors into their decisions and maintain these considerations across successive hearings. Defendants whom the court credits with making considerable progress but who maintain treatment resistance are nevertheless perceived as constituting an unmanageable risk threshold. Judges subsequently voice "concerns," reference ongoing "instability," and advise defendants to embrace treatment before the subsequent hearing to expect a different verdict. In involuntary commitment cases, judges may declare, for example, that they might have rejected the petition—or that the duration of involuntary detention could have been reduced—had the defendant consented to medication.

Paternalistic strategies are predominantly displayed by judges, though they can also be witnessed among certain defense attorneys. Frequently invoking what psychiatrists and social workers "consider beneficial," through declarations such as "everyone here seeks your best interests," they reframe judicial proceedings in therapeutic language while actually concealing the underlying coercion. This approach portrays the courts as advocating for defendants while presenting judges as distinguished and commanding figures. Some defense lawyers voice their personal convictions during proceedings about what they consider beneficial for their clients, often citing the duration of their professional relationship and asserting their dedication to defendants' welfare, while expressing convictions that occasionally differ from defendants' preferences. In interviews, these attorneys explained that offering their opinion to the court constitutes part of their ethical responsibility to prioritize clients' well-being, even when this assessment contradicts received instructions. In their view, mental health legal work diverges from standard legal practice and permits—or even necessitates—such approaches. Nevertheless, this interpretation contradicts the ethical and professional standards governing legal practice; I will address this issue more comprehensively in the next chapter. Judges typically do not object to this practice. Some express gratitude for the contributions of defense lawyers and overlook the disconnect between their stated opinions and their clients' directives. In certain cases, judges and defense lawyers jointly discuss the well-being of defendants in front of them. In others, judges reprimand defendants for their "lack of maturity" or "lack of willpower," expressing the hope that they will "finally take responsibility for themselves." After hearings, psychiatrists may reiterate the judge's statements in efforts to convince defendants to consent to treatment. In interviews, some psychiatrists explained that the fact that the judge does not know the defendant personally, combined with the prestige and authority of the court, makes judicial statements particularly persuasive for some defendants.

Confusion concerning the courts' actual authority is generated and maintained by several legal practitioners, psychiatrists, and social workers. Most proceedings occur without providing defendants with clear explanations about the hearings' purpose, applicable legal criteria, or relevant legal framework. Regarding treatment, multiple elements foster the impression that courts possess decision-making authority: treatment constitutes the most consistently addressed subject during hearings; judicial participants continually stress its significance, and defendants are informed that treatment refusal will directly influence judicial decisions. In numerous instances, judges make declarations that could lead someone without legal training to believe that involuntary treatment has been ordered.

This confusion is maintained after the hearings, as the practices of psychiatric institutions and child welfare services are not always consistent with the legal framework and judicial orders, as reported by defense lawyers. It should be noted that the staff of these institutions receive little legal training, particularly regarding its technical and procedural aspects. In formal interviews, psychiatrists affirmed they have difficulty obtaining clear legal information from their hospital's legal services, and my discussions with professionals during fieldwork observations confirm widespread misunderstanding of court authorities, especially regarding involuntary treatment. Multiple psychiatrists and nurses mistakenly believed defendants could receive involuntary medication under Review Board authority, while social workers wrongly assumed parents must comply with Youth Division treatment orders.

Defense lawyers indicated that their clients often struggle to understand the limits of judicial power and the scope of the orders issued against them—particularly when multiple orders are involved. In interviews, they described how defendants often repeatedly believe they are legally mandated to undergo therapy, even though this may not be legally accurate. They point out that even when the court holds no power over treatment, non-compliance still generates substantial legal consequences, as judges consider treatment refusal in their decisions. Defendants therefore keenly understand that recovering their children's custody, shortening detention or involuntary hospitalization periods, or otherwise enhancing their legal position, necessitates therapeutic compliance. Contributing to these pressures is the judiciary's symbolic authority, with the courtroom experience itself frequently causing intense anxiety for defendants.

Mental health courtroom ethnographic observation demonstrates that judicial practices, rather than functioning as protective mechanisms for rights, frequently expand and consolidate the institutional frameworks of psychiatric and child welfare systems. Beyond psychiatric paradigm adherence, the therapeutic justice approach reconfigures—and deforms—core legal principles, including treatment consent rights, making them pliable and substantively hollow. Treatment consent—a key rights battlefield in psychiatry in recent decades—has become ceremonial rather than meaningful, effectively remaining beyond reach for marginalized populations facing psychiatric coercion under right-to-treatment rhetoric. The practical denial of treatment refusal through judicial means, eliminating genuine autonomy, alongside the corporeal violence of psychiatric coercion, defines judicial narratives of alterity. These narratives reveal the existence of an "other" who may be coerced in the name of a treatment right that belongs exclusively to them.

References

Beaupert, F., & Brosnan, L. (2021). Weaponizing absent knowledges: Countering the violence of mental health law. In B. Russo & J. Sweeney (Eds.), *The Routledge international handbook of mad studies* (pp. 119–131). Routledge.

Beresford, P., & Russo, J. (Eds.) (2021). The Routledge international handbook of mad studies. Routledge.

Bernheim, E. (2024a, November 14). *Why involuntary admission and treatment won't solve homelessness. The Conversation Canada*. https://theconversation.com/why-involuntary-medical-admission-and-treatment-wont-solve-homelessness-243428 (accessed August 9, 2025).

Bernheim, E. (2024b). Extending the boundaries of the psychiatric hospital: The use and misuse of psychiatric coercion during the Covid-19 pandemic in Quebec and Ontario. In Flood, C., Chen, Y.Y. B., Deonandan, R., Halabi, S. & S. Thériault (Eds.), *Borders, Boundaries and Pandemics*, Routledge (pp. 273–280). doi:https://doi.org/10.4324/9781003394006.

Bernheim, E., Ferron-Parayre, A., & Gauthier-Boiteau, D. (2025). To consent and to refuse electroconvulsive therapy: A study of consent documents and court orders in the province of Quebec. *Canada. Ethical Human Psychology & Psychiatry, 27*(1), 25–45. https://doi.org/10.1891/EHPP-2024-0011

Bernstein, D. E. (2007). Expert witnesses, adversarial bias, and the (partial) failure of the Daubert revolution. *Iowa Law Review, 93*, 451–490.

Boyle, S., Walsh, T., & Nelson, L. (2021). A study into the operation of the Queensland mental health review tribunal. *Medical Law Review, 29*(1), 106–127. https://doi.org/10.1093/medlaw/fwaa043

Brosnan, L., & Flynn, E. (2017). Freedom to negotiate: A proposal extricating "capacity" from "consent." International Journal of Law in Context, 13(1), 58–76. doi:https://doi.org/10.1017/S1744552316000471.

Canale, D. (2021). The opacity of law: On the hidden impact of experts' opinion on legal decision-making. *Law and Philosophy, 40*(5), 509–543. https://doi.org/10.1007/s10982-021-09408-8

Case, P. (2016). Dangerous liaisons? Psychiatry and law in the court of protection—Expert discourses of "insight" (and "compliance"). *Medical Law Review, 24*(3), 360–378. https://doi.org/10.1093/medlaw/fww027

Faulkner, A. (2017). Survivor research and mad studies: The role and value of experiential knowledge in mental health research. *Disability & Society, 32*(4), 500–520. https://doi.org/10.1080/09687599.2017.1302320

Fazel, S., Singh, J. P., Doll, H., & Grann, M. (2012). Use of risk assessment instruments to predict violence and antisocial behaviour in 73 samples involving 24 827 people: Systematic review and meta-analysis. *BMJ, 345*, e4692. https://doi.org/10.1136/bmj.e4692

Gatowski, S., Dobbin, S. A., Richardson, J. T., Ginsburg, G., Merlino, M. L., & Dahir, V. (2001). Asking the gatekeepers: A National Survey of judges on judging expert evidence in a post-*Daubert* world. *Law and Human Behavior, 25*(5), 433–458. https://doi.org/10.1023/A:1012899030937

Haack, S. (2004). Truth and justice, inquiry and advocacy, science and law. *Ratio Juris, 17*(1), 15–26. https://doi.org/10.1111/j.0952-1917.2004.00252.x

Henwood, B. (2008). Involuntary inpatient commitment in the context of mental health recovery. *American Journal of Psychiatric Rehabilitation, 11*(3), 253–266. https://doi.org/10.1080/15487760802186337

Hiday, V. A. (1981). Court decisions in civil commitment: Independence or deference? *International Journal of Law and Psychiatry, 4*(1–2), 159–170. https://doi.org/10.1016/0160-2527(81)90026-1

Hood, C. (1991). A public Management for all Season? *Public Administration, 69*(1), 3–19. https://doi.org/10.1111/j.1467-9299.1991.tb00779.x

Jobling, H. (2019). The legal oversight of community treatment orders: A qualitative analysis of tribunal decision-making. *International Journal of Law and Psychiatry, 62*, 95–103. https://doi.org/10.1016/j.ijlp.2018.12.002

Kovera, M. B., Russano, M. B., & McAuliff, B. D. (2002). Assessment of the commonsense psychology underlying Daubert: Legal decision makers' abilities to evaluate expert evidence in hostile work environment cases. *Psychology, Public Policy, and Law, 8*(2), 180.

Lesse, S. (1982). The psychiatrist in court-theatre of the absurd. *American Journal of Psychotherapy, 36*(3), 287–291. https://doi.org/10.1176/appi.psychotherapy.1982.36.3.287

Oaks, D. W. (2011). The moral imperative for dialogue with organizations of survivors of coerced psychiatric human rights violations. In Kallert, T. W., Mezzich, J. E. & Monahan, J. (Eds.), *Coercive treatment in psychiatry: Clinical, legal and ethical aspects* (pp. 185–211). doi:https://doi.org/10.1002/9780470978573.

Pilling, M. D., Daley, A., Gibson, M. F., Ross, L. E., Zaheer, J. (2018). Assessing "insight," determining agency and autonomy: Implicating social identities. In Kilty, J., Dej, E. (Eds.), Containing madness: Gender and "Psy" in institutional contexts (pp. 191–213). Palgrave Macmillan. doi:https://doi.org/10.1007/978-3-319-89749-3_9.

Porter, D. (2013). Establishing normative validity for scientific psychiatric nosology: The significance of integrating patient perspectives. In J. Paris & J. Phillips (Eds.), *Making the DSM-5: Concepts and controversies* (pp. 63–74). Springer. https://doi.org/10.1007/978-1-4614-6504-1_5

Reyes, M. (2017). Danger! The Defendant is "Disturbed." Risks of Using Psychiatric Assessments to Predict Future Dangerousness. Connecticut Public Interest Law Journal, 17, 141–168.

Russo, J. (2023). Psychiatrization, assertions of epistemic justice, and the question of agency. *Frontiers in Sociology, 8*, 1092298. https://doi.org/10.3389/fsoc.2023.1092298

Skurka, S., & Renzella, E. (1998). Misplaced trust: The courts' reliance on the behavioural sciences. *Canadian Criminal Law Review, 3*, 269–284.

Stefan, S. (1992). Leaving civil rights to the experts: From deference to abdication under the professional judgment standard. *Yale Law Journal, 102*, 639–718.

Sunkel, C., & Sartor, C. (2022). Perspectives: Involving persons with lived experience of mental health conditions in service delivery, development and leadership. *BJPsych Bulletin, 46*(3), 160–164. https://doi.org/10.1192/bjb.2021.51

Sutherland, E. E. (2005). Undue deference to experts syndrome. *Indiana International & Comparative Law Review, 16*, 375–422.

Swanson, J. W., McGinty, E. E., Fazel, S., & Mays, V. M. (2015). Mental illness and reduction of gun violence and suicide: Bringing epidemiologic research to policy. *Annals of Epidemiology, 25*(5), 366–376. https://doi.org/10.1016/j.annepidem.2014.03.004

Szmukler, G., & Appelbaum, P. S. (2008). Treatment pressures, leverage, coercion, and compulsion in mental health care. *Journal of Mental Health, 17*(3), 233–244. https://doi.org/10.1080/09638230802052203

Thom, K., & Nakarada-Kordic, I. (2014). Mental health review tribunals in action: A systematic review of the empirical literature. *Psychiatry, Psychology and Law, 21*(1), 112–126. https://doi.org/10.1080/13218719.2013.790004

Veldmeijer, L., Terlouw, G., Van Os, J., Van Dijk, O., & Van't Veer, J., & Boonstra, N. (2023). The involvement of service users and people with lived experience in mental health care innovation through design: Systematic review. *JMIR mental health, 10*, e46590. https://doi.org/10.2196/46590

Wangmo, T., Seaward, H., Pageau, F., Hiersemenzel, L. P., & Elger, B. S. (2021). Forensic-psychiatric risk evaluations: Perspectives of forensic psychiatric experts and older incarcerated persons from Switzerland. *Frontiers in Psychiatry, 12*, 643096. https://doi.org/10.3389/fpsyt.2021.643096

White House. (2025, July 24). *Ending crime and Disorder on America's Streets*. Executive Orders. https://www.whitehouse.gov/presidential-actions/2025/07/ending-crime-and-disorder-on-americas-streets/(accessed August 9, 2025).

8
The Judicial Violence

I enter the room, which is small and dirty. It is a storage area where a table and chairs have been placed in the middle of the place. The room is extremely depressing. In addition to being tucked away at the end of what feels like a labyrinthian "madhouse," both the corridor and the staff area, as well as the room we are in, are dilapidated and in need of cleaning and a fresh coat of paint. I feel great discomfort. I can't believe this place even exists. It feels anachronistic and nightmarish. To park someone here is to condemn them to an ill fate. How can you stay sane (if that really means anything) in a place like this? It seems to me that if you are not out of your mind when you arrive, you quickly become so. The difference compared to first time I came here is that I now know the Review Board better. The attitude of the judges, their questions, their smiles, their comments.—Excerpt of personal observation notes, Review Board hearing, Department of Psychiatry, General Hospital.

What I have come to understand through my research is that the "mental health crisis" is in fact a crisis of inequality, domination, and power relationships. Beyond the traditional structures of domination—of elites over marginalized people, wealthy over poor, white over

E. Bernheim, *Therapeutic (In)justice and the Shadow Carceral State*, The Politics of Mental Health and Illness, https://doi.org/10.1007/978-3-032-16186-4_8

racialized, men over women—what takes place in mental health courtrooms is a struggle to preserve privilege and uphold the status quo. It is a contest over who holds the authority to define what is right, good, and moral. The judicial narrative on mental health is, above all, a discourse on who the bearers of legitimate experiences and opinions are, and on who is entitled to exercise authority and coercion over whom. It does not concern itself with alleviating suffering or providing support to those in need. It remains silent on the structural neglect faced by marginalized populations. And it generally does not engage with the question of rights.

The "mental health crisis" is, in practice, a "rights crisis." Defendants I met during their hearings or in interviews reported that accessing information about their rights is difficult. Echoing Amélie and Clara, they described being poorly informed or not informed at all or even in some cases misled by hospitals or child welfare services. Many expressed fears about asserting their rights: fear of retaliation, of being kept institutionalized longer, of being humiliated, or of permanently losing their children. They recounted being told that they would be "looked down upon" by psychiatrists and social workers if they inquired about their rights or acted assertively in court. Several noted that other defendants often choose not to appear in court, hoping this might result in shorter periods of detention or commitment, more successful negotiations around medication, or better chances of seeing their children. According to many, refraining from asserting their rights does not lead to a reduction in coercion. These accounts are corroborated by psychiatrists and defense lawyers who reported in formal interviews that the institutional cultures of certain facilities do not support the implementation of rights and, in many cases, actively discourage it through informal coercion, lack of access to quality information, and the discrediting of rights advocacy groups, which are at times portrayed as "extremist," "radical," or "anti-psychiatric." My findings, in this respect, are consistent with those of studies conducted in other jurisdictions (Munt & Littlechild, 2024; Furgalska, 2023).

The defendants I met in the corridors of the courthouse, or whom I formally interviewed, declared almost universally that their attorneys failed to explain the nature of the judicial proceedings they faced—let alone their legal protections. For them, inadequate information and hearing preparation represented merely one manifestation among many of the "scorn," "dismissal," and routine indignities they endure as they live in society. Many asserted that "rights aren't meant for us," or that rights exclusively belong to "rich people," to those with power. Several defendants told me that judges are out of touch with their reality, do not understand the impact of their decisions, and are not impartial. Those with multiple court appearances qualify this observation by noting that "it hinges on which judge your encounter. You might be extremely fortunate or profoundly unfortunate."

Defendants participating in advocacy organizations have different experiences. They acquire knowledge of their rights, and of the significance and implementation of those rights, through peer solidarity, one-on-one support, educational workshops, and documentation. For them, rights bear minimal connection to courts and legal professionals; they concern dignity, mutual support, respect, and agency. Their learning about their rights thus become an experience of collective and political resistance.

In the defendants' perspectives, psychiatric institutions, child welfare services, and the courts constitute a network of institutions that mirror each other, function collaboratively, and seem interchangeable. This perception reflects these institutions' increasingly tight cooperation within the continuum of care I explored in the second chapter, and my findings demonstrate that courts, while embracing the psychiatric paradigm, operate within the continuity of other institutions along the continuum. From this standpoint, the violence inherent in therapeutic justice constitutes one dimension of the institutional violence characterizing neoliberal societies. This commonplace violence is, however, enhanced by the authority and power inherent in judicial institutions, symbolized by ritualism of hearings and the ceremonial of the procedures, and by the concrete and symbolic coercion associated with judicial orders.

Judicial violence also involves broken promises. The judicialization of mental health procedures was the bulwark against the abuses of the asylum era. It was meant to ensure strict procedure, defense rights, and decision-making by an impartial third party. However, as studies have demonstrated, the judicial institution failed in this task from the outset

(Appelbeaum, 1997; Hiday 1990, 1988, 1977). Today, in the neoliberal context and under the impetus of therapeutic jurisprudence, mental health courtrooms are a lucrative market for some, and a trap for others.

The Mental Health Justice Market

With the growing judicialization of mental health over the past several decades, an entire market of related legal and non-legal services has emerged. It includes, among other roles, specialized judges, defense lawyers, in-house counsels from the increasingly expanding legal departments of hospitals and child welfare services, liaison officers bridging courts and psychiatric or social service providers, court clerks assisting family members in filing petitions, and community organizations tasked with implementing and monitoring therapeutic programs. While I will focus specifically on judges and defense lawyers, a broader inquiry is warranted to fully understand the scope and implications of this expanding field.

Throughout ethnographic fieldwork, echoing observations made by other researchers—particularly concerning court diversion programs (Collins, 2020; Nolan, 2020)—I noted the strong devotion of some legal practitioners to mental health courtrooms. Some judges, for instance, request to be assigned to mental health cases, while others deliberately avoid them. Those who are more engaged often describe being emotionally affected by defendants and their stories and express a belief that they can "make a difference" in these individuals' lives. These judges frequently emphasize that they make decisions through emotion rather than rational deliberation. They often assert a capacity to relate to defendants, to understand their experiences, and to persuade them to adopt different life choices. Their self-representation is that of judicial actors seeking to do things differently, to reform institutional practices, and to render justice more accessible and responsive to individual needs. Some adopt strategies to reduce the perceived intimidation of the courtroom: by choosing not to wear their robes, or by modifying procedural rules, for example, not requiring defendants to take the witness stand or to stand when testifying. In both formal interviews and informal conversations during hearing observation, certain judges reported adjusting their demeanor and the conduct of proceedings to the particulars of each case and the characteristics of each defendant. These adaptations are made in an effort to meet defendants "where they are," while still maintaining the minimum decorum and formality required by the judicial context. Broadly speaking, the judges most invested in mental health courtrooms tend to believe in the intrinsic therapeutic value of judicial processes. They regard the courtroom itself—and the legal process it enacts—as capable of producing therapeutic effects. Compared to their colleagues who are less involved in mental health courtrooms, they demonstrate increased propensity to deploy the treatment refusal thwarting strategies delineated in the preceding chapter—specifically undue pressure and paternalistic interventions.

Judges who are more deeply invested in mental health courtrooms tend to hold a conception of their role—and of mental health justice more broadly—that presupposes a collaborative stance on the part of lawyers, particularly defense lawyers. In formal interviews or during observation sessions, discarding an adversarial system wherein parties present their evidence and arguments, these judges emphasized that a more flexible procedure is required to promote what they consider defendants' best interests. They affirmed that defense counsels must go beyond client instructions and adopt positions regarding their clients' therapeutic needs, both to inform the court and to persuade defendants. They approved of situations where defense attorneys voice perspectives that differ from their clients' positions when necessary, utilizing their personal knowledge of defendants to justify such approaches. From these judges' perspective, addressing client's best interests constitutes not simply a professional obligation for lawyers practicing in mental health law but an ethical—even moral—imperative that overrides conventional legal ethics. They reported expecting defense lawyers to exhibit empathy and solicitude toward clients, similar to the behaviors observed in a supportive relationship. Conversely, they tended to critique defense attorneys who advocate strictly according to client directives—especially when, from their perspectives, defendants require treatment. For these judges, attorneys should refrain from vigorously advocating positions that contravene their clients' best interests, regardless of client preferences.

In preceding chapters, I discussed the difficult working conditions under which defense attorneys are required to practice in the field of mental health. These include the urgency of cases, the last-minute disclosure of evidence, the difficulty—often the impossibility—of securing expert opinions, high caseloads, and back-to-back hearings, as well as the frustration, confusion, and distress of defendants, some of whom are often repeatedly subjected to legal proceedings. To these already challenging conditions is added the fact that defense lawyers almost always lose their cases. In Chapter 4, I presented available data on the proportion of decisions that side with defendants, even partially; the figures are concerningly low. Beyond the outcomes themselves, my observations revealed that the time allocated to presenting defendants' evidence and arguments amounts, on average, to only one-quarter of the time granted to hospitals and child welfare services. Consistent with the logic of judges invested in mental health courtrooms, most lawyers, describe their role as "hybrid," fully embrace the mental health practice. For them, urgency, lack of resources, overwhelming caseloads, and institutional pressure are inherent features of mental health courtrooms. They describe mental health as a distinct area of legal practice, situated at the intersection of law and clinical work, oriented toward their clients' best interests, and requiring—indeed justifying—alternative approaches. According to both my observations and interviews, these attorneys rarely make legal arguments during hearings, instead adopting a posture of cooperation with psychiatrists and social workers.

These perspectives are not shared by several of legal practitioners. In interview and during observation sessions, judges expressed concern that many defense lawyers fail to present legal arguments—or even put forward arguments that are detrimental to their clients—during hearings. They reported observing practices in mental health courtrooms that they do not encounter in other areas of law, some recounting that they themselves have suggested to defense lawyer arguments or legal points in favor of their clients' rights. From their standpoint, mental health cases do not differ procedurally from other legal matters, nor do they exempt lawyers from their professional and ethical obligations. They noted that many defense lawyers appear to be poorly prepared, inadequately informed, or entirely unfamiliar with their cases and clients.

For few of the defense lawyers interviewed, the condition of practice in mental health courtrooms is profoundly demoralizing. They reported feeling instrumentalized, reduced to playing a nominal role. In their view, mental health courtrooms resembled a performance, a charade, in which they are cast in a marginal role. They observed that little space is typically devoted to law and rights, despite their efforts to steer courtroom discourse back toward legal reasoning. Over my fifteen years of research in the mental health courtrooms, the few lawyers involved in defending defendants' rights have all left the practice.

Compared to other legal domains, mental health practice involves a relatively narrow pool of attorneys. In the Montreal judicial district, a team of around seven public lawyers handle cases involving involuntary commitment, involuntary treatment, and Review Board hearings. Public lawyers in child welfare matters are exclusively dedicated to representing children. Private lawyers remunerated by legal aid also take on involuntary commitment, involuntary treatment, Review Board, or child welfare cases. As the number of cases subject to judicialization has increased, hospitals and child welfare services have expanded their in-house legal departments, and some of their lawyers have become specialized in these types of proceedings. Given that the number of judges presiding over these matters is also relatively limited, most legal actors in this field know one another—particularly since some of the current judges previously practiced in these fields as lawyers before being appointed to the bench. This situation raises an important issue of trust for the defendants, which I have already discussed. The narrow circle of lawyers and judges, along with the closed-door nature of several procedures, generates an insular environment where practices become routinized, minimally monitored, and rarely challenged. I observe that, when defense lawyers unfamiliar with this practice appear in mental health courtrooms, they are quickly reprimanded for failing to conform to established practices. They are accused of wasting the court's time pleading law and rights, as well as of "not understanding how things work here." For a lawyer who entered a mental health courtroom for the first time and whom I met in the course of courtroom observations, the experience appeared "surreal." Referring to the judicial process as "a circus," they declared that they would "waste no more time on this kind of case."

In the context of the scarce funding dedicated to mental health and child welfare cases, these courtroom practices tend to repel certain lawyers while drawing others. One public lawyer indicated during a formal interview that they felt "like the only one swimming against the current." They reported being aware of their poor reputation among judges and colleagues due to their thoroughly prepared cases and detailed legal arguments—so much so that some judges had even complained about them to their supervisors, claiming they did not understand the nature of practice in mental health courtrooms. They observed that both judges and lawyers often remarked that "these aren't landmark cases," or that the mental health law is "not complicated," while, in many situations, they often seemed to be unfamiliar with the applicable legal frameworks—something I noted repeatedly during both courtroom observations and interviews. For this attorney, their role is to make institutions understand that illegal practices would not be tolerated, protecting their clients, but also indirectly all those subjected to coercion in psychiatry. Yet they also expressed a sense of loss of meaning in judicial proceedings where, as they put it, "we've forgotten the role we're supposed to play as legal practitioners, to shelter and protect people we see as vulnerable." From their perspective, it is essential to remind the courts that defendants are rights-bearing individuals: "If I, with the position I currently hold as a public lawyer, don't do it—who will? Who will?" A few months after this interview, they resigned from their position as a public lawyer and left mental health law practice altogether. This attorney quitting mental health law practice is, as implied above, far from an isolated case. A few years earlier, another lawyer from the same office had resigned, nearing burnout not only due to excessive workload but also because of the very nature of mental health practice.

While public law offices are marked by significant turnover, private firms specializing exclusively in mental health or child welfare law have emerged in response to increasing demand. Over the fifteen years of my field research, the number of private lawyers in these areas has grown substantially. Arguing that the practices of public lawyers infringe upon defendants' rights, particularly by denying them the freedom to choose their own counsel, some private attorneys have adopted various strategies to increase the number of cases in which they are retained. While legal-aid mandates offer low remuneration—often failing to compensate for case preparation, for example—they can become highly profitable in a high-volume practice model, in which lawyers handle back-to-back hearings throughout the day. In cases of involuntary commitment, for example, where a dozen of unrepresented defendants appears in court each morning, these lawyers position themselves strategically within the courthouse. One typically waits at the elevator exit to meet individuals as they arrive, while another—or sometimes several—stands farther down the hallway, ready to receive the clients referred by the first. This practice has proven to be lucrative. An access to information request revealed that, in 2021, a private attorney charged the legal-aid office $156,600 for 605 involuntary commitment cases (Legal Services Commission, 2022). Lawyers practicing in this field also take on involuntary treatment and Review Board cases, which suggests that this sum was not this lawyer's overall income. During the same period, the average income of a Quebec lawyer was between $90,000 and $110,000 (Quebec Bar, 2022). This practice could be a violation of the Code of Professional Conduct of Lawyers, which states that a "lawyer who offers [their] professional services" must not "seek to take advantage of a person who is vulnerable, particularly due to age or physical or psychological condition." Defendants facing involuntary commitment petition find themselves in a position of considerable vulnerability. In interviews or during hearings, defendants reported feeling helpless when appearing alone at the courthouse, uncertain of what awaited them. The presence of counsel provided reassurance to many. In retrospect, several reported having felt that their lawyer served no purpose, was complicit, or even that they had been taken advantage of by their lawyer. The practice is well known among several judges, who denounce a form of "ambulance chasing." Nevertheless, it has expanded substantially over the past two decades without any significant repercussions for the private lawyers who practice it. Although some of them expressed discomfort with the situation, none of the judges interviewed or observed reported having brought these issues to the attention of the Bar.

This is not the only questionable practice observed during my research. A criminal defense attorney I encountered at a Review Board proceeding, for instance, described how one of their clients had requested continued representation following a verdict of not criminally responsible due to mental disorder. This deviates from standard Quebec practice, where criminal lawyers ordinarily withdraw at that juncture, with mental health law practitioners assuming representation before the Review Board. Unlike involuntary commitment proceedings, Review Board hearings are pre-scheduled several months in advance, as defendants appear either after receiving an unfit to stand trial or not criminally responsible verdict, or during their mandated annual hearing. The attorney explained that when they tried to enroll as counsel on the case, the Review Board's clerk notified them that the defendant already had recorded legal representation—a private lawyer who was a regular in mental health courtrooms. They reached out to their client to confirm whether they had selected different counsel; the client replied that they had not and were unfamiliar with the referenced lawyer's name. This incident reveals that the lawyer had secured hearing information from a source other than the defendant, whether from hospital staff or from Review Board personnel. This further indicates that defendants who fail to proactively secure legal representation may find themselves represented by such private attorneys merely by default upon reaching their hearing, without intentional selection.

From my observations and interviews with psychiatrists and lawyers, this kind of practice is neither rare nor uncommon, nor it is work of a single individual. I observed various interactions between attorneys and their clients—whether in courthouse hallways while awaiting hearings or during the proceedings themselves—that showed that defendants had given no instructions to their lawyers and, occasionally, that lawyers and defendants seemed to have never interacted prior to the hearing. In one hearing, for example, the judge had to insist that the defense lawyer meet with the defendant—their own client—after realizing that the defendant had no understanding of the nature of the proceedings or the content of the psychiatric report. In another case, the defense lawyer informed the client only after a hearing of the Review Board that "we'll request a discharge at the next hearing [in twelve months]." In matters of involuntary commitment or involuntary treatment, where defendants are frequently absent from their hearings, some lawyers manage to be appointed by the court as counsel without ever having spoken to the defendant. Some psychiatrists and lawyers reported in interview that certain private lawyers give gifts to nurses in psychiatric department, and that some hospital legal departments directly refer defendants to these lawyers.

Before the Review Board, where defendants must appear every twelve months unless they are granted an unconditional discharge, I repeatedly observed defense practices that raised serious concerns about potential conflicts of interest. Some private lawyers regularly oppose their client's unconditional discharge—even against their client instructions, sometimes against the recommendations of attending psychiatrists, and at times despite the absence of evidence that the defendant poses a significant threat to the safety of the public. In Chapter 6, I described a hearing involving a defendant who had been under Review Board supervision for eight years and was seeking an unconditional discharge, while their psychiatrist was recommending detention to address their gambling problems. During the hearing, the defense lawyer aligned themself with the psychiatrist, stating, "You've heard my client? He wants to be discharged. In my opinion—having known them for eight years—he should be incarcerated." At another hearing involving a 22-year-old man charged with robbery and assault in a grocery store—their first offense—the psychiatrist recommended an unconditional discharge, describing the incident as "a mistake" and affirming that the defendant posed no significant threat to the safety of the public, a position the defendant himself shared. The defense lawyer opposed the discharge, instead advocating for a conditional release "to keep an eye" on the defendant. In the hallway, during the tribunal's deliberation, the psychiatrist—clearly frustrated—told the lawyer that they "didn't understand their own role." In yet another case, a psychiatrist testified that the defendant did not pose a significant threat to the safety of the public but stated that they would "prefer" the defendant remain under Review Board supervision "just in case." The defense lawyer, contradicting the defendant's wish for an unconditional discharge, pleaded for a conditional release, stating that the defendant would only have to behave well to avoid an involuntary commitment or a detention. From the perspective of a private defense counsel, a conditional release by the Review Board necessitates a subsequent hearing within twelve months, thereby extending the legal mandate, whereas an absolute discharge terminates the proceedings entirely—a procedural distinction that bears no monetary consequences for public lawyers. The observed practices of private lawyers suggest that, in some cases, their own financial interests may influence the services they provide to the defendants and the arguments they make before the courts.

In interviews, some private lawyers also reported problematic practices, such as demanding illegal payment from defendants in exchange for taking on their legal-aid cases, failing to adequately inform defendants about the nature and course of the proceedings, or deliberately allowing defendants to make statements during hearings that result in outcomes contrary to their expressed wishes. Despite the seriousness of these practices—solicitation in courthouse hallways, strategic client acquisition, conflicts of interest, and illegal fees—and the fact that they are well known among many actors in the mental health and child welfare systems, these lawyers are rarely held to account. It is exceptional for judges to intervene during hearings to call lawyers to order. Complaints to the Bar's disciplinary council are rare and, when filed, generally do not result in consequences. It is worth noting that such complaints must come from individuals, excluding advocacy groups that, based on the experiences of their members, might otherwise be in a position to compile compelling cases. During interviews, defendants voiced apprehension about possible retribution following the submission of complaints against their attorneys. Such concerns are grounded in practical considerations: defendants understand they may require future legal services and recognize that should this attorney remain the exclusive available counsel, it is more prudent to maintain good relations with them. These statements mirror Amélie's earlier assertions, referenced in the introduction, regarding the need to engage in strategic decision-making to secure the most favorable future circumstances.

The emergence of a mental health justice market manifests not merely through expanded legal service provision, but also by a phenomenon of *serial judicialization*—the repeated subjection of individuals to judicial processes. This judicial intensification has positioned courts and legal practitioners as essential stakeholders within psychiatric and child welfare systems. Professional alliances have consolidated among psychiatrists, social workers, lawyers, and judges, with earlier professional ambivalence toward the consequences of inter-professional cooperation on the distinct expertise and authority of the different parties involved having largely dissipated. Psychiatrists generally frame judicialization as instrumental to their practice, with several revealing in interviews their deliberate pattern of subjecting specific patients—who are characterized by some as "more ill" or "more complex," but also "more criminally inclined"—to recurrent court proceedings, believing that "exposure to uniform judicial messaging from different judges" would ultimately secure patient acquiescence—or submission.

Is a Defense Possible?

During involuntary commitment and treatment hearings, I observed that cases are generally poorly prepared, both by hospital and defense lawyers. In addition to deficiencies in legal argumentation and scientific support, factual findings are often imprecisely constructed, prompting certain judges to voice concern in interviews about the substandard quality of case materials submitted for their consideration. While the urgency typically associated with these cases may partially explain this situation, cases scheduled weeks in advance are not necessarily better prepared. For instance, I witnessed a defense lawyer who had been assigned to a case for over a month appear at an involuntary treatment hearing without a copy of the hospital's petition. They first requested it from opposing counsel, then from a family member of the defendant present in the courtroom and finally stated that they had no questions for their client. In another case, noting the absence of a defendant at a hearing already postponed twice, the judge asked the defense lawyer whether their client would attend, to which the lawyer replied that they had no idea because they had not spoken to them.

In all four mental health courtrooms I investigated, the questions posed by defense lawyers to psychiatrists, social workers, and defendants are generally similar—if not identical—from one case to another. This lack of individual attention is compounded by structural constraints and, in some instances, a lack of understanding of applicable law, which results in defense lawyers failing to oppose questionable practices by hospitals and child welfare services. Examples include systematic requests for deadline extensions under statutory provisions; petitions lodged with the court in anticipation of future developments, or in violation of prescribed legal norms; contravention of existing court orders, such as keeping defendants in custody despite conditional release orders, or denying authorized contact between parents and children. Hospitals and child welfare services justify these practices by citing shortage of resources, the burdensome and time-consuming nature of judicial procedures, or efforts to adapt legal processes to clinical needs. Some hospital lawyers even described some of these practices as attempts at "legal innovation." Despite the negative impact on their clients, defense lawyers rarely challenge these practices, nor do they raise concerns about the legal or procedural irregularities involved, or the potential violations of defendants' rights. In interviews, they reported either lacking any real leverage to contest such practices—how can one object to a missed deadline when the hospital or child welfare services lacks the resources to meet it?—or genuinely believing that complying with such practices was in their client's best interest.

Due to a loss of trust, some defendants choose to retain the services of private lawyers who are not regulars in mental health courtrooms, and sometimes experts. They describe spending hours preparing their cases, having to "brief" their lawyer who often knows very little about mental health law. The involvement of an expert can make an important difference; one defendant interviewed was thus able to win five of the six involuntary treatment trials they endured in the past ten years. Such advocacy, however, entails substantial temporal and particularly financial expenditures that remain inaccessible to many. During an interview, a defendant engaged in a multi-year "legal battle" against child welfare services disclosed:

> Me, the lawyer, the rights—do you realize my accumulated costs? I've stopped calculating. I call the bank, requesting: "Do something, I need to pay the lawyer." [...] I have to sit down and look at my finances, I have to look at how I got into debt, what needs to be paid and all that. Right now, I'm too stressed, I don't do it.

Court observation revealed that defendants often receive more effective assistance when appearing without counsel than when represented by inadequately prepared attorneys. In unrepresented proceedings, judges exercise a more directive role through detailed questioning that facilitates fact-finding. In interviews, judges indicated expectations that counsel will identify and address case-specific legal issues, leading to assumptions that attorney passivity reflects case adequacy, resulting in interpretations of counsel silence as confirmation of procedural sufficiency. Many judges characterized regular mental health court lawyers as field experts, despite the problematic professional conduct discussed above.

Beyond counsel-related challenges, defendants encounter multiple barriers to effective defense presentation, many previously examined in preceding chapters: procedural urgency limiting preparation time, diminished credibility assessments, deliberate destabilization tactics by institutional legal representatives, and the emotional gravity inherent in cases with life-altering implications. Defendants also encounter institutional sanism—widespread judicial assumptions that psychiatric conditions inherently compromise predictability and safety, preclude capacity for self-determination, and necessitate therapeutic intervention. Additionally, defendants confront judicial risk-aversion driven by concerns about public safety and institutional legitimacy. Numerous judges expressed anxiety that favorable rulings regarding defendant liberty or child custody could result in catastrophic outcomes—self-harm or violence against others—following court decisions. Interview included references to recent incidents or to the experiences of colleagues that validate these anxieties. Such concerns produce judicial decision-making paralysis, with some judges openly declaring they consistently rule in favor of hospitals and child welfare services and other expressing anticipated self blame for adverse post-ruling outcomes. Judges also express additional concern about the erosion of public confidence in judicial institutions. This judicial caution mirrors psychiatric institutional behavior, particularly in commitment and detention contexts. In interviews, some psychiatrists expressed similar liability concerns, citing cases where post-discharge deaths or violent incidents resulted in legal litigations against healthcare institutions and individual clinicians. For them, judicial decision-making functions as professional liability shielding, with some psychiatrists acknowledging systematically advocating for maximum restrictive interventions pending judicial decision, operating under the assumption that subsequent judicial release decisions transfer professional responsibility from medical to legal authorities.

However, the primary barrier to substantive defense in mental health adjudication stems from legal interpretation and judicial practices. From the very outset of their testimony, defendants are required to take a clear position on their mental health situation. Because the courts are convinced that defendants suffer from mental health problems, defendants are effectively presented with merely two possible positions: acknowledgment or denial. Both positions yield identical conclusions: implicit deductive reasoning regarding defendant dangerousness, public threat, or incapacity necessitating therapy; only the persuasive strategy varies. When defendants concede mental health difficulties, counsel and judges endeavor to convince them that cooperation and treatment compliance constitute their pathway to recovery, predominantly through paternalistic discourse or pressure. When defendants maintain denial, they confront them with perceived contradictions, contrasting their statements with those of mental health professionals or social workers. These strategies can be more aggressive, involving threats, intensified pressure, or more forceful moral lectures. In either scenario, deliberate ambiguity may be maintained about the court's authority and the nature of its orders, especially regarding involuntary treatment. This dichotomous judicial practice effectively circumvents any substantive arguments defendants might advance by constraining them to binary positions of either accepting or denying institutional allegations from hospitals and child welfare services. Such practice contradicts multiple Supreme Court of Canada precedents. The Court has established that psychiatric diagnostic acceptance or rejection cannot constitute evidence of mental disorder or incapacity (Starson, 2003). Across criminal and civil jurisprudence, danger, threat, or incapacity cannot be presumed exclusively from psychiatric diagnosis or assessment. Courts must also examine factual evidence, particularly regarding defendants' informational comprehension and preference articulation, or concrete behaviors demonstrating actual—rather than speculative—risk or incapacity (Starson, 2003; Molodovic, 2000; Winko, 1999). The Supreme Court has consistently reaffirmed judicial roles as procedural protections against state interventions potentially violating defendant rights in mental health adjudication (Ontario (Attorney General), 2020; Pinet, 2004; Swain, 1991).

In mental health courtrooms, beyond flexible interpretation of substantive and procedural legal frameworks and professional ethical standards, core legal principles frequently receive inconsistent application—or are met with complete disregard. Courts exercise significant discretionary authority to render decisions they consider appropriate, including notification waivers, provisional orders and *ex parte* proceedings—proceedings conducted with only one-party present. Regarding evidentiary standards, tribunals regularly permit hearsay testimony, mid-hearing evidence introduction, and extensions for strengthening deficient or incomplete documentation. While statutory interpretation should prioritize individual rights protection, judges frequently rationalize such decisions by citing general civil procedure principles, contending that petitioners—hospitals or child protection agencies—possess assertable rights, or that default judgments may be entered against non-responsive defendants. Nevertheless, child welfare services, while intervening when parental conduct threatens children's welfare, possess no fundamental "right" to family disruption or child removal, just as hospitals lack fundamental "rights" to involuntary commitment, detention, or treatment. These represent exceptional state powers exercisable solely under extraordinary circumstances through stringent procedural frameworks. Defendants—parents, patients—constitute the actual rights-holders. Judicial orders encompassing involuntary commitment, involuntary treatment, detention, conditional release, child removal, or parental contact limitation minimally relate to rights enforcement. Instead, they sanction rights violations for risk management and protection objectives, in a cost-benefit balancing exercise.

Judgment-writing practices follow the same logic. In involuntary commitment and involuntary treatment hearings, "draft judgments"—pre-written decisions submitted by the plaintiff for the court's use—are almost always filed. In civil matters, it is generally accepted that plaintiffs may submit draft judgments when the defendant does not respond to the petition and the court is expected to render a default judgment, i.e., without hearing from the defendant. In these matters, however, draft judgments are routinely filed when the defendant is present and submits a defense. Based on my observations, these drafts are signed by judges with minimal or no revisions in roughly three-quarters of the cases. This widespread practice has significant consequences for the rights of the defense. These drafts, often copied and pasted from previous templates, are short, generic and fail to disclose the judicial reasoning underlying each decision. This renders the process opaque both for defendants in their individual cases and for those seeking to rely on case law in preparing a defense. This practice illuminates why legal doctrine in these areas remains rudimentary, even after more than three decades of statutory existence and continuously expanding litigation. It also contradicts the guidance of higher courts, which have held that regardless of whether defendants are present or not at their involuntary commitment or treatment hearing, judges must independently conduct legal analysis and provide reasons for their decisions, explicitly rejecting any form of automatic or formulaic judgment writing (Centre intégré universitaire de santé et de services sociaux de la Capitale-Nationale, 2017; C.R., 2017; F.D., 2015). An analysis of court files relating to forced treatment orders in a district outside Montreal revealed that many of the draft judgments signed by the court contained significant errors, such as the omission of the duration of the order (Bernheim et al., 2024), which raises the question of whether the judges read the draft judgments. These findings indicate that, operationally, courts frequently operate not as substantive decision-makers in involuntary commitment or treatment matters, but as ceremonial endorsement bodies for rubber-stamping determinations manufactured by hospital legal staff.

In child welfare cases and in the Review Board, the practices differ. Child welfare services, as plaintiffs, and the treating psychiatrist designated as a witness by the Review Board, typically submit extensive written documents that directly address the central issues of the hearings—namely, the danger to the security or development of the child, and the threat to public safety. Judicial decisions are generally based on these documents, incorporating long excerpts and relying heavily on the analyses provided by psychiatrists, social workers, or other experts, where applicable. These decisions typically do not summarize or engage with the defense's arguments, making it difficult to determine whether such arguments were presented at all, and if so, what their legal relevance is. The consequences of this practice are similar to those associated with the use of draft judgments: it is often difficult to discern the court's reasoning, and thus the legal basis for the orders issued.

Judicial approaches to procedural, evidentiary, and judgment-writing practices tend to overlook the context of pronounced power imbalance and fundamental rights at stake, paralleling ordinary civil litigation or administrative adjudication. Even though they are consistent with civil procedure principles requiring flexible procedural application, these practices exacerbate inter-party power disparities and benefit hospitals and child welfare services. For instance, they predominantly benefit from deadline extensions for evidence completion; allegations of previously undisclosed facts typically generate surprise effects during hearings that disadvantage defendant and their counsel; and hearsay admission generally strengthens institutional evidence by permitting reliance on unverified third-party statements. More broadly, mental health court practices, including notification waivers and *ex parte* proceedings, constitute derogations from defense rights and compromise judicial oversight functions.

In certain instances, fundamental legal principles are simply disregarded, as exemplified by an involuntary electroconvulsive therapy (ECT) hearing I attended and later discussed with the defense attorney in interview. The case involved a defendant whose ECT had been limited to twelve sessions by an appellate court ruling six months prior. The medical institution filed a subsequent petition regarding the same individual, seeking twelve additional ECT sessions and 52 maintenance treatments. During opening proceedings, defense counsel referenced the appellate decision and invoked *res judicata* doctrine—the principle that a matter already decided by a court cannot be relitigated. The defense lawyer later described the exchange: "I argued, 'Judge, the appellate court established twelve sessions as the limit. That ruling is binding. If my opposing counsel disagreed with the judgment, their option was Supreme Court appeal. We cannot simply circumvent established precedent, especially with only six months elapsed.' The judge replied: 'Counsel, here it's not about law.' I say, 'Because in a courtroom, that's what I thought it was about.'" I documented similar incidents repeatedly throughout observational fieldwork, when several attorneys and judges explained that legal requirements should not impede psychiatric and social work practice. This perspective parallels psychiatric professional arguments, claiming that legal procedures are excessively complex and time-consuming, diverting clinical resources from therapeutic activities.

Although these judicial practices contradict basic legal principles, defendants rarely initiate appellate proceedings. Higher court decisions in these areas are scarce, particularly in relation to the substantial volume of lower court orders. Multiple factors account for this phenomenon, primarily defendants' limited awareness of their legal entitlements. For individuals navigating multiple legal proceedings, procedural variations between courts compound comprehension difficulties regarding their legal position. Interview evidence confirm defendants' confusion about whether they had appeared before superior or provincial courts, or whether they were governed by involuntary treatment orders or guardianship arrangements, for example. Most remained unaware that appellate remedies existed for their matters. Defense attorneys described lacking adequate time and resources for appellate work, requiring brief preparation and repeated court appearances. They indicated that formerly available public appellate legal divisions had been eliminated, with personnel reassigned to disparate offices. Appeals must consequently be prepared during public lawyers' personal time, and their court appearances create service interruptions that colleagues must assume in trial-level courts, generating additional workload burdens for the team. For private counsel, legal-aid fee structures fail to compensate for appellate preparation demands. Accordingly, some of them provide such representation pro bono—without compensation. The minority of public and private defense lawyers pursuing appeals reported in interview selecting cases with capacity to "strengthen legal precedent." They identified concerning practices and institutional rights violations they seek to challenge through appellate mechanisms, awaiting "ideal cases"—those where factual foundations support legal positions and enhance judicial persuasion. Within contexts of restricted appellate volume, this strategy can produce systemic modifications by transforming practices advantaging all defendants. This approach implies, however, that viable and potentially successful appeals may remain unpursued.

In practice, defendants' rights work against them both in presenting defenses within judicial proceedings and in advocacy activities in public or political contexts. As detailed in Chapters 5 and 6, courts tend to interpret defendants' rights assertions as indicators of aggressiveness or denial of mental health problems. The same pattern occurs when defendants report rights violations or discrimination they experience in their contacts with public institutions or society generally. Generally, they are not believed. They are perceived as manipulative or paranoid. This dynamic extends to public and political discourse. First, the existence of defendants' rights and remedies paradoxically suggests that involuntary commitment, treatment, detention, or child removal results either from their failure to exercise available rights or from the legal incorrectness of their position. This perception reflects the fundamental nature of litigation: producing winners and losers. Second, demonstrating structural rights violations through case-by-case analysis proves extremely challenging; judicial processes are inherently case-specific, combined with typically closed proceedings, and result in minimal systemic data compilation—and in even less public disclosure. Furthermore, alleging rights violations by courts—institutions presumed impartial and law-implementing—presents inherent contradiction and argumentative complexity in a context where public confidence in the Canadian judicial system is generally robust (Crandall & Lawlor, 2022).

Asking whether substantive defense occurs in mental health courtrooms, my research establishes it commonly constitutes procedural symbolism. Justice in mental health courtrooms is predominantly performative rather than substantive; it functions as a vehicle for psychiatric paradigm, emphasizing therapeutic rather than legal goals—commencing with treatment imperatives. Investigation of mental health courtrooms indicates that when judicial procedures are directed toward extra-legal ends, the core concept of defense representation becomes ambiguous, arguably meaningless: within therapeutic paradigms, there is no defense to be made—cooperation is the only viable option.

The Judicial Trap and the Shadow Carceral State

For defendants, the experience of mental health courtrooms often feels Kafkaesque, with predetermined outcomes. In interviews, they reported, alongside profound powerlessness within the judicial setting, that "whatever you say, it's held against you," that "they are four, five against you." They expressed feeling subjected to prejudgment and questioned judicial neutrality. Many entered hearings with modest expectations; they confirmed that proceedings developed exactly as they had pessimistically anticipated.

Yet judicial procedures produce ramifications extending considerably beyond hearings and court orders. According to my observations, judicialization—especially *serial judicialization*—is fundamentally characterized by cascading losses. Tangible losses—employment termination, income reduction, housing displacement—and relational losses—family dissolution, social disconnection, friendship erosion—systematically undermine individuals and their support networks where they exist. These losses frequently become the foundation for subsequent social service, psychiatric, and law enforcement interventions. Yet, since underlying structural determinants—poverty, discrimination, inequality—remain unaddressed, they create perpetual cycles of intervention from which individuals can hardly extricate themselves (Paik, 2021). These cumulative interventions produce additional judicial proceedings, causing further losses and requiring more interventions.

Serial judicialization frequently begins with tangible losses. Eviction, or residential or employment losses can activate child welfare service responses or psychiatric institutional interventions, generating multiple contacts with health, social, and police services when immediate housing solutions remain unavailable. As interventions and judicial processes multiply, losses accumulate progressively, generating what are labeled "chronic" conditions—chronic mental health issues, chronic homelessness, chronic substance abuse. While defendants are forced, often by court order, to access health and social services, they are characterized as "frequent service users," and are sometimes accused of abusing services through their persistent requests. Although procedural combinations may vary, essential outcomes remain substantially equivalent.

Some defendants I met in the course of my research fieldwork experienced judicialization affecting every life dimension: housing, family relationships, social benefits, immigration status, and healthcare access. In some cases, defendants, especially those with child welfare involvement backgrounds, have been subject to serial judicialization throughout their entire life span from childhood, as Clara, whose story I recounted in Chapter 5, did. I encountered numerous such individuals in mental health courtrooms, which is logical, as violence exposure or child welfare intervention in childhood constitutes risk predictors for adult violence and parental incapacity within assessment tools. During formal interview or observations, they expressed feeling "systematically abandoned" and experiencing complete powerlessness. They reported institutional distrust and uncertainty about escape routes from their circumstances. They contended that behaviors subject to judicial blame—instability, unpredictability, aggressiveness—mirror their institutional treatment throughout their lives.

Among the most significant research findings is the comprehensive surveillance apparatus governing defendants under mental health civil or administrative orders within community settings. Ethnographic observation reveals that extensive professional and community networks participate in this monitoring framework—occasionally including family members and close relationships—spanning law enforcement officers, medical institutions, social services, pharmacists, community outreach workers, and group home or shelter staff. This surveillance system facilitates judicial orders compliance, such as condition breach reporting, but routinely exceeds these boundaries, especially regarding treatment adherence. During hearings, psychiatrists consistently described receiving reports from residential workers about defendants' substance use or medication non-compliance, pharmacist notifications about missed prescription collections, or the ability to locate defendants by contacting group homes or shelter. In multiple cases, defendants were not subject to involuntary treatment orders, yet psychiatrists indicated such information assisted them in "building grounds" for obtaining such court decisions. Multiple social workers and psychiatrists' testimonies confirmed that inter-professional collaboration encompasses systematic defendant information sharing, particularly with police services.

Defendants describe experiencing relentless monitoring, and feeling imprisoned within an "institutional matrix" where initial contact creates permanent capture. Senior participants describe a shift that emerged around the early 2010s when previously reliable support systems—community groups, shelters, community outreach workers—initiated cooperation with police forces, social services, psychiatric institutions, and courts. Several defendants reported declining further involvements with these institutions, concerned about data sharing practices and the related coercion. Therefore, they avoid shelter and housing services, even throughout brutal winter seasons.

My fieldwork data cannot establish the precise proportion of defendants experiencing serial judicialization, nor determine the number of concurrent judicial orders affecting these individuals. Nevertheless, approximately one-quarter of observed hearings contained references to at least one additional judicial proceeding, indicating this phenomenon extends beyond isolated cases. This pattern appears to be escalating alongside increasing judicial caseloads over the past two decades. These findings support the conclusion that for a substantial subset of defendants, civil and administrative judicialization represents a primary—if not the predominant—intervention mechanism yet manifestly fails to resolve underlying structural issues. As courts have become fully integrated within the continuum of care, surveillance, reporting, and judicialization have become normalized practices, embodying the shadow carceral state (Beckett & Murakawa, 2012).

References

Appelbaum, P. S. (1997). Almost a revolution: An international perspective on the law of involuntary commitment. *Journal of the American Academy of Psychiatry and the Law Online, 25*(2), 135–147.

Beckett, K., & Murakawa, N. (2012). Mapping the shadow carceral state: Toward an institutionally capacious approach to punishment. *Theoretical Criminology, 16*(2), 221–244. https://doi.org/10.1177/1362480612442113

Bernheim, E., Grisé, A.-D. Perreault, E. (2024). Les pratiques des contentieux des Centres intégrés de santé et de services sociaux en matière d'autorisation de soins et les droits des parties défenderesses: une étude des dossiers judiciaires de Longueuil. In Quebec Bar training department (pp. 90–116). La protection des personnes vulnérables, Yvon Blais.

Centre intégré universitaire de santé et de services sociaux de la Capitale-Nationale v.D.M., 2017 QCCA 1333.

Code of Professional Conduct of Lawyers, CQLR c B-1, r 3.1. (n.d.)

C.R. v. Centre intégré de santé et de services sociaux du Bas-Saint-Laurent. (2017). *QCCA*, 328.

Collins, E. R. (2020). The problem of problem-solving courts. *University of California Davis Law Review, 54*, 1573–1630.

Crandall, E., & Lawlor, A. (2022). Public support for Canadian courts: Understanding the roles of institutional trust and partisanship. *Canadian journal of Law and society/La revue canadienne droit et société, 37*(1), 91–112. https://doi.org/10.1017/cls.2021.28

F.D. v. Centre universitaire de santé McGill, (Hôpital Royal-Victoria). (2015). *QCCA*, 1139.

Furgalska, M. (2023). "Informed consent is a bit of a joke to me:" lived experiences of insight, coercion, and capabilities in mental health care settings. *International Journal of Law in Context, 19*(4), 456–474. https://doi.org/10.1017/S1744552323000174

Hiday, V. A. (1990). Dangerousness of civil commitment candidates: A six-month follow-up. *Law and Human Behaviour, 14*(6), 551–567. https://doi.org/10.1007/BF01044881

Hiday, V. A. (1988). Civil commitment: A review of empirical research. *Behavioral Sciences & the Law, 6*(1), 15–43. https://doi.org/10.1002/bsl.2370060104

Hiday, V. A. (1977). Reformed commitment procedures: An empirical study in the courtroom. *Law & Society Review, 11*(4), 651–666. https://doi.org/10.2307/3053176

Legal Services Commission. (2022). *Demande d'accès à l'information—réponse, N/dossier*, 77181/14. https://www.csj.qc.ca/IntranetUploads/CSJ/Francais/DemandeDAcces/DTCD-14.pdf

Munt, C., & Littlechild, B. (2024). The lived experience of coercion. In *Coercion and violence in mental health settings: Causes, consequences, management* (pp. 3–25). Springer Nature. https://doi.org/10.1007/978-3-031-61224-4

Nolan, J. L., Jr. (2020). The cultural constraints of legal transplantation a ten-year retrospective. *Cardozo Journal of Conflict Resolution, 21*, 641–662.

Ontario (Attorney General v. G., 2020 SCC 38, [2020] 3 SCR 629.

Paik, L. (2021). *Trapped in a maze*. University of California Press.

Pinet v. St. Thomas Psychiatric Hospital, [2004] 1 SCR 528.

R. v. Molodowic, [2000] 1 SCR 420.

R. v. Swain, [1991] 1 SCR 933.

Quebec Bar (2022). *Barreau-Mètre: la profession en chiffre.* https://www.barreau.qc.ca/media/gadfrlil/barreau-metre-2022-faits-saillants.pdf (accessed August 9, 2025).

Starson v Swayze, [2003] 1 SCR 722.

Winko v. British Columbia (Forensic Psychiatric Institute), [1999] 2 SCR 62.

9

Conclusion: Beyond Rights—The Political Struggle

Analytically and politically, the mere act of criticizing human rights does little to provide useful alternatives to human rights frameworks, regimes, and movements that might succeed in areas where human rights have failed—in part because human rights are (so far) not designed to succeed in those areas. To bring the limited aims and often glancing successes of human rights movements into focus is simply to demand another politics to supplement goals that are inadequate in the first place and strategies that rarely work, especially in the socioeconomic domain. A threatening enemy, rather than a powerless companion, is what market fundamentalism demands.—Samuel Moyn, 2017: 169.

My ethnographic studies within mental health courtrooms have illuminated the systemic violence of therapeutic justice, which, clothed in rhetorics of individual agency, best interests, and therapeutic intervention, suppresses voices and masks the inherently coercive character of its mechanisms and adjudications. Although certain legal practitioners served as vigorous and successful advocates for mental health rights in the 1960s–70s, and although courts functioned as pioneering institutions in recognizing and safeguarding these rights, contemporary practices

E. Bernheim, *Therapeutic (In)justice and the Shadow Carceral State*, The Politics of Mental Health and Illness, https://doi.org/10.1007/978-3-032-16186-4_9

within mental health courtrooms suggest quite different patterns. A retrospective analysis is necessary to illuminate these phenomena.

In a 1981 paper, Phil Brown contends that mental health rights recognition hinged upon endorsement from powerful stakeholders, especially mental health professionals. In the context of transinstitutionalization, the involvement of mental health professionals, along with people with psychiatric experience in advocating for rights proved indispensable for guaranteeing that emerging institutional and legal transformations would advance their professional objectives. However, they consistently failed to recognize or validate critiques of psychiatry regarding the discipline's precarious and contentious scientific basis and treatment modalities, notably coercive interventions (Oaks, 2011). While publicly championing the cause of rights (hospitals and professional bodies endorsed rights prior to formal legal recognition), mental health professionals predominantly regarded the movement as jeopardizing their professional standing and pursued more aggressive strategies to maintain dominance, which notably operates through the power to decide and implement coercion. One such strategy involved the rhetoric of right to treatment, which developed in the aftermath of the mental health rights movement as I outlined in the second chapter. The right-to-treatment doctrine perpetuates mental health professional authority over patients by exclusively empowering them to define patients' best clinical interests, thus constructing an intrinsic epistemic hierarchy consistent with the historical foundations of coercive practices—namely danger and risk paradigms. However, employing rights discourse instead of coercion terminology transforms the narrative from control to protection.

Judicial systems have generally aligned with this approach. By recognizing that the detention of a person with mental illness constitutes cruel and unusual punishment and violates constitutional rights, while simultaneously maintaining that therapeutically motivated detention does not, courts have effectively disavowed that rights infringements can result from therapeutic mechanisms. When pushed to its logical conclusion, the belief that therapy cannot be inherently coercive undermines the fundamental meaning of rights, especially the rights to treatment consent and refusal—and the connection to bodily autonomy and physical integrity—while similarly diminishing defense rights. A 2016 Ontario

Court of Appeal decision in Canada elaborates this reasoning. The case originated from a legal challenge by the Empowerment Council, Systematic Advocates in Addictions and Mental Health, an advocacy coalition representing mental health and addiction service users, disputing the community treatment order (CTO) regime. Ontario's framework permits individuals meeting involuntary commitment criteria to consent to CTOs for community treatment; however, they risk involuntary admission whenever physicians suspect treatment non-adherence. The advocacy groups contended this arrangement precludes authentic consent to treatment since involuntary commitment constitutes the only alternative. The Court dismissed this argument through three rationales that represent, from my perspective, the implicit cornerstones of therapeutic justice: 1) coercion denial—coercion is not the law's purpose but merely its collateral effect, which makes it, through legal fiction, a non-coercive regulatory mechanism; 2) right to treatment—mandating potentially beneficial treatment for individuals incapable to consent to treatment fulfills state responsibilities under *parens patriae* authority; and 3) legitimacy of pressured consent in therapeutic settings—since individuals qualify for involuntary commitment, providing "less restrictive" and "consensual" alternatives cannot constitute coercion (Thompson, 2016: 56). This legal rationale embodies the foundational logic of the practices I witnessed in mental health courtrooms. However, it renders standard challenges founded on rights to freedom, bodily autonomy, and contractual integrity essentially unviable. By denying the coercive aspects of therapeutic interventions, it effectively blocks the practical application of constitutional rights and their attendant legal and procedural protections. Through its grounding in rights to treatment doctrine, this legal rationale inherently prioritizes clinical best interests in mental health above all other considerations. Finally, by validating consent obtained under pressure as legally sound, it diverges from established practices in contract law and informed consent in physical medicine. This judicial rationale finds itself considerably distanced from the 1960s–70s movement driven by people with psychiatric experience and appears to legally embody the movement's cooptation by mental health professionals and the political establishment that Phil Brown (1981) documented.

It is essential to note initially that whereas legal and academic scholarship frequently references a "psychiatric patient rights movement," lived-experienced-authored literature speaks rather of the "liberation movement," "liberation front," or "Mad liberation" (Frazer-Carroll, 2023; Starkman, 2012; Chamberlin, 1978). This distinction is crucial. The liberation movement objectives, advocacies, and visions were inherently political—it pursued liberation, empowerment, and social changes—not legal ones. Although law may act as a lever for social transformation, it is certainly not the sole resource—while the movement impacted law, particularly human rights legislations, through involvement in reform and in litigation, its magnitude far surpasses legal contexts. Originally formed through alliances with "radical therapists," the movement gained strength and political identity through self-help groups. These entities prioritized consciousness-raising, community education, democratic participation, and mutual support that people had been denied within psychiatric institutions (Starkman, 2012; Chamberlin, 1978). Although mental health professionals and academics have frequently minimized these groups as "therapeutic alternatives" that leave the status quo unchanged, research demonstrated that most of them, in the United States, aimed to address "social injustices that [we]re seen as no longer tolerable" (Emerick, 1996: 156). The political orientation of the liberation movement was commonly portrayed as antagonistic toward mental health professionals, even as antipsychiatric—however, "anti-psychiatry is largely an intellectual exercise of academics and dissident mental health professionals. There has been little attempt within anti-psychiatry to reach out to struggling ex-patients or to include their perspective" (Chamberlain, 1990: 324). Consistently, the antipsychiatry label is used to discredit arguments and those who advocate them (Szasz, 2010; Schramme, 2004).

The liberation movement joined and drew inspiration from other liberation or solidarity movements, such as feminism, the rebellion of gay men against psychiatrization, and community solidarity that existed until the nineteenth century (Starkman, 2012). It operated within an anti-establishment perspective, criticizing structural oppression, and focused on the power inequalities within a "giant industrial complex in which thousands of people, many of them with professional status, earn large salaries at the expense of those who are defined as mentally ill" (Ginsberg, 1974: 4). Fundamentally, the liberation movement constituted a movement by and for psychiatric survivors—excluding people without psychiatric experience in the writting. It privileged the knowledge gained from lived experience and worked toward the abolition of coercion, especially by asserting recognition of treatment consent and refusal rights.

Various authors, including people involved in the movement, argue that the liberation movement's political dimension diminished through the inclusion of mental health professionals or public representatives, as well as by receiving government funding, and by members of the movement accepting invitations to advisory committees and professional organization meetings (Starkman, 2012; Chamberlin, 1990; Brown, 1981). These circumstances compelled individuals and organizations to adopt either cooperative or confrontational stances. Critical voices were utilized to sideline activists and groups perceived as unproductive or polarizing, and their political claims became progressively diluted. However, there is little evidence to suggest that liberation movement participation and cooperation achieved concrete results. The *Convention on the Rights of People with Disabilities* (CRPD, 2006) serves as a compelling illustration: despite emphasis on the inclusion of people with psychiatric experience in the writting, formal coercion prohibition was discarded, although it was fundamental to the liberation movement since its inception, in favor of rights frameworks (Wilson, 2022). It is significant that contemporary scholarship tends to reduce liberation movement activism to its juridical dimensions. This reductionist approach may stem from the fact that legal achievements represent the aspect of their efforts that garners the widest agreement.

According to Neil Milner (1986: 105), while liberation requires direct political action, the liberation movement instead embraced the "myth of rights," "an ideology emphasizing the effectiveness of litigation as a strategy for social change." In pursuing this path, while the movement generally characterized the psychiatric system as oppressive, it positioned the legal system and legal professionals as emancipatory allies. Litigation and judicialization was thus regarded as a practical and effective vehicle for social transformation, although it necessarily entailed reformulating issues as matters of law and excluding individuals in favor of legal practitioners, thus dispossessing people with lived experience of the narrative and depoliticizing the struggle. Litigation and judicialization also represent a break from the political democracy and solidarity framework promoted during the movement's foundational phase. Most importantly, litigation and judicialization have predominantly failed to produce results: they have not managed to prohibit coercion or secure survivor damages, as courts have rejected recognizing the use of coercion as professional malpractice. As my research shows, they have not achieved a departure from the psychiatric paradigm or successfully confronted the structural issues that underlie coercive practices. Perhaps more fundamentally, neither litigation nor judicialization has succeeded in adjudicating between the rights to consent to and refuse treatment and the right to treatment promoted by mental health professionals. In other words, in mental health contexts, it has proven unattainable to successfully establish that legally acknowledged rights hold superior value and evidentiary force compared to "moral rights" (Birnbaum, 1960). In practice, the legal community has not served as an ally to the liberation movement, save for rare exceptions. As demonstrated earlier, even the initial judicial decisions in favor of the liberation movement harbored the foundational premises of therapeutic justice and reflected a judicial embrace of the psychiatric paradigm.

Judi Chamberlin, a psychiatric survivor and pioneer of the liberation movement, and author of the authoritative book "On Our Own: Patient-Controlled Alternatives to the Mental Health System," contended in 1995 that rights will never be practically granted unless structural issues and discrimination are acknowledged and addressed:

> Rehabilitation, in its truest sense, must mean not only assisting our readaptation to society but recognizing the ways in which social practices prevent that readaptation. Stigma and discrimination must be honestly faced and fought. Inadequate incomes and housing must be changed, or we can never live decent and comfortable lives. And unless the questions of power and powerlessness are dealt with in an open and frank way, we

shall never be accorded our basic human dignity and our fundamental human and citizenship rights.

Mental health rights are recognized in principle—yet they remain considerably distant from the rights Judy Chamberlin envisioned. However, they have fueled extensive academic work and sustained activism. Five decades following the first national legislative reforms and twenty years after the CRPD, as psychiatric coercion use escalated markedly, debates continue over whether the CRPD could end coercive practices (Davidson, 2025), whether statutory changes might eliminate discrimination (Dawson & Szmukler, 2021), or how to implement a rights-based approach in psychiatric care (Cosgrove et al., 2021). The central work of advocacy groups essentially involves rights promotion, rights education, and defending rights codified in mental health laws. The myth of rights is thus alive and well.

Nevertheless, the focus on rights is still far from having produced durable systemic change. Justice and rights have not only failed to ensure access to basic needs, including housing, food, education, and healthcare, or to protect against coercion and oppression; they have individualized what were fundamentally collective issues. Even the acknowledgment of systemic rights violations failed to produce system-wide change, with the burden of enforcement continuing to fall on individuals. For example, in British Columbia, Canada, the Office of the Ombudsperson found that the province had failed to respect key elements of its own mental health legislation, including the right to consent to treatment. A rights advisory service was subsequently recommended (Office of the Ombudsperson, 2019). While systemic violations were recognized, the response remained individual in nature, expecting involuntary committed patients to be informed and to pursue legal recourse—a strategy that has proven unsuccessful in several jurisdictions. Meanwhile, psychiatric institutions and the provincial government escaped increased regulatory oversight, accountability structures, and the duty to provide reparations to the thousands of people whose rights were transgressed. In Quebec, Canada, a class-action lawsuit recently forced the government to offer compensation to individuals illegally detained in psychiatric institutions (The Canadian Press, 2024). Nevertheless, multiple obstacles persist in impeding access to compensation money, beginning with the essential condition that affected persons be informed of the class-action and that they satisfy the requisite criteria. Considering that people are frequently inadequately informed regarding their rights, it remains highly uncertain whether they recognize that their detention was unlawful—much less whether they possess the means to demonstrate it. In this case as well, no one faced consequences, no institutional surveillance was instituted, and no systemic modifications are anticipated. More broadly, the Ombudsperson's work as well as the judicial ruling fail to acknowledge the power relations and discrimination intrinsic to these practices. Although rights violations are systemic in nature, they tend to be treated as the aggregation of individual situations.

The progress that had been accomplished in the aftermath of civil rights movements and legislative reforms is being eroded incrementally—both in mental health and across all spheres of social law. The escalating use of coercion despite laws remaining mostly unchanged suggests that the progress achieved was less due to rights than political will or the convergence of the interests of various groups. Rights may therefore be viewed as "reformist reforms"—as they operate within the boundaries of the status quo, implementing changes that preserve rather than challenge the dominant institutional logics (Ben-Moshe, 2020). Much like deinstitutionalization, the mental health law reforms of the 1960s and 1970s were shaped through negotiated consensus among actors with fundamentally divergent interests: the state, the mental health professionals, and liberation movement activists (Brown, 1984). Through the institutionalization of rights, the political demands of the liberation movement were largely neutralized, power relationships remained unaltered, and the use of coercive practices has persisted.

Liat Ben-Moshe (2020: 16) argues that "improvements or progressive alternatives is the core problem with reform and not abolition-based approaches. It increases the scope of incarceration, and instead of making the system more just, it spreads an unjust system to more people" (Ben-Moshe, 2020: 16). The abolitionist position—central to the psychiatric liberation movement—calls for political action rooted in self-determination and reparation. Engaging in a broader social conversation that addresses the structural dynamics of power and domination requires moving beyond the rhetoric of rights (Scheingold, 2004). Such a shift involves questioning the hegemony of law, legal rights, and justice as the primary framework for regulating behavior and relations, as well as adjudicating matters related to coercion. Following my research and that of other researchers, it is reasonable to question the preeminent role granted to legal practitioners in mental health matters, as well as the meaning and pertinence of a judicial process that claims to be more therapeutic than legal.

In this regard, it appears essential to speak about and make coercion visible. Coercion, whether psychiatric or not, is a political question of power. As with any political issue, the main challenge is the control over the narrative. The judicial system, encompassing civil and administrative courts, possesses coercive power; however much it may seek to be "therapeutic" or "compassionate," to "adapt" or "individualize," it remains fundamentally an institution that constrains. It is perceived as such and operates in multiple ways. The semantic drift we presently witness, which permeates the entire care continuum, whereby coercion poses as compassion, protection, or rights, represents a political transformation of the narrative consistent with the political climate and the current or anticipated reforms I addressed in Chapter 2 regarding people experiencing homelessness, encampments, and forced treatment. However, coercion is not "compassion," it is not "rights-based," it is not "protection." Coercion is inherently violent. It constrains, it forces, it threatens. Lived experiences reveal how it traumatizes, dehumanizes, and destroys, as described, for example, by David W. Oaks:

> I was exposed to a variety of coercive acts while in psychiatric institutions. For instance, upon admission my basic rights were immediately taken a way, and then slowly given back as privileges for behaviour that was considered appropriate. My every movement was monitored and controlled. Any seemingly peaceful rebellion by me—such as questioning staff—could be misinterpreted as violent, and result in another forced drugging. [...]
>
> The subjective experience of being forcibly injected with psychotropic drugs and left isolated has created one of my longest-standing recurring nightmares. There I was, a confused and frightened young person. I felt at the time that I needed respite, advice, support and comfort. Instead,

> the impact of the coerced psychiatric drug felt like a wrecking ball to the cathedral of my mind, a mind which was indeed troubled, but which I valued nonetheless. While on coerced neuroleptic psychiatric medication, also known as antipsychotics, the more I tried to focus and think, the more difficult I found the task. I developed a number of physical side effects to the medications that some might consider trivial, but that I found upsetting, such as muscle contortions in my neck and blurry vision. All in all, I felt humiliated, disrespected and defiant. I certainly did not feel a high level of trust with my mental health providers that might have been more conducive to a therapeutic relationship. (Oaks, 2011: 190)

The experiences of people I encountered in my research, and that others have similarly documented, reveal that psychiatric coercion mirrors coercion more broadly, whether from the criminal justice system, social services, or other sources—a predictable outcome given that coercive psychiatric methods are directly borrowed from penal institutions (Foucault, 2006). The serial judicialization, the repeated interactions with police, social services, and health services, and the expansion of community-based surveillance challenge claims about mental health difference. Coercion is multidimensional; it manifests in various forms and operates through different systems; it targets and strikes marginalized individuals in multiple ways. Regardless of the specifics of the system, there is invariably a justification for coercion—be it punishment, protection, risk, or all these reasons combined—but it remains fundamentally similar, trespassing upon freedoms, autonomy, and integrity. I contend that the current political issue concerns coercion as a whole, starting with acknowledging it for what it actually is—a form of institutional violence embedded in discrimination, profiling, and colonialism.

History shows that structural transformation has typically emerged from broad political mobilizations. This has been the case in mental health, when psychiatric survivors formed alliances with other groups in solidarity against oppression. The student protests of the 1960s, the critique of capitalism in Italy, and democratic movements in Argentina during the 1980s were pivotal in challenging the power structures, including asylum systems and psychiatric coercion. These political mobilizations gave rise to the development of community-based care models (Badano, 2024; Mauri & Barcala, 2020). Community-based care has represented and continues to embody a political commitment that reconceptualizes mental health care service users as "community members" rather than as "mentally ill." This approach tends to rectify power disparities, with relationships between professionals and users paralleling those in physical medicine.

Italy's Trieste mental health system stands as the best-known and most successful example of these approaches. Implemented since 1971 under psychiatrist Franco Basaglia's direction, it consists of round-the-clock community services including group homes, home care services, and small hospital units used for emergencies but generally not hospitalizing beyond 24 hours. Services are delivered by peers and carers most often within people's living environments, promoting community integration and social inclusion. Operating without restraints or locked doors and not risk-driven, the system has witnessed substantial decreases in crisis interventions, while Trieste's involuntary admission and Community Treatment Order rates—implemented in open facilities—remain one of the lowest in the North global countries. Although Trieste invested heavily in developing community services, its system costs amount to 60% of former psychiatric hospital expenses (Sashidharan, 2022; Sade, Goljevscek & Corradi-Webster, 2020; Mezzina, 2016). Research indicated that Trieste inhabitants, mental health workers included, demonstrated diminished sanist prejudices relative to populations in more institutionally oriented legal frameworks, including more comfort with community-based crisis intervention (Vicente et al., 1993).

Despite being hailed as one of the "most innovative and progressive" mental health systems (Sashidharan et al., 2019: 95), the Trieste model has generated criticism and resistance, particularly through the characterization of psychiatrist Franco Basaglia's work as "antipsychiatric," "idealistic," or lacking an evidence-based foundation (Guaiana et al., 2019). According to psychiatrist Sashi Sashidharan and colleagues, these arguments mask political motivations designed to preserve the status quo:

> the dismissal of Basaglia's work was more about protecting the prevailing norms of psychiatry at the time than any commitment to the canon of evidence-based medicine, as there was strong evidence that his work in

> Gorizia and Trieste had led to great improvements in mental healthcare, substantial clinical benefits for patients, greater satisfaction of families and local communities, and active endorsement and participation by mental health staff (Sashidharan et al., 2019: 95).

Even though developments in research appear to support the Trieste model, it currently faces considerable political pushback. In 2021, an open letter (Asquini et al., 2021) and accompanying petition (Change.org, 2021), signed by several international experts, condemned "a new right wing regional government that, on poorly informed and ideological grounds is fast and impulsively dismantling Trieste's wonderful system of community care" (Change.org, 2021). Following the pattern established by neoliberal governments—particularly under Ronald Reagan (Sashidharan, 2022)—the new administration, as part of its healthcare privatization agenda, seeks to eliminate what it frames as "politically left-wing psychiatry" (Frances, 2021).

The attempted dismantling of Trieste's community care model mirrors criminal justice trajectories, while since the 1980s, neoliberal political shifts in several countries have produced more punitive criminal legislation and, in the case of the United States, prison system privatization. As a result, the number of incarcerated people has generally escalated in these countries (Tonry, 2022).

The United States, as a principal pioneer and driving force behind global neoliberal policies, provides a particularly compelling case for examining the systematic coherence of coercive policies across institutional domains. Between the 1960s and 1980s, following the closure of asylums, the United States established "the best system of community psychiatry in the world" (Sashidharan, 2022: 53). It was, actually, a stay in the United States that inspired Franco Basaglia's Trieste model. Since the mid-nineteenth century, American practices of rehabilitation, probation, parole, and juvenile courts were the most progressive worldwide, and the United States had a relatively stable incarceration rate (Tonry, 2022). Following a social debate concerning child removal by child welfare services, where the racist and classist dimensions and overuse of that practice were highlighted, a policy aimed at providing services directly to families to prevent removals was implemented in 1980 (Raz,

2020). Upon assuming the US presidency in 1981, Ronald Reagan embarked on major political changes. He reduced or eliminated several social programs, including child and family services, community-based mental health services, and criminal justice rehabilitation programs, continued the privatization of several federal institutions, and increasingly delegated services such as childcare, healthcare, and correctional services to profit-making organizations (Raz, 2020; Tingle, 1988). These changes provoked, or contributed to, clear trends toward coercion. The incarceration rate quadrupled over the next five decades (Leigh, 2020); between 1983 and 1990 alone, the number of children placed in foster care rose from 280,000 to 400,000 (Raz, 2020), a pattern that was sustained throughout subsequent decades (Goetz, 2020); although statistics are not available nationally, studies demonstrate a 60 to 150% increase in psychiatric beds administered by private corporations in the 1980s, with involuntary admission rates around 90% in these facilities (Hutchins, Frank & Glied, 2011; Mechanic et al., 1998; Samson, 1990). Consequently, whereas hospital admissions in public psychiatric facilities decreased, in private institutions, they rose. These data demonstrate that, in the aftermath of transinstitutionalization, state coercive capacity expanded significantly and remains so at present.

Inter-movement solidarity, Trieste's model, and the US example illuminate the vast potential, but also the imperative, for transcending conventional systems and structures to reconceptualize coercion—as well as the abolition of coercion. Drawing on Foucault (2008, 2003), this exercise positions coercion as a violent population management mechanism targeting marginalized groups through a child welfare-psychiatry-prison pipeline. Beyond the political implications of this conclusion, research must urgently acknowledge these realities. Scholarship contributing to "mental health crisis" narratives, psychiatrizing social problems, notably homelessness, and advocating rights-based approaches and therapeutic justice abounds (Wilson, 2023; Ben-Moshe, 2017; Mills, 2015). Yet this literature not only frequently fails to illuminate the evident shortcomings of such approaches, but generally overlooks the economic, political, and social dimensions of these social issues. It neglects to expose how policies of abandonment and structural neglect generate social crises, or the relationship between wealth concentration and widespread precarity. Confronting coercive mechanisms in neoliberal contexts demands both transcending traditional research silos—criminal justice, mental health, homelessness, child welfare, housing—and crucially reclaiming critical thought, semantic clarity, and repositioning power as the central analytical framework for understanding social relations. In essence, to awaken politically (Bassett, 2020).

References

Asquini, M. et al. (2021, May 27). Trieste Mental Health Service Model under threat. International Mental health Collaborating Network. https://imhcn.org/news/call-to-add-your-support-for-trieste/ (accessed August 7, 2025).

Bassett, M. T. (2020). Tired of science being ignored? *Get political. Nature, 586*(7829), 337–338. https://doi.org/10.1038/d41586-020-02854-9

Ben-Moshe, L. (2020). *Decarcerating disability: Deinstitutionalization and prison abolition*. University of Minnesota Press.

Ben-Moshe, L. (2017). Why prisons are not "the new asylums". *Punishment & Society, 19*(3), 272–289. https://doi.org/10.1177/1462474517704852

Birnbaum, M. (1960). The right to treatment. *American Bar Association Journal, 46*, 499–505.

Brown, P. (1984). The right to refuse treatment and the movement for mental health reform. *Journal of Health Politics, Policy and Law, 9*(2), 291–313. https://doi.org/10.1215/03616878-9-2-291

Brown, P. (1981). The mental patients' rights movement and mental health institutional change. *International Journal of Health Services, 11*(4), 523–540. https://doi.org/10.2190/CU8G-D0RJ-YY54-UC3F

Convention on the Rights of Persons with Disabilities, A/RES/61/106, 12 December 2006.

Chamberlin, J. (1995). Rehabilitating ourselves: The psychiatric survivor movement. *International Journal of Mental Health, 24*(1), 39–46. https://doi.org/10.1080/00207411.1995.11449302

Chamberlin, J. (1990). The ex-patients' movement: Where we've been and where we're going. *The journal of Mind and Behavior*, 323–336. https://www.jstor.org/stable/43854095

Chamberlin, J. (1978). *On our own: Patient-controlled alternatives to the mental health system.* McGraw-Hill.
Change.org (2021, June 8). Save Trieste's Mental Health System. https://www.change.org/p/international-mental-health-collaborating-network-save-trieste-s-mental-health-system. (accessed August 9, 2025).
Cosgrove, L., Morrill, Z., Karter, J. M., Valdes, E., & Cheng, C. P. (2021). The cultural politics of mental illness: Toward a rights-based approach to global mental health. *Community Mental Health Journal, 57*(1), 3–9. https://doi.org/10.1007/s10597-020-00720-6
Davidson, L. (2025). Swinging the pendulum from 'a necessary evil'to 'the dignity of risk': Can new UN legislative guidance help to end psychiatric coercion? *International Journal of Law and Psychiatry, 102*, 102102. https://doi.org/10.1016/j.ijlp.2025.102102
Dawson, J., & Szmukler, G. (2021). The "fusion law" proposals and the CRPD. In M. Stein, F. Mahomed, V. Patel, & C. Sunkel (Eds.), *Mental health, legal capacity, and human rights (pp. 95–108).* Cambridge University Press. https://doi.org/10.1017/9781108979016
Emerick, R. E. (1996). Mad liberation: The sociology of knowledge and the ultimate civil rights movement. *The Journal of Mind and Behavior*, 135–159. https://www.jstor.org/stable/43853695
Foucault, M. (2008). *The birth of biopolitics: Lectures at the Collège de France, 1978–1979.* Palgrave Macmillan.
Foucault, M. (2006). *Psychiatric power: Lectures at the Collège de France, 1973–1974* (first published in 2003). Picador.
Foucault, M. (2003). *Abnormal: Lectures at the college de France 1974–1975.* Verso.
Frances, A. (2021). Save Trieste's mental health system. *The Lancet Psychiatry, 8*(9), 744–746.
Frazer-Carroll, M. (2023). *Mad world: The politics of mental health.* Pluto Press.
Goetz, S. L. (2020). From removal to incarceration: How the modern child welfare system and its unintended consequences catalyzed the foster care-to-prison pipeline. *University of Maryland Law Journal of Race, Religion, Gender & Class, 20*, 289–305.
Guaiana, G., Bastiampillai, T., Allison, S., & O'Reilly, R. (2019). Basaglia's impact. *The lancet. Psychiatry, 6*(2), 94–95.
Ginsberg, L. H. (1974). The mental patient liberation movement. *Social Work, 19*(2), 3–103. https://www.jstor.org/stable/23712159

Hutchins, E. C., Frank, R. G., & Glied, S. A. (2011). The evolving private psychiatric inpatient market. *The Journal of Behavioral Health Services & Research, 38*(1), 122–131. https://doi.org/10.1007/s11414-009-9199-6

Leigh, A. (2020). Estimating long-run incarceration rates for Australia, Canada, England and Wales, New Zealand, and the United States. *Australian Economic History Review, 60*(2), 148–185. https://doi.org/10.1111/aehr.12194

Mechanic, D., McAlpine, D. D., & Olfson, M. (1998). Changing patterns of psychiatric inpatient care in the United States, 1988-1994. *Archives of General Psychiatry, 55*(9), 785–791. https://doi.org/10.1001/archpsyc.55.9.785

Mezzina, R. (2016). Creating mental health services without exclusion or restraint but with open doors Trieste. *Italy. L'information psychiatrique, 92*(9), 747–754. https://doi.org/10.1684/ipe.2016.1546

Mills, C. (2015). The Psychiatrization of Poverty: Rethinking the Mental Health–Poverty Nexus. Social and Personality Pschology Compass, 9(5), 213–222. doi:https://doi.org/10.1111/spc3.12168.

Milner, N. (1986). The dilemmas of legal mobilization: Ideologies and strategies of mental patient liberation groups. *Law & Policy, 8*(1), 105–129. https://doi.org/10.1111/j.1467-9930.1986.tb00372.x

Moyn, S. (2014). A powerless companion: Human rights in the age of neoliberalism. *Law and Contemporary Problems, 77*(4), 147–169. https://www.jstor.org/stable/24244651

Oaks, D. W. (2011). The moral imperative for dialogue with organizations of survivors of coerced psychiatric human rights violations. In Kallert, T. W., Mezzich, J. E. & Monahan, J. (Eds.), *coercive treatment in psychiatry: Clinical, legal and ethical aspects* (pp. 185-211). https://doi.org/10.1002/9780470978573

Raz, M. (2020). *Abusive policies: How the American child welfare system lost its way*. University of North Carolina Press. *Yale Law & Policy Review, 6*, 229–258.

Rose, N. (1985). Unreasonable rights: Mental illness and the limits of the law. *Journal of Law & Society, 12*, 199–218. https://doi.org/10.2307/1410128

Sade, R. M. S., Goljevscek, S., & Corradi-Webster, C. M. (2020). Intensive home support for mental health crises: Experience of the Trieste territorial crises team, in Italy. *Saúde e Sociedade, 29*, e190831. https://doi.org/10.1590/S0104-12902020190831

Samson, C. (1990). Inequality, the new right and mental health care delivery in the United States in the Reagan era. *Critical Social Policy, 10*(29), 40–57. https://doi.org/10.1177/026101839001002903

Sashidharan, S. P. (2022). Why Trieste matters. *The British Journal of Psychiatry, 220*(2), 52–53. https://doi.org/10.1192/bjp.2021.149

Sashidharan, S. P., Mezzina, R., Saraceno, B., Rosen, A., Davidson, L., Frances, A., & Kendall, T. (2019). Basaglia's impact. *The lancet. Psychiatry, 6*(2), 95–96.

Schramme, T. (2004). The legacy of antipsychiatry. In T. Schramme & J. Thome (Eds.), *Philosophy and psychiatry* (pp. 94–119). Walter de Gruyter.

Scheingold, S. (2004). *The politics of rights: Lawyers, public policy, and political change* (2nd ed.). University of Michigan Press.

Starkman, M. (2012). The movement. In B. A. LeFrançois, R. Menzies, & G. Reaume (Eds.), *Mad matters: A critical reader in Canadian mad studies* (pp. 27–37). Canadian Scholars.

Szasz, T. (2010). Psychiatry, anti-psychiatry, critical psychiatry: What do these terms mean? *Philosophy, Psychiatry, & Psychology, 17*(3), 229–232.

The Canadian Press (2024, October 27). Settlement over preventive detentions in Quebec worth $8.5 million. *Montreal Gazette*. https://www.montrealgazette.com/news/provincial-news/article560149.html (accessed August 9, 2025).

The Office of the Ombudsperson. (2019, March). *Committed to Change: Protecting the Rights of Involuntary Patients under the Mental Health Act*. Special Report N°42. https://bcombudsperson.ca/assets/media/OMB-Committed-to-Change-FINAL-web.pdf (accessed August 9, 2025).

Thompson v. Ontario (Attorney General), 2016 ONCA 676.

Tingle, M. L. (1988). Privatization and the Reagan administration: Ideology and application.

Tonry, M. (2022). Punishments, politics, and prisons in western countries. *Crime and Justice, 51*(1), 7–57. https://doi.org/10.1086/721278

Vicente, B., Vielma, M., Jenner, F. A., Mezzina, R., & Lliapas, I. (1993). Users' satisfaction with mental health services. *International Journal of Social Psychiatry, 39*(2), 121–130. https://doi.org/10.1177/002076409303900205

Wilson, A. (2023). An alternative spotlight. Colonial legacies, therapeutic jurisprudence, and the enigma of healing. In A. Aliverti, H. Carvalho, A. Chamberlen, & Sozzo, m. (Eds.), *Decolonizing the criminal question*. Oxford University Press. https://doi.org/10.1093/oso/9780192899002.003.0018

Wilson, K. (2022). The CRPD and mental health law: The conflict about abolition, the practical dilemmas of implementation and the untapped potential. In *Disability law and human rights: Theory and policy* (pp. 171–197). Springer. https://doi.org/10.1007/978-3-030-86545-0_9

Index

E. Bernheim, *Therapeutic (In)justice and the Shadow Carceral State*, The Politics of Mental Health and Illness, https://doi.org/10.1007/978-3-032-16186-4

FSC
www.fsc.org
MIX
Papier | Fördert
gute Waldnutzung
FSC® C083411

Kolibri 360 GmbH
Ferdinand-Jühlke-Straße 7
99095 Erfurt, Deutschland
produktsicherheit@kolibri360.de